Sopris West®

Step Up to Writing in Math

Maureen Auman and Debbie Valette

All Levels
Grades K–12

Explicit, Effective, Math-Focused Writing Strategies

Sopris West®
EDUCATIONAL SERVICES

A Cambium Learning® Company

BOSTON, MA · LONGMONT, CO

ISBN-13: 978-1-60218-684-2
ISBN-10: 1-60218-684-7

Printed in the United States of America
Published and Distributed by

Sopris West®
EDUCATIONAL SERVICES

A Cambium Learning® Company

4093 Specialty Place • Longmont, CO 80504
303-651-2829 • www.sopriswest.com

169316/326/06-15

Dedication

To our families and friends, who encourage us and believe in the work we are doing.

To teachers and their students who have accepted the challenge to improve communication skills in their math classes.

Acknowledgments

A number of people at Sopris West Educational Services helped make this book possible:

- Michelle LaBorde, Rob Carson, and Annette Reaves shared their expertise and talents. We appreciate their time, patience, and guidance as our editors and product managers.
- Holly Bell, Geoff Horsfall, and the rest of the Enriching Literacy and Math (ELM) product group contributed in numerous ways throughout the process.
- We are especially thankful to Caela Tyler and Sherri Rowe, who helped with graphics and design.

Several important individuals helped both of us behind the scenes; we appreciate their work and enthusiastic support:

Elke Adler, John Auman, Jim Auman, Katie Connaughty-Auman, Lin Kuzmich, Jill Yarberry-Laybourn, Sharon Nealeigh, Lynn Utzmann-Nichols, Rodney Peffer, Alain Valette, Francis Valette, Sally Valette, and Marilyn A. Whitman.

About the Authors

Maureen E. Auman, M.A., is the author of *Step Up to Writing*, a nationally-recognized, research-based writing program designed for primary, intermediate, and secondary educators to help students become proficient and effective writers. Maureen has spent the last 20-plus years focused on creating successful teaching strategies for diverse populations of students, including gifted and talented, special education, at-risk, and English language learners. She is a speaker at local, regional, and national literacy conferences where she presents hands-on, multisensory writing strategies for teachers across the curriculum. Additionally, Maureen works with district and school administration teams, and curriculum specialists to develop school-wide writing plans.

Maureen began her 19-year teaching career in 1979 as a language arts teacher with the Archdiocese of Denver and later worked in the Cherry Creek School District in Colorado. She received her master's degree in administration, supervision, and curriculum from the University of Colorado at Denver in 1989. Currently, Maureen serves as an instructor of literacy strategies at Adams State College; owner of ReadWriteConnection LLC, an educational consulting company; and author of the *Step Up to Writing* program. Her program publications include *Step Up to Writing 3rd Edition*, *Handy Pages* (for Primary, Intermediate, and Secondary levels), *Classroom Reproducibles*, *Step Up to Writing Poster Sets*, and the co-authored texts, *Primary Steps*, *Write at Your Doorstep*, and *Step Up to Writing in Math*.

Maureen and her husband divide their time between Florida and Northern Colorado.

Debbie Valette has taught extensively in at-risk schools with linguistically and culturally diverse populations. Her company, Literacy Unlimited, LLC, is dedicated to helping educators in all content areas empower students through literacy. Debbie has more than 10 years of experience sharing *Step Up to Writing* strategies with students and K–12 colleagues locally and nationally. As an independent educational consultant, she customizes workshops that equip educators and administrators with strategies to help their students meet district and state literacy standards.

Debbie received her B.A. in Spanish Literature from the University of Illinois and her M.Ed. in Bilingual/ESL Education from the University of Illinois in Chicago.

Debbie, her husband, and their two daughters live in Boulder, Colorado.

CONTENTS

What Is *Step Up to Writing in Math?*

Step Up to Writing in Math expands on the approach to writing in math introduced in *Step Up to Writing* (Auman, 2008). It provides practical strategies that improve students' ability to communicate about their math knowledge and understanding.

The National Council of Teachers of Mathematics (NCTM) has identified communication as an essential part of mathematics education. Not only does the ability to write about math help students demonstrate their comprehension of math concepts, but it also helps them better analyze and evaluate ideas and retain the math content that they learn for longer periods of time. In addition, students are increasingly being required to write about math on state and national assessments—sometimes even to write full-page answers about a math concept.

Math standards vary from state to state, and math assessments look slightly different from district to district, but the emphasis on writing in the math classroom is consistent nationwide. Math students in all grades and at all ability levels have to explain, compare, describe, justify, evaluate, analyze, argue, predict, and apply what they have learned.

Writing has become a regular and important part of math instruction because when students write they:

- reflect on their learning;

- clarify, refine, and organize their thinking;

- discover errors or solutions;

- give meanings to words by using them in an appropriate context;

- make their thinking concrete;

- deepen their understanding;

- demonstrate what they have learned;

- analyze and evaluate their ideas; and

- retain what they've learned.

Writing strategies are important in all math classes. Students who excel at working math problems may not be very good at articulating the thinking behind their answers. And those who struggle with math often find that using a straightforward process to explain their answers clarifies concepts that they didn't previously understand. All types of students who use the *Step Up to Writing in Math* strategies show almost immediate improvement in their work because the strategies require them to organize ideas and information, demonstrate comprehension, plan before they begin writing, and provide specific examples and evidence in their responses.

Although being able to write quickly and accurately about math content is becoming more and more important, time to teach and assign math-related writing, unfortunately, is still scarce. That is why the *Step Up to Writing in Math* tools and techniques are designed to save time for both teachers and students. They require minimal preparation time because the structure they present for writing is very visual, hands-on, and sequential. They are practical and are easy to teach and learn. In addition, the program includes a method for grading writing assignments that makes scoring easier and more defensible for teachers who do not specialize in language arts.

Students of all ages and skill levels can use the strategies in this book. The writing examples and practice items are divided into three levels: primary (first through third grades), intermediate (third through sixth grades), and secondary (sixth through twelfth grades).

A Multisensory Approach

Step Up to Writing in Math strategies incorporate multisensory instruction. Many of the activities require folded or cut paper, colors, lists, symbols, and/or practice guides.

Students learn to visualize the steps needed to complete a number of important writing tasks by:

- watching teachers demonstrate the strategies;

- participating in active, hands-on guided lessons;

- practicing each skill independently or in pairs or small groups;

- using strategies regularly as a way to learn new concepts and content, and to prepare for local and state assessments;

- analyzing, reviewing, and/or improving each strategy during discussions with teachers and classmates; and

- referring to scoring guides that show specific criteria for improving writing.

For students who struggle with math, with writing, or simply with writing about math concepts, the multisensory *Step Up to Writing in Math* approach improves both communication about and comprehension of math subject matter. Students who balk at complex problems learn to break them down into manageable chunks. Students for whom numerical answers come easily learn to visualize and verbalize the process they use to reach their answers. All students learn to communicate mathematical information and relate the concepts they are learning to their lives outside of math class.

A Common Language for Reading, Writing, and Speaking About Math

Students learn best in schools where administrators and teachers set common goals and standards for success and where teachers, administrators, support staff, families, tutors, and community members share a common language for teaching and assessing basic literacy skills.

With the *Step Up to Writing in Math* methods, students at all grade levels learn similar strategies, and all students are held to the same high standards regardless of the subject matter. The common language that this approach encourages among those inside and outside of schools helps students deliver quality work in all of their classes.

The more they use the *Step Up to Writing in Math* strategies, the more ingrained these techniques become. Students begin to wield these tools to finish assignments that don't explicitly call for a *Step Up to Writing in Math* approach, or even to meet personal goals. They also feel empowered to share the strategies with others.

A Means of Encouraging Independence and Creativity

When students begin to use *Step Up to Writing in Math* tools, they learn specific steps and structures for different kinds of writing assignments. However, they understand, even as they learn these structures, that all good writing strategies are flexible. They quickly make the *Step Up to Writing in Math* strategies their own, making changes as needed to fit different assignments and goals.

Students learn that creativity means molding what they know about a math concept or math content into something new. It means being able to solve problems. It means being able to explain ideas and processes to others. *Step Up to Writing in Math* strategies make this possible.

Strategies That Meet the Needs of All Students

- **Reluctant writers.** Students who do not see themselves as writers are willing to try the *Step Up to Writing in Math* strategies because they seem doable. These students are often surprised by the results, and they become willing to try writing again.

    Reluctant writers who lack patience are drawn to *Step Up to Writing in Math* strategies because they produce good results while taking little time to master.

- **Beginning writers.** Beginning writers like to know what is expected of them in an assignment. They also like knowing that they have the guidance and guidelines they need to complete the task.

These writers appreciate the opportunity to repeat a task over and over again until they have developed confidence and skills. They respond well to *Step Up to Writing in Math* because the program's strategies are meant to be used over and over again until they become automatic.

In addition, the strategies are presented in small steps with the support that beginning writers need.

- **Students with learning disabilities.** Students with learning disabilities want (and need) to feel like they are part of a class—doing what the other students are doing. Strategies in *Step Up to Writing in Math* can easily be adjusted to fit the needs of all learners. Tools like practice guides and framed responses give extra help to students who need it.

   At the same time, multisensory instruction makes learning easier. The multisensory strategies of *Step Up to Writing in Math* help students remember the steps they need to take and visualize the answers to math problems.

   The strategies also help students with learning disabilities complete their work more quickly and, therefore, keep up with their peers. These strategies decrease frustration and increase success. They are especially important for students who are working to increase their processing speed.

- **English language learners (ELLs).** The *Step Up to Writing in Math* strategies help students learn the academic language of writing generally, as well as the more specific academic language they need to communicate about math concepts and content.

   The strategies quickly and clearly show the basic patterns of writing in English. The numerous writing examples provided as tools for instruction can help ELLs with reading and writing. As students read (or listen to) the examples, they learn about sentence and paragraph structures.

   The multisensory, active, hands-on lessons make learning English more fun and rewarding.

   Most important, the strategies can be used to ensure that students with limited English speaking or writing skills are challenged and that expectations for their math comprehension are high.

   Step Up to Writing in Math strategies work in any language; ELLs can practice the strategies in their first language.

- **Remedial and at-risk students.** As students listen to and participate in guided lessons, they relearn literacy skills they have forgotten. During teacher demonstrations and in small-group activities, they find opportunities to ask questions and get clarification about math content as well as writing methods.

Some remedial students have not learned to communicate about what they understand and what they do not understand. All *Step Up to Writing in Math* strategies are designed to help students communicate about their comprehension of math concepts.

For many students, math class may be an ideal place to improve writing skills. Math teachers often explain processes in simple, clear ways, so students who have not learned from their other teachers how to organize their thoughts and express themselves in writing may find a math teacher's explanation of writing strategies easier to understand. Remedial and at-risk students may also respect the efforts of the math teacher to teach and encourage these skills.

- **Typical students.** Students who consistently do well with math computation and problem solving may have difficulty writing about how they reach their answers. Because they are motivated to do well, they like learning strategies that improve their communication skills. They are also looking for ways to save time. They appreciate any guidance they get that saves them time. Therefore, they embrace the *Step Up to Writing in Math* strategies, which are designed to help students complete work quickly and accurately.

  Typical students also like the specific feedback that the *Step Up to Writing in Math* scoring guides provide. They like knowing what they must do to earn a specific grade, and they appreciate the examples of responses, explanations, paragraphs, and reports.

- **Advanced or gifted/talented students.** Sometimes those who do extremely well in math class are unaware of all of the steps they actually take as they solve problems. Because answers come quickly for them, students identified as advanced may become frustrated when they are asked to explain their problem-solving processes. *Step Up to Writing in Math* strategies help because they force students to think in slow motion, which makes it easier for them to explain a process.

  Some students identified as gifted/talented struggle with organizing their ideas. All of the *Step Up to Writing in Math* strategies teach organization. Many gifted/talented students are relieved to find that such strategies exist. Other gifted/talented students write very well. When they use the tools and strategies, they are challenged to try new methods and to perfect their skills.

How *Step Up to Writing in Math* Supports Key Principles of Math Education

Step Up to Writing in Math helps teachers meet the principles and standards of the NCTM.

The Equity Principle

> *Excellence in mathematics education requires equity—high expectations and strong support for all students.**

Step Up to Writing in Math offers step-by-step strategies that help all students understand and master content. Each of the strategies requires students to move beyond memorization and use higher-order thinking skills to accomplish tasks.

The Curriculum Principle

> *A curriculum is more than a collection of activities; it must be coherent, focused on important mathematics, and well-articulated across the grades.**

The strategies in *Step Up to Writing in Math* are generic and can be used at all grade levels. As students move from class to class and from grade to grade, they hear similar messages about communicating in math, and they are held to the same high standards by all teachers. Students become comfortable with the strategies, and they use them to master and retain math content.

Using these strategies across grade levels supports students in mastering the processes of math: problem solving, reasoning and writing of proofs, communicating math concepts, drawing connections, and accurately illustrating their ideas.

The Teaching Principle

> *Effective mathematics teaching requires understanding what students know and need to learn, and then challenging and supporting them to learn it well.**

Every strategy in *Step Up to Writing in Math* asks students to communicate, orally or in writing, about their thinking process. When students communicate, they reveal what they know and what they need. In addition to asking them to communicate, these strategies support students by giving them systems for reasoning that make complex tasks more

---

* Reprinted with permission from *Principles and Standards for School Mathematics*, copyright 2000 by the National Council of Teachers of Mathematics. All rights reserved.

manageable. When students feel empowered, they are more likely to reach their learning potential.

The Learning Principle

*Students must learn mathematics with understanding, actively building new knowledge from experience and previous knowledge.**

When students use the strategies in *Step Up to Writing in Math*, they engage in communication and critical thinking. In order to successfully communicate, they must grapple with their ideas until they can clearly articulate what they want to say. Through this process, students clarify their thinking and gain understanding. Students who can effectively communicate about concepts are more likely to retain them, creating a stronger base of prior knowledge on which to build future learning.

The Assessment Principle

*Assessment should support the learning of important mathematics and furnish useful information to both teachers and students.**

The element of assessment is inherent in every strategy in *Step Up to Writing in Math*. Because these strategies require communication, students are routinely revealing their way of thinking and teachers are providing immediate feedback. Whether the communication is written or oral, it provides teachers with the information necessary to assess the students' learning. This two-way communication also gives students the opportunity to reflect on their own learning. When students communicate, they grow as mathematicians, and they keep teachers abreast of their level of understanding.

Step Up to Writing in Math also provides practical, time-saving scoring guides for assessment. All parts of the scoring guides are easy to remember and incorporate as students write. The scoring guides help student writers see what is needed to reach proficient and advanced levels.

The *Step Up to Writing in Math* scoring guides scream "Welcome to success!" They show students exactly what they need to fix to move up the 16-point scale from the below-basic and basic levels to the proficient and advanced levels. The scoring guides empower student writers to be independent and to take control of the final scores they receive.

---

* Reprinted with permission from *Principles and Standards for School Mathematics*, copyright 2000 by the National Council of Teachers of Mathematics. All rights reserved.

The Problem Solving Standard

Instructional programs from prekindergarten through grade 12 should enable all students to monitor and reflect on the process of mathematical problem solving.*

Step Up to Writing in Math includes strategies that help students describe their problem-solving processes. These concrete tools give students the guidance they need to confidently explain what they are thinking. Because their explanations are shared in a coherent, recognizable pattern, teachers can more easily gain insight into students' train of thought, and students are better able to monitor and reflect on their own processes and those of others.

The Reasoning and Proof Standard

Instructional programs from prekindergarten through grade 12 should enable all students to develop and evaluate mathematical arguments and proofs.*

To develop reasoning, students need to engage in mathematical conversations. The tools in *Step Up to Writing in Math* facilitate math conversations—both oral and written.

The Communication Standard

Instructional programs from prekindergarten through grade 12 should enable all students to:
- *organize and consolidate their mathematical thinking through communication;*
- *communicate their mathematical thinking coherently and clearly to peers, teachers, and others;*
- *analyze and evaluate the mathematical thinking and strategies of others; and*
- *use the language of mathematics to express mathematical ideas precisely.**

Step Up to Writing in Math offers concrete, practical, step-by-step strategies for teaching students to communicate effectively, both orally and in writing. With repeated use of these strategies, students learn to communicate—and, in the process, they more thoroughly learn the math content. In addition, these strategies help students understand the thinking of others. The training tools in this book make the invisible aspects of communication visible.

Step Up to Writing in Math includes a variety of strategies to build students' math vocabulary, which is essential to effective communication. These strategies work with

---

* Standards are listed with the permission of the National Council of Teachers of Mathematics (NCTM). NCTM does not endorse the content or validity of these alignments.

students of all ages and ability levels; students master these strategies by using them from grade level to grade level and by applying them across content areas.

The Connections Standard

Instructional programs from prekindergarten through grade 12 should enable all students to recognize and apply mathematics in contexts outside of mathematics.*

Step Up to Writing in Math offers vehicles by which students can communicate their understanding of how to apply math concepts in contexts outside of the math classroom. The questioning strategies require students to think about real-life applications for the math content they're learning. Students also learn to use journals or formal reports to demonstrate how they apply math concepts in their everyday lives.

Strategies can easily be applied to activities and assignments in science, geography, social studies, music, art, and so on.

The Representation Standard

Instructional programs from prekindergarten through grade 12 should enable all students to create and use representations to organize, record, and communicate mathematical ideas.*

Step Up to Writing in Math includes suggestions for ways students can create and use visual aids to represent data and meaning. The advice covers the use of representations to communicate about math vocabulary; about the meanings of graphs, tables, or charts; and about problem-solving processes.

Step Up to Writing in Math addresses the Representation Standard in several ways. First, students learn strategies for reading and solving word problems that include making sketches, charts, tables, graphs, and so on as a way to encourage thinking and show reasoning.

Students also make representations in note taking and while learning new math terms. Representations become part of the students' notes, and they are used to show (step-by-step) through pictures/representations what is needed to solve a problem.

A third method involves reading, analyzing, and writing about graphs. Students use these strategies with graphs that have already been created and with the graphs that they create.

Finally, students are encouraged to add visual pieces, samples, color, markings, charts, sketches, and so on as they work independently, with peers, or in teacher guided lessons.

---

* Standards are listed with the permission of the National Council of Teachers of Mathematics (NCTM). NCTM does not endorse the content or validity of these alignments.

Implementing *Step Up to Writing in Math*

What role does *Step Up to Writing in Math* play in my classroom?

- It is an important supplemental resource.

- The strategies in the book are meant to help you more effectively teach your curriculum and meet your district's and/or state's math standards.

- It contains a smorgasbord of strategies. Pick and choose the strategies you find most helpful.

- If your school uses *Step Up to Writing*, this book can help you reinforce the common language and common strategies that your students and fellow teachers are already using.

How do I use *Step Up to Writing in Math*?

- This book contains a collection of generic strategies that should be introduced, practiced, and used repeatedly at all grade levels.

- The book is not chronological. Use strategies on an "as needed" basis. Read through the book, scanning the strategies and the associated tools. Try a few strategies. Then add more to your repertoire to empower students to communicate about math.

- Strategies can be used together or separately.

- The book has three components: a Teacher's Guide, Math Tools, and a CD-ROM.

  - The Teacher's Guide includes directions and examples to aid in the instruction of each strategy.

  - The Math Tools, found at the end of each section, are included to facilitate the teaching and learning of a strategy. Tools are used by students with teachers as they learn, practice, and apply strategies. The tools are divided into three sections: Primary, Intermediate, and Secondary. Each tool is discretely labeled with a P, I, or S so that you can comfortably use samples from any level.

  - The CD-ROM contains 8.5" x 11" printable copies of all the tools that appear at the end of each section.

When do I use *Step Up to Writing in Math*?

- The strategies should be integrated into your math instruction.

- They can be used anytime that students are asked to communicate about math—on a daily basis or for special assignments and assessments.

- The strategies can work well at the beginning of a unit, during a unit, or at the end of a unit (as an assessment piece).

How do I integrate *Step Up to Writing in Math* into my curriculum?

- If your school has adopted *Step Up to Writing*, find out which strategies teachers use on a regular basis. Highlight these strategies in your *Step Up to Writing in Math* table of contents.

- Review your curriculum and math standards.

- Cross-reference your curriculum expectations and math standards with the table of contents in *Step Up to Writing in Math*.

- Make note of the strategies that will help you meet your expectations and standards.

- When possible, work with teachers in your department, at your grade level, or on your team to determine which strategies will have the greatest impact on student learning. In "*Step Up*" schools, some of the strategies you choose will be ones that your colleagues have already implemented and students have already used. Using common language and common strategies will empower you and your students.

- After experimenting with each strategy, meet with fellow teachers to share your successes, concerns, and modifications. It is easier to integrate new strategies into a curriculum when teachers work together to make decisions and share ideas.

- Use the strategies on a regular basis so that you and your students have ample opportunity to master them.

- Display a list of strategies you plan to teach and use. The list will serve as a reminder to you and your students.

How do I get started?

- If you work on a team, consider partnering with another content-area teacher to implement a strategy.

- Keep your end goal in mind when choosing a strategy.

  1. Start small, trying out one strategy at a time.

  2. Start with a simple strategy that you foresee using on a regular basis.

  3. Read the directions, choose the appropriate tools, and try out the strategy before introducing it to the class.

4. Tell students the purpose of the activity/strategy and make your expectations clear.

5. Use several examples and step-by-step directions to introduce the strategy.

6. Practice the strategy with your students, using easy or familiar content.

7. Once students demonstrate understanding, ask them to practice independently or with peers.

8. Assess whether the strategy has helped students reach the intended goal. Use assessments to inform instruction.

- Although *Step Up* strategies save time in the long run, they initially require an investment of time for modeling and guided practice. It is often necessary "to move slowly in the beginning in order to move quickly later on." No matter how simple a strategy may seem, students benefit from modeling and repeated practice.

Using *Step Up to Writing* in Math Materials

Teacher's Guide

- Your Teacher's Guide includes seven sections. Teachers often start with vocabulary and reading strategies because they take only a few minutes to introduce and can be applied to lessons throughout the year.

- Strategies in sections like the assessment section should be shared early in the year and reviewed often. This way students will master the strategies, feel confident, and be able to use them effectively during an assessment.

- The lesson samples and directions in the Teacher's Guide are generic and written to meet the needs of a large audience. There are no absolute right or wrong ways to introduce a strategy. Practicing a strategy on your own will help the most. As you learn the strategy, you will discover your best way of presenting it to your students.

Math Tools

- Your sets of Math Tools are included at the end of each section and on the CD found at the back of the book.

- Math Tools are labeled only with the letters P, I, and S—not with Primary, Intermediate, and Secondary. This makes it easy to use tools with students at any level. Primary tools, for example, are often appropriate (and fun) to share with older students. They learn concepts and methods quickly when examples are simple and easy to follow.

- Math Tools are used for initial instruction, practice, review, assessment, and application. Many tools can be copied to become a part of the students' math notebooks for use throughout the year.

CD-ROM

- Your CD-ROM contains all of the tools included with each section. These may be copied for students' use, turned into overhead transparencies to use during class lessons, and displayed using your computer.

Examples in the Teacher's Guide

- Examples for *Step Up to Writing in Math* strategies are included with directions in the Teacher's Guide. These examples vary. Some are secondary; others are more primary. The examples in the Teacher's Guide will help you see and learn each strategy quickly.

- You may decide to share these examples with your students, but their primary purpose is to help you as you try each strategy before teaching it to your students.

Examples on the Math Tools

- Examples for *Step Up to Writing in Math* strategies are marked with P for primary, I for intermediate, and S for secondary but can be used at any level if they fit your lesson and work with your students.

- Read through all examples a couple of times before you share them with students. This will help you anticipate questions that students might have. This will also help you make the best use of the tool itself.

Using *Step Up to Writing in Math* Teacher's Guide

SECTION **3** SUMMARIZING TEXT AND WRITING ABOUT GRAPHS

Each of the seven sections is clearly marked at the top of the page and is further divided into subsections by topic or concept. The subsections correspond to the labels on the accompanying Tools pages.

A strategy overview is provided at the beginning of each subsection. The overview includes a synopsis of the teaching strategy, a list of accompanying Tools pages, and connections to other aspects of the Teacher's Guide.

Examples illustrate the strategies and give readers a visual reference to guide classroom implementation.

3-5 Framed Paragraphs for Writing About Graphs

A framed paragraph can help students (both typical students and those with limited writing skills) learn to explain or analyze a graph, chart, table, or other graphical representation. Framed paragraphs can also save time. Teachers can create frames, make copies, and have them handy for responses when only a few minutes are available for writing.

Framed paragraphs are an effective way to give students more practice writing about graphs. They also work well for homework assignments and when students work with substitute teachers.

However, they should be used along with the strategies and tools from **3-1 Four-Step Summary Paragraph** and **3-3 Writing to Explain a Graph**. Framed paragraphs are not a substitute for direct instruction and guided practice. It is important that students learn to work independently as they interpret and write about graphs.

Use **Math Tool 3-5** as an example. Make an overhead transparency and student copies as needed. In a guided lesson, complete the work with input from students.

Tool S-3-5

Use the following examples as guides when you create your own framed paragraphs:

Math Tools are labeled in the text, below the thumbnail, and again at the end of each section.

Page 540 Line Graph

The line graph on page 540 shows _____
_____. First, _____
_____. It also
_____
_____. Finally, _____
_____.

The Dean Family Trip

The table showing the miles per gallon of gasoline that the Dean family used on their car trip gives _____. First, _____
_____. Second, _____
_____.

---

112   *Step Up to Writing in Math*

Before a Lesson and **During a Lesson**, included in each section, offer suggested steps for preparing and presenting each strategy.

Additional Ideas are included for each strategy to extend the students' learning and provide ideas for adaptations and accommodations.

During a Lesson

- Display Math Tool I-6b. Explain that concept maps show everything a student knows about a particular term. These maps also serve as an outline that students can use to write a definition paragraph of the term.

- Read through the example in Math Tool I-6b and the accompanying extended definition. Explain to students that once they have created a concept map, they can write a paragraph or short-report definition of the term based on the concept map. They should create sentences by using the information from each box to define and tell more about the concept or term.

- Using Math Tool I-6a, create a new concept map with help from students. Discuss the strategy with students, providing time for them to practice alone or with a peer, and then to share results. If time permits, turn the contents of the concept map into a detailed definition paragraph.

Additional Ideas

- Give students a partially completed concept map as an assessment. Ask them to fill in the remainder of the map, then write a detailed definition paragraph.

- Use Math Tool I-6a for individual or group quizzes.

- Offer an alternative concept map format, or ask students to design a new format. For example:

- Post concept maps on the wall; add to them as students progress in their understanding throughout a unit of study.

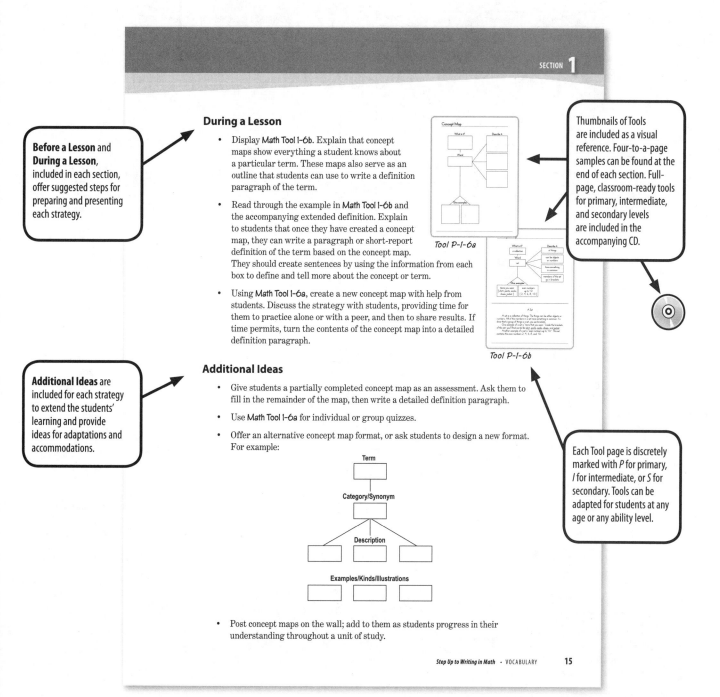

Tool P-I-6a

Tool P-I-6b

Thumbnails of Tools are included as a visual reference. Four-to-a-page samples can be found at the end of each section. Full-page, classroom-ready tools for primary, intermediate, and secondary levels are included in the accompanying CD.

Each Tool page is discretely marked with *P* for primary, *I* for intermediate, or *S* for secondary. Tools can be adapted for students at any age or any ability level.

Step Up to Writing in Math · VOCABULARY **15**

Using *Step Up to Writing in Math* Math Tools

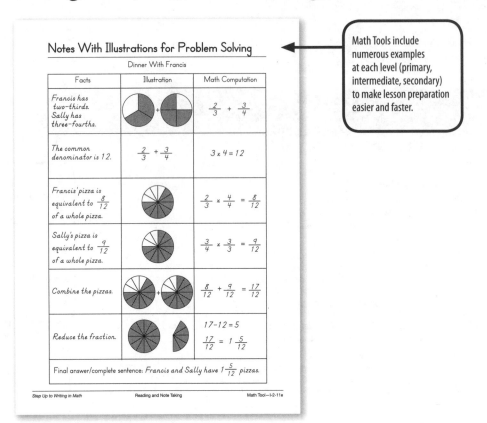

Notes With Illustrations for Problem Solving

Dinner With Francis

Facts	Illustration	Math Computation
Francis has two-thirds. Sally has three-fourths.		$\frac{2}{3}$ + $\frac{3}{4}$
The common denominator is 12.	$\frac{2}{3}$ + $\frac{3}{4}$	$3 \times 4 = 12$
Francis' pizza is equivalent to $\frac{8}{12}$ of a whole pizza.		$\frac{2}{3}$ × $\frac{4}{4}$ = $\frac{8}{12}$
Sally's pizza is equivalent to $\frac{9}{12}$ of a whole pizza.		$\frac{3}{4}$ × $\frac{3}{3}$ = $\frac{9}{12}$
Combine the pizzas.		$\frac{8}{12}$ + $\frac{9}{12}$ = $\frac{17}{12}$
Reduce the fraction.		$17-12 = 5$ $\frac{17}{12}$ = $1\frac{5}{12}$

Final answer/complete sentence: *Francis and Sally have $1\frac{5}{12}$ pizzas.*

Step Up to Writing in Math   Reading and Note Taking   Math Tool—I-2-11e

> Math Tools include numerous examples at each level (primary, intermediate, secondary) to make lesson preparation easier and faster.

Three-Column Notes for Problem Solving

Word Problem: _____

Question: _____

Steps (Tell what to do.)	Reasons (Explain why.)	Work (Solve the problem.)

Final answer in a complete sentence:

Math Tool—P-2-12a   Reading and Note Taking   Step Up to Writing in Math

> Primary Tools are intended for first- and second-grade readers and writers. All strategies, however, can be used orally with kindergarten students. They can learn and rehearse strategies orally in small- and whole-group guided lessons.

> Templates can be used for students, for overhead transparencies, or with computer projectors.

Using *Step Up to Writing* in Math Scoring Guides

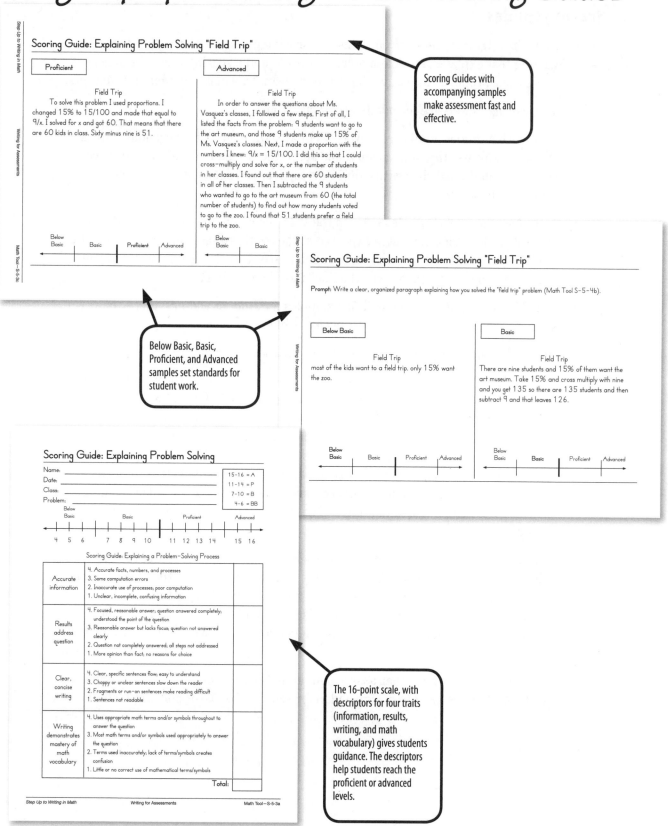

Scoring Guide: Explaining Problem Solving "Field Trip"

Proficient

Field Trip

To solve this problem I used proportions. I changed 15% to 15/100 and made that equal to 9/x. I solved for x and got 60. That means that there are 60 kids in class. Sixty minus nine is 51.

Advanced

Field Trip

In order to answer the questions about Ms. Vasquez's classes, I followed a few steps. First of all, I listed the facts from the problem: 9 students want to go to the art museum, and those 9 students make up 15% of Ms. Vasquez's classes. Next, I made a proportion with the numbers I knew: 9/x = 15/100. I did this so that I could cross-multiply and solve for x, or the number of students in her classes. I found out that there are 60 students in all of her classes. Then I subtracted the 9 students who wanted to go to the art museum from 60 (the total number of students) to find out how many students voted to go to the zoo. I found that 51 students prefer a field trip to the zoo.

> Scoring Guides with accompanying samples make assessment fast and effective.

> Below Basic, Basic, Proficient, and Advanced samples set standards for student work.

Scoring Guide: Explaining Problem Solving "Field Trip"

Prompt: Write a clear, organized paragraph explaining how you solved the "field trip" problem (Math Tool S-5-4b).

Below Basic

Field Trip

most of the kids want to a field trip. only 15% want the zoo.

Basic

Field Trip

There are nine students and 15% of them want the art museum. Take 15% and cross multiply with nine and you get 135 so there are 135 students and then subtract 9 and that leaves 126.

Scoring Guide: Explaining Problem Solving

Name: _____
Date: _____
Class: _____
Problem: _____

| 15-16 = A |
| 11-14 = P |
| 7-10 = B |
| 4-6 = BB |

Below Basic — Basic — Proficient — Advanced
4 5 6   7 8 9 10   11 12 13 14   15 16

Scoring Guide: Explaining a Problem-Solving Process

Accurate information	4. Accurate facts, numbers, and processes 3. Some computation errors 2. Inaccurate use of processes; poor computation 1. Unclear, incomplete, confusing information	
Results address question	4. Focused, reasonable answer; question answered completely; understood the point of the question 3. Reasonable answer but lacks focus; question not answered clearly 2. Question not completely answered; all steps not addressed 1. More opinion than fact; no reasons for choice	
Clear, concise writing	4. Clear, specific sentences flow; easy to understand 3. Choppy or unclear sentences slow down the reader 2. Fragments or run-on sentences make reading difficult 1. Sentences not readable	
Writing demonstrates mastery of math vocabulary	4. Uses appropriate math terms and/or symbols throughout to answer the question 3. Most math terms and/or symbols used appropriately to answer the question 2. Terms used inaccurately; lack of terms/symbols creates confusion 1. Little or no correct use of mathematical terms/symbols	
		Total:

Step Up to Writing in Math   Writing for Assessments   Math Tool—S-5-3a

> The 16-point scale, with descriptors for four traits (information, results, writing, and math vocabulary) gives students guidance. The descriptors help students reach the proficient or advanced levels.

Scoring Guides

- *Step Up to Writing in Math* contains two scoring guides: a scoring guide for writing that explains a problem-solving process and a scoring guide for generic paragraphs, reports, or essays that explain or analyze math content and concepts.

- The scoring guides are included in the Math Tools.

- The scoring guides at all three levels (Primary, Intermediate, Secondary) work the same way, use the same format, and serve the same purpose. The sentence structures and word choices are different to meet the needs of students at different grade levels.

- Introduce the scoring guides early in the year. They are simple to use and give students a clear idea of what is expected at the proficient and advanced levels. Let students know that all writers, at some point, are at the basic level but that you will be helping them reach "over the line" into the upper levels.

- With the scoring guides you will find samples for student writers; these show students what writing at all four levels looks like.

Note: Assessment for writing in math is important, but it does not need to be time consuming.

- The National Mathematics Advisory Panel (2008) encourages the use of formative assessment. "Formative assessment—the ongoing monitoring of student learning to inform instruction—is generally considered a hallmark of effective instruction in any discipline" (46). Instructions and additional suggested activities in the Teacher's Guide include numerous hints for assessing students quickly and effectively using things like index cards, self-stick notes, small strips of paper, and so on. This gives students a chance to respond quickly about their learning. Teachers can read responses quickly to see what students have and have not learned.

- The scoring guides for writing about content and writing to explain problem solving are designed to save teachers time and to give students the feedback they need to improve their work. These can be used for formal department, school, district, or state assessments, but they also work well for informal assessments in the classroom. Students can use these independently and when they work in small groups.

- The scoring guides and other assessment activities are good tools to use when grade-level teams meet to design a plan for school-wide assessment in math.

SECTION 1 VOCABULARY

Math teachers at all grade levels know that communicating about math is essential to mathematics education; improving students' math vocabulary is a crucial part of the curriculum. To effectively communicate about math, students need a solid grasp of math language. Having a strong math vocabulary gives them the power to understand and articulate math concepts.

According to the National Council of Teachers of Mathematics' *Principles and Standards for School Mathematics*, students in the early grades should be expected to communicate their math ideas using everyday words. However, as students progress, the teacher's role is to connect students' own language with more formal, sophisticated mathematical vocabulary.

The NCTM's communication standard stipulates that instructional programs should enable students "to use the language of mathematics to express mathematical ideas precisely" (60).* *Step Up to Writing in Math* supports this goal by providing strategies that help students master, retain, and use precise mathematical terms and concepts.

The communication standard also states that "instructional programs from prekindergarten through grade 12 should enable all students to communicate their mathematical thinking coherently and clearly to peers, teachers, and others" (60).* Strategies within Section 1 of *Step Up to Writing in Math* require students to speak and write about their understanding of math terms and concepts. They also ask students to use terminology in context—helping improve the precision and accuracy of their math vocabulary.

---

* Standards are listed with the permission of the National Council of Teachers of Mathematics (NCTM). NCTM does not endorse the content or validity of these alignments.

Step Up to Writing vocabulary strategies can be used informally as part of a math lesson or more formally when terms are introduced before a lesson. Pre-teaching vocabulary at the beginning of a unit helps students recognize what they already know (background knowledge) and helps them set a purpose for reading about and learning new words. Pre-teaching vocabulary will empower students to tackle math content and math problems.

Objectives

- Help students master and retain math vocabulary

- Increase students' ability to understand and communicate about math

- Build students' confidence and skills for writing about math

- Provide strategies for writing on math assessments

- Give students strategies to work with independently and with their peers

1-1 Math Vocabulary Lists

Students can use a math vocabulary list as a quick spelling reference or as a tool to remind them of math terminology. The goal is for students to refer to the list on a daily basis. As they do so, their spelling of common math terms will improve. More important, they will feel empowered to write; when they struggle to find the right math term, the list will help.

The use of math vocabulary lists will improve students' oral and written responses in class. It will also help on tests. Students are ordinarily not able to use word lists in formal assessments. However, if they refer to the list on a regular basis, they are more likely to remember each word and spell it correctly on exams. Also, the more comfortable students are with math terms, the more fluent their writing will be.

Before a Lesson

- Review the math vocabulary list on **Math Tools 1-1a** to **1-1c** for your grade level. Make overhead transparencies and student copies as needed. If these lists do not work with the content you are currently covering, or if they do not meet the needs of your students, add words to them or create your own vocabulary list.

- Consider making extra copies of your vocabulary list for students to use at home, to keep in the school's writing lab, to share when lists get lost, and/or to use in small-group sessions.

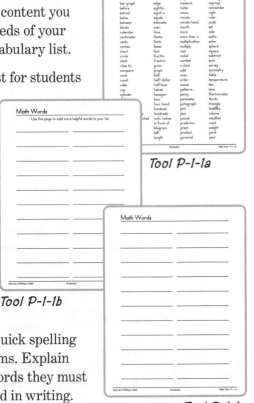

Tool P-1-1a

Tool P-1-1b

Tool P-1-1c

During a Lesson

- Give students directions for keeping math vocabulary lists.

- Hand out copies of the math vocabulary list you want them to use. Read through the list with students, emphasizing the pronunciation of each word.

- Explain to students that they can use this list as a quick spelling reference and as a reminder of acceptable math terms. Explain that these are their non-negotiable math words—words they must know how to spell and use in context, both orally and in writing.

- To build students' confidence, have them peruse the list again to determine how many words they already understand and know how to spell.

- Give students time to ask questions. Encourage them, and remind them that professional writers rely on books and lists of words to help them complete their work.

- Tell students that even though they will not be able to use their vocabulary list on formal assessments, they will remember and be able to use more math terms if they refer to their list regularly.

- Make plans for adding words to the list.

Additional Ideas

- Throughout the year, model the precise use of math language in your questions and explanations. You may have to use informal language from time to time, but always use it in conjunction with formal math language. The more students are exposed to math terminology, the more likely they are to use and understand it.

- Require students to use precise math language when they explain their thinking, reasoning, and processes. Once again, they may need to give explanations in their own words at first. Show them how to translate their words into math language.

- Ask students to check the list periodically to see whether they need to review any words for spelling or meaning.

- Create a word chart for the particular words associated with the unit you are teaching. The words on this chart will change from unit to unit, but all will remain on students' overarching math vocabulary list throughout the year.

- Consider creating math vocabulary notebooks. Students are more likely to learn, use, and remember math terms when they must keep all of the vocabulary organized and handy as a reference. Students will be less likely to "throw away this week's list" if they are required to keep and use notebooks.

- Encourage writing across content areas. Share the math vocabulary lists with science and social studies teachers. The more students refer to the list the more they master these terms.

1-2 Tips for Introducing New Words

These simple tips for introducing new terms in the math classroom will help students make the words their own.

Before a Lesson

- Develop a system for students to record new math terms and their meanings in their math vocabulary notebook.

- Select words that are critical for student understanding of the current lesson or unit.

- Write words on the board or overhead projector. Breaking new words into syllables can be helpful, as small chunks of information are easier to remember. Breaking words into syllables will help students with punctuation and spelling. For example:

pro por tion	prop er ty	pol y gon
pro duct	pe rim e ter	par al lel o gram

- Look for words with root words. Point out the root word, suffix, and/or prefix.

During a Lesson

- Pronounce new words several times, and ask students to echo your pronunciation. Familiarity with the pronunciation of math terms makes students more confident when they answer questions, give responses, and participate in discussions.

- Ask students to record the new words in their math vocabulary notebook.

- Ask students whether they are already familiar with the terms being introduced. Ask them to share their knowledge with the whole group.

- Provide examples of the new terms in context. Flyers that come with telephone, electric, gas, or water bills often contain math terms. You may also be able to find math vocabulary words in newspapers, magazines, advertisements, catalogs, and other literature. Ask students to try to figure out the meaning of a word based on its use in these materials.

- Remind students that they will be expected to spell and use math terms correctly.

1-3 Breaking Down Definitions

This strategy helps students make sense of definitions by breaking them down into smaller chunks that are easy to read and remember. It is useful for comprehending and mastering new terms.

Breaking down a definition involves four steps:

1. Print **Math Tool 1-3a**, or else fold notebook paper into three columns, with the label "Math Term (Word)" above the first column, "Definition" at the top of the middle column, and "Example" above the last column.

2. In the first column, write the term that students are learning.

3. Outline the definition in the second column using dashes and dots along with words or short phrases. If the word you're defining is a noun, the first item in the definition breakdown (identified with a dash) should be the category of the word; if the term you're defining is a verb, the first item should be a synonym (a word that means the same thing). The other words in the middle column explain the specifics of the word.

4. Add an example of the term in the third column. (Examples work well; math sentences, personal connections, and illustrations are also effective.)

So, for example, to break down the term fraction, you would begin with the definition: *A fraction is the ratio or comparison of two numbers, written as A/B. The value of A is called the numerator, and the value of B is the denominator. The value of B can never be zero.*

The key components of this definition could be broken down as:

Math Term (Word)	Definition	Example

fraction	- ratio or comparison
	  • of two numbers
	  • written as $\frac{A}{B}$
	- value of A
	  • called the numerator
	- value of B
	  • called the denominator
	  • can't equal zero	

Similarly, to break down the verb *to estimate*, you would start with its definition: *To estimate means to make a good guess, a guess based on knowledge, a guess that is reasonable.*

Then you would pull out the key components:

Math Term (Word)	Definition	Example

to estimate	- to guess
	  • using knowledge
	  • being reasonable	

After you've filled in the third column, these broken-down definitions would look something like:

Math Term (Word)	Definition	Example

fraction	- ratio or comparison
	  • of two numbers
	  • written as $\frac{A}{B}$
	
	- value of A
	  • called the numerator
	
	- value of B
	  • called the denominator
	  • can't equal zero
		$\frac{1}{4}$
		
		→ $\frac{2}{8}$
		
		$\frac{4}{16}$ ←

to estimate	- to guess
	  • using knowledge
	  • being reasonable
		I estimate (guess) that there are 5,000 people in the stands.

Before a Lesson

- Make overhead transparencies and student copies of Math Tools 1-3a, 1-3b, and 1-3c as needed. Read and review these tools.

- Select words to use for demonstration and modeling.

- Write the words and definitions on a transparency or chart paper for use during demonstrations.

- If you use words from the students' textbook glossary, make them available or remind students to bring them to class.

During a Lesson

- Show students several words and their definitions from class dictionaries or textbooks. Emphasize how difficult it might be to read and remember long, detailed definitions.

- Tell students that breaking down definitions is a reading strategy that will help them read and remember definitions, both in math class and in their other classes. Explain that many people need help learning to read definitions.

- Display **Math Tools 1-3b** and **1-3c**. Explain the three columns in the examples of broken-down definitions. Explain that remembering smaller chunks of information is easier than remembering complete sentences. Tell students that you will help them learn how to set up definitions in this way.

- Using a word that you have selected, teach students the process for breaking down definitions. Read the definition with the class. Model for students how to find the category for the word (or a synonym if the term is a verb or adjective). Explain that the category or synonym is the most important part of the definition because it tells what type of math term the word you're defining is. The category for *cow* would be *animal*; the category for *formula* would be *method*; the category for *inch* would be *unit* of measure.

- Review the process with another math term. Share several more examples in a guided lesson format, asking students to provide the information for the three columns.

- Ask students to explain the meaning of words that you have broken down. Have them use the information in the broken-down definitions as a way to check the effectiveness of this strategy.

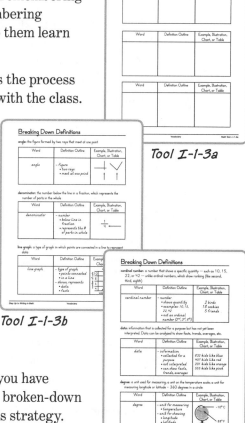

Tool I-1-3a

Tool I-1-3b

Tool I-1-3c

At first, breaking down definitions will take time. However, after only a few sessions, students become proficient and capable of participating in class demonstrations. As their skills improve, students can take an active role. Give pairs of students two or three words and an overhead transparency with an overhead marker. Have these small groups prepare their words in the Breaking Down Definitions style, and share them with the class. Provide guidance, directions, and encouragement as they share. Model this strategy and help clarify terms each time new vocabulary is introduced. Have students complete vocabulary definitions independently only when they have mastered this skill.

Note: Another way to use categories to help students learn vocabulary is to help them separate a list of terms into categories. This will help them see connections and relationships.

Additional Ideas

- Set the expectation that students should record vocabulary words and their definitions in the Breaking Down Definitions format in their math vocabulary notebooks.

- Remind students that they will be expected to use their broken-down definitions to explain the meaning of words in complete thoughts.

- Teach students how to use the three-column notes from this strategy to study their vocabulary words. Just fold column three over column two to create a study guide.

- Have students practice articulating definitions. Ask them to form two concentric circles, with the same number of people in each circle. Instruct one circle to stand still (the listeners) while the other rotates (the speakers). Ask the students to rotate. When you say "Stop!" the rotating students must explain the meaning of a word to the students across from them.

- Ask students for ideas for using or improving the Breaking Down Definitions strategy.

1-4 Homonyms, Homophones, and Homographs

Use homonyms, homophones, and homographs to help students see the connections and differences between words they use in everyday life and words they use in math.

EXAMPLES:

Homonyms are two words that are identical in spelling and pronunciation but different in meaning.	• palm (tree) and palm (of your hand) • loaf (of bread) and loaf (to be lazy)
Homophones are words that are alike in pronunciation but different in meaning and sometimes spelling.	• night and knight • here and hear
Homographs are words that are alike in spelling but different in meaning and pronunciation.	• bass and bass • wound and wound

Looking at math vocabulary words and their homonyms, homophones, or homographs can help students remember new words.

Before a Lesson

- Determine which words you would like students to compare. Students need to be familiar with the definitions of the words in order to compare them. Select words from the students' textbooks, the list provided in **Math Tool 1-1**, or the list below.

addition	base	commission
cone	constant	cube
difference	digit	face
figure	interest	odd
pattern	pie	plane
powers	slope	scale
order	range	set
sign	table	yard

- Make an overhead transparency and student copies of **Math Tool 1-4** as needed.

- Jot down examples to use as you demonstrate the strategy. For instance:

mean	In math, the mean is the average of a set of numbers. In everyday life, "mean" can refer to being rude or cruel.
median	In math, the median is the middle number in a series of numbers. In everyday life, the median is the concrete structure in the middle of the road.
mode	In math, the mode is the number that occurs the most times in a series of numbers. In everyday life, "mode" can refer to the manner in which you do something or to a popular style or fashion.

- If appropriate, ask students to note homonyms, homophones, or homographs in the third column when breaking down definitions.

- Consider adding an art element to your lesson. Ask students to create sketches showing the difference between the ways a word can be used. For example, students might create mini posters showing the difference between a table at home and a table created for a math lesson.

During a Lesson

- Review the meanings of the terms homonym, homophone, and homograph.

- Display **Math Tool 1-4.** Share the example(s) on the tool. Ask students to suggest other math terms that are also everyday terms.

- Using one of the pairs of homonyms, homophones, or homographs that you have selected, demonstrate how you would write about the two words.

- Take this strategy further by showing students how they can draw analogies to show similarities and differences between the two terms. For example, they can master the definition of median by remembering that it is the "middle" number, just as the concrete median is in the "middle" of the road. Similarly, a student can use the word "popular" from the everyday meaning of mode to remember that the mode is the most "popular" number in a series.

- Give students time to practice this skill individually or with partners. Provide time for them to share and to discuss how homonyms, homophones, and homographs can help them remember math vocabulary.

Tool S-1-4

1-5 **Word Webs**

A word web illustrates the connections between different math terms.

Here is an example of a word web that uses the word *triangles* as a starting point:

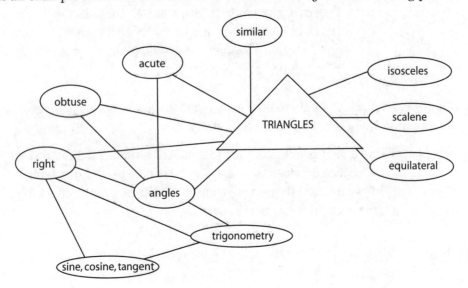

Use word webs at the beginning of a unit to tap into students' prior knowledge. Use them at the end of a unit to allow students to demonstrate what they know and to recognize relationships among the math terminology.

Before a Lesson

- Determine which concept or word you will have students walk through in your demonstration.

- Draw an example of another word web (or use the triangles example) on chart paper or the board.

- Designate space for other word webs that you will create during the demonstration.

During a Lesson

- Model the Word Web strategy by explaining the example you have already created.

- With help from students, create a new word web based on a term that they are studying or will cover in an upcoming unit.

- Once the web is complete, ask students to give their reasons for adding words to the web or placing words in a particular place. Encourage student participation by asking leading questions. For example:

Teacher	Why did you add the word "angles" to the web?
Student	I added the word "angles" because triangles are made up of angles.

- Encourage students to ask for clarification regarding entries in the web. (See **Section 4-6 Empowering Students With Questioning Skills** for ideas to use to empower students to ask questions.)

Additional Ideas

- Use word webs at the end of a unit to determine which concepts you need to revisit.

- Ask students to create word webs in small groups, share ideas, and explain the rationale behind their entries.

- Ask students to reorganize an existing word web, grouping related entries into clusters to show how they are related. Again, ask students for their reasoning.

- Encourage students to add drawings, symbols, and color to enhance the word webs.

1-6 Concept Maps

This strategy enables students to demonstrate a thorough understanding of a concept or term. A concept map places a word, its category (for nouns) or a synonym (for verbs), descriptive terms, and examples in a chart-like format.

From the concept map, students can write an extended definition of the term. For example:

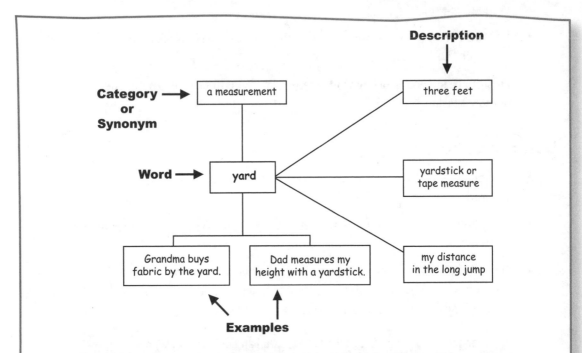

Category or Synonym → a measurement

Description → three feet

Word → yard

yardstick or tape measure

my distance in the long jump

Grandma buys fabric by the yard.

Dad measures my height with a yardstick.

Examples

A yard is one way to measure. A yard is three feet long. You can measure a yard with a yardstick or a tape measure. A yard is about as far as I can jump in the long jump in gym.

When Grandma buys fabric at the store to make curtains or a dress, she asks for the fabric in yards. The clerk cuts just as many yards as she needs.

When Dad measures how tall I am, he uses a yardstick. A yardstick shows the feet and inches on it, and it is exactly one yard long.

Concept maps can help students understand and retain new concepts by giving them a visual process for analyzing vocabulary. Students can build them over time or use them at the end of a unit of study to review key concepts. They also work well for a quick assessment.

Before a Lesson

- Make overhead transparencies and student copies of Math Tools 1-6a and 1-6b as needed.

- Select which math terms you will use during the demonstration.

During a Lesson

- Display **Math Tool 1-6b**. Explain that concept maps show everything a student knows about a particular term. These maps also serve as an outline that students can use to write a definition paragraph of the term.

- Read through the example in **Math Tool 1-6b** and the accompanying extended definition. Explain to students that once they have created a concept map, they can write a paragraph or short-report definition of the term based on the concept map. They should create sentences by using the information from each box to define and tell more about the concept or term.

- Using **Math Tool 1-6a**, create a new concept map with help from students. Discuss the strategy with students, providing time for them to practice alone or with a peer, and then to share results. If time permits, turn the contents of the concept map into a detailed definition paragraph.

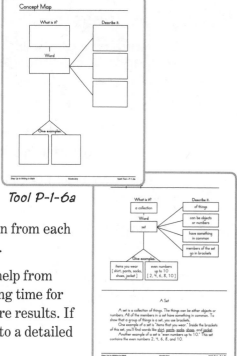

Tool P-1-6a

Tool P-1-6b

Additional Ideas

- Give students a partially completed concept map as an assessment. Ask them to fill in the remainder of the map, then write a detailed definition paragraph.

- Use **Math Tool 1-6a** for individual or group quizzes.

- Offer an alternative concept map format, or ask students to design a new format. For example:

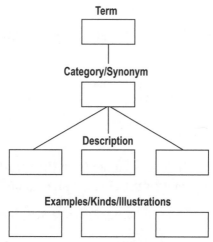

- Post concept maps on the wall; add to them as students progress in their understanding throughout a unit of study.

1-7 Word Banks

A word bank is a set of related terms grouped together in a bubble. In this strategy, the teacher gives students a word bank of related terms; then students use the words from the bubble to write sentences that demonstrate their knowledge and understanding of that term or concept.

Word banks help students see relationships between words. They also give students a chance to practice using math language to define terms or explain processes.

Use this strategy for assignments or assessments after students are familiar with the vocabulary in a unit.

Examples:

number
divided
division

dividend:

The dividend is the number that is divided in a division problem. For example, in the division problem 12 divided by 3, the number 12 is the dividend.

comparison
written
quantities

ratio:

A ratio is a comparison of two quantities by division. A ratio can be written in words (two to three), with a colon (2:3), or as a fraction ($\frac{2}{3}$).

Before a Lesson

- Review the examples of word banks on **Math Tools 1-7b** and **1-7c**.

- Make overhead transparencies and student copies of **Math Tools 1-7a, 1-7b,** and **1-7c**, as needed.

- Select banks of words to use for demonstration. Choose words that all students know and can use comfortably when you are introducing this strategy. Keep in mind that the number of words in a bank can vary; choose examples that fit your students and their ability levels.

- Write two or three word bank assignments on the board or on an overhead transparency to use for demonstration, modeling, and/or practice. For example:

  - Using the terms in the word bank, define *symmetry*.

  - Using the terms in the word bank, explain how to multiply fractions.

During a Lesson

- Display **Math Tools 1-7b** and **1-7c**. Explain the word bank activity and describe the examples.

- Using the transparency for **Math Tool 1-7a**, write a word bank example for students.

- Have students use **Math Tool 1-7a**; ask them to copy one of the word bank assignments from the board. Have them complete the word bank response and share their results.

- Discuss the activity and its effectiveness. Give students hints for writing better responses. Encourage them to write in complete sentences, use all words from the bank, and include examples when appropriate. Explain that writing a response that includes every word from the word bank does not guarantee success. Using each word in a way that illustrates its meaning or purpose is important, as is being mathematically precise.

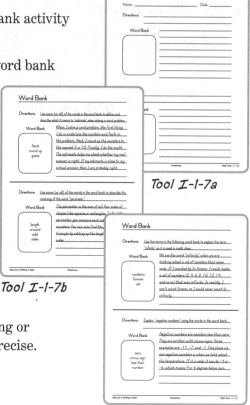

Tool I-1-7a

Tool I-1-7b

Tool I-1-7c

Additional Ideas

- Create a word bank that includes words that don't belong. Challenge students to find them.

- Ask students to create word bank assignments for a unit of study or for their peers to complete. Suggest that they refer to their broken-down definitions to find groups of words to fill the bubbles. (See **1–3 Breaking Down Definitions**.)

- Give students a list of terms (see **Math Tool 1-1** for vocabulary words that are good word bank candidates) and a set of empty word bank bubbles. Ask them to sort the terms into appropriate bubbles. Once they are finished sorting, ask the students to justify their grouping of terms.

- Challenge students further by using the Circle Once, Underline Twice strategy with the word bank. Circle the category or synonym in the definition and underline at least two distinguishing characteristics. Put the circled and underlined words in the word bank bubble in any order. For example:

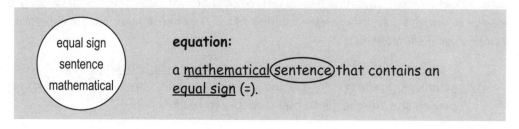

1-8 Meaningful Sentences

A meaningful sentence "paints a picture/image" in the reader's mind, and it demonstrates the writer's mastery of the word (C.I.R.C. 1989). Writing meaningful sentences that include vocabulary words helps students better understand and remember those words. This strategy encourages students to use their knowledge and imagination to create sentences that demonstrate their mastery of math terms. Use the Meaningful Sentences strategy with words that students have already studied but that are hard to remember or commonly misused.

Meaningful sentences show a vocabulary term and its definition in context. Students can learn which sentences are meaningful by comparing the four types of sentences that are most frequently written as part of vocabulary lessons:

- **Pointless sentence.** This sentence has no value because it does not reflect the meaning of the word. For example, a pointless sentence for the vocabulary term *add* might look like:

  > I can <u>add</u>.

- **Replace (substitution) sentence.** This kind of sentence may sound good. In fact, it may even be long and detailed. However, it does not demonstrate an understanding of the vocabulary word. If another word were substituted for the vocabulary word, the sentence could still make sense. For example:

  > In math class yesterday, I <u>added</u> lots of numbers to find an answer.

- **Dictionary sentence.** This is a sentence that simply restates the definition of the term. A student can write a good dictionary sentence and still not understand the meaning of the word. For example:

  > To <u>add</u> means to combine the value of two or more numbers to find a total value.

- **Meaningful sentence.** A meaningful sentence (a sentence filled with meaning) demonstrates understanding of the vocabulary word and paints a picture or creates a "mind movie" for the reader. Students who write meaningful sentences convince the reader that they understand and can correctly use the vocabulary word. For example:

  > Jerry scratched his head twice as he <u>added</u> his phone bill, credit card bill, insurance payment, and health club dues; he wondered whether the total would exceed his weekly paycheck.

Note: Meaningful sentences can also show the word and its definition in context. Students can circle the vocabulary term, then underline all the words and phrases in the sentence that help define it. For example, if the vocabulary word were *interest*, a meaningful sentence might look like this:

> As Beth <u>deposited</u> another <u>$85</u> into her <u>savings account</u>, she hoped that the bank's (interest) rate would <u>increase</u> so that she would have <u>enough money</u> when she turned 16 to buy a good used car.

This exercise helps students write meaningful sentences and helps them determine whether a sentence is meaningful, or whether it falls into one of the other sentence categories.

Before the Lesson

- Select words to use for demonstration and modeling.

- Practice creating and analyzing your own meaningful sentences.

- Make overhead transparencies and student copies of **Math Tools 1-8a** to **1-8e**, as necessary.

Tool S-1-8a

During a Lesson

- Explain that the meaningful sentence strategy is a way of setting a high standard for writing sentences for math vocabulary terms.

- Display **Math Tools 1-8b** and **1-8c**. Show students the examples of the four usual types of vocabulary sentences. Explain why a meaningful sentence is the most effective way of demonstrating mastery of a math term. Tell students that dictionary sentences can be deceiving. Sometimes people may be able to write a dictionary sentence that sounds good, even if they do not really understand the definition of the vocabulary word. Meaningful sentences, on the other hand, show mastery and understanding.

Tool S-1-8b

Tool S-1-8c

- Using **Math Tool 1-8a**, demonstrate the four-sentence approach to writing a meaningful sentence. Define the terms as you write, answering questions and clarifying the differences among the four sentence types.

Tool S-1-8d

- Have students practice (alone or in groups) using **Math Tool 1-8a**. Remind them to use relevant words from the definition to help them create their meaningful sentences.

Tool S-1-8e

- Present **Math Tools 1-8d** and **1-8e** as an alternative method for writing and evaluating meaningful sentences. Share several examples of this approach. Help students compare the two methods.

- Point out that the goal for both methods is to improve vocabulary sentence writing. Expect meaningful sentences whenever you ask students to write using math terms.

Additional Idea

- Create your own fill-in-the-blank meaningful sentences. Share them aloud or in a written form, leaving out the math terms. Ask students to suggest words for the blank spaces and explain their rationale. Use terms that students are currently studying in class. For example:

> On the roller rink floor, the _____ of the chain of children grew as one more person attached himself to the game of crack the whip. (radius)

> In the not-so-distant future, a high-speed train may travel on a track that takes the shortest possible path from the North Pole to the South Pole, stopping briefly to catch a glimpse of the center of the earth. The train will travel along the earth's _____. (diameter)

> The skateboarding math whiz looked at the half-pipe and realized that the geometric shape he was skating on was a _____. (parabola)

1-9 Word Maps

Use a word map when you want students to demonstrate and apply everything that they know about a word. Once students learn the parts of a word map and practice with their classmates, they feel empowered to tackle word maps on their own. You can encourage students to use word maps whenever they're confronting a new math term, whether or not you've formally given them a word map as an assignment. Students who master this technique, which ties together several of the strategies presented in other sections of this book, will not only be better at building their math vocabulary, but will also be better at learning and retaining words outside of the math classroom.

A word map has four quadrants. In the top left quadrant is the word's broken-down definition, attained using the strategy presented in **1-3 Breaking Down Definitions**.

In the bottom left quadrant, students write a sentence demonstrating how the vocabulary word connects to their own life. For example:

> **Perimeter**—My uncle asked me to help him install new baseboards in his dining area. We had to figure the <u>perimeter</u> of the room, subtracting for openings for the doors, before he headed out to buy the materials.

Average—Last week my mom kept track of how many diapers my twin sisters used each day. She recorded the number every evening for a week because we needed to know the <u>average</u> number of diapers they use in a day. We are planning a camping trip in the hills where there are no stores, so we want to be prepared.

In the top right quadrant of the word map, students provide pictures or examples of the word. The pictures, illustrations, and/or examples should be clear and helpful to students. Students should always be able to explain their drawings.

Finally, in the bottom right quadrant of the word map, students create a sentence using the word. They can use the lessons from **1-8 Meaningful Sentences** to write quality sentences for their word maps.

Here is what a word map looks like:

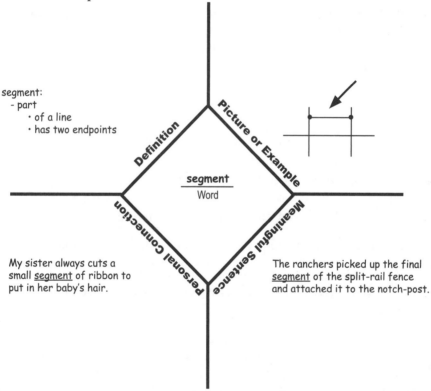

Before a Lesson

- Review strategies **1-3 Breaking Down Definitions** and **1-8 Meaningful Sentences**.

- Come up with some examples of connections you can make between math vocabulary and your own life. Seeing your examples will help students make their own personal connections.

- Make student copies and transparencies of Math Tools 1-9a, 1-9b, and 1-9c, as necessary.

During a Lesson

- Start by reviewing the strategy **1-3 Breaking Down Definitions** for student review.

- Display **Math Tools 1-9b** and **1-9c**. Explain the contents and intent of each section in these word maps. Take time for questions. If applicable, ask students to describe other word maps that they have completed in other classes.

- Using **Math Tool 1-9a**, create a word map with the class. Stop and ask for input. Explain each step you take; give students reasons for your choices. Reread and discuss the final product.

- Ask students to complete a word map of their own using **Math Tool 1-9a**. Students enjoy working with peers on this activity. Share and display the students' work.

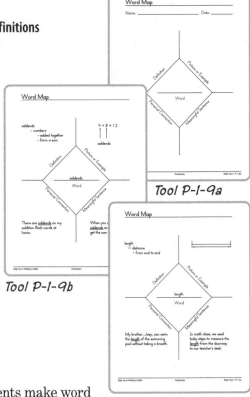

Tool P-1-9a

Tool P-1-9b

Tool P-1-9c

Additional Ideas

- Before or during a unit, have small groups of students make word maps for important terms. Have students re-create the word map form on large pieces of paper. Encourage high-quality work (printing, arrangement, accuracy, design, and color). Display the word maps as a way to help students learn the words and prepare for assessments.

- Create word maps in the computer lab, using graphics programs that are available for students.

- Challenge students to create a word map style of their own and teach it to their classmates.

1-10 Riddles

Have some fun! You and your students will enjoy writing and solving riddles. Use this strategy to write riddles about the words or concepts you are covering in class. Creating and solving riddles is a great way to increase student retention of the meaning of words or concepts.

Riddles meet five standard criteria:

1. Riddles are written in first person: I have all the right angles.

2. Riddles give facts: My sides are all the same length.

3. Riddles give hints: You may find me on cookies, candy bars, and crackers.

4. Riddles all end in the same question: What (or who) am I?

5. Riddles often have only four lines but can have five or six if needed.

In addition to being fun, writing a riddle about a word or concept requires knowledge, the ability to synthesize information, and creativity. It is actually quite challenging.

Before a Lesson

- Review **Math Tool 1-10a**.

- Make an overhead transparency and student copies of **Math Tool 1-10a** as needed.

- Create other riddles to share during class demonstrations of this strategy.

- Plan for a way to collect and keep all riddles for use throughout the year. (For example, you could format riddles using a word processing program, have students illustrate or decorate them, and then store the final products in a three-ring binder for all to enjoy.)

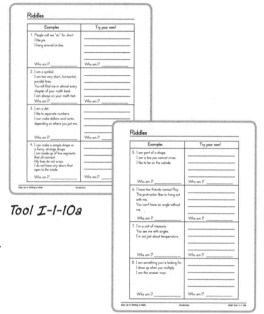

Tool I-1-10a

Tool I-1-10b

During a Lesson

- Ask students to solve a riddle at the beginning of class to get them thinking about math.

- Explain the five characteristics of a riddle pattern by dissecting one of the riddles on **Math Tools 1-10a** and **1-10b** or a riddle of your own.

- Demonstrate the pattern by writing a riddle with or for the class.

- Give students time to try their hand at riddle writing; provide suggestions and support as needed.

- Consider giving students riddles with only a few of the lines completed. Ask students to complete the riddles.

- Share successes, and give students time to help one another. Often students can write part of a riddle but get stuck. Peer support and input helps.

Answers to the example riddles on Math Tools 1-10a and 1-10b

Primary:	Intermediate:	Secondary:
1. sum	1. circumference	1. exponent
2. inch	2. equal sign	2. the number i
3. octagon	3. decimal point	3. slope
4. centimeter	4. polygon	4. mode
5. difference	5. edge	5. percent
6. calculator	6. vertex	6. multiple
	7. degree	7. perimeter
	8. product	8. radian

Additional Ideas

- Help students find ideas for a riddle by creating a word web (**1-5 Word Webs**) related to words the students are learning.

- Provide lists of math words that your students know and that you think will help them create a riddle. Consider using **Math Tools 1-1a, 1-1b, and 1-1c** as resources.

- Help students start a riddle; ask them to finish it.

- Share (and have students share) riddles often to keep students thinking and to serve as models for student writing.

- Involve family members and/or the school's administrative support team.

- Keep the process fun; expect and celebrate success.

- Help students create a book of riddles, and illustrate their riddles.

Math Tools: Primary

Math Words

above	division	less than <	quart
add	dollar	liter	quarter
addend	dollar sign	mark	quarter hour
after	doubles	maybe	rectangle
bar graph	edge	measure	regroup
before	eighths	meter	remainder
behind	equal =	minus	right
below	equals	minute	ruler
between	estimate	minute hand	scale
blocks	even	month	set
calendar	face	more	side
centimeter	factor	more than >	sixths
cents	facts	multiplication	solve
certain	fewer	multiply	sphere
chart	foot	next	square
circle	fourths	nickel	subtract
clock	fraction	number	sum
close to	gram	o'clock	survey
compare	graph	odd	symmetry
cone	half	ones	table
count	half–dollar	order	temperature
cube	half hour	ounce	ten
cup	halves	patterns	tens
cylinder	hexagon	penny	thermometer
date	hour	perimeter	thirds
decimal point	hour hand	pictograph	triangle
degree	hundred	pint	twelfths
degrees Celsius	hundreds	plus	volume
degrees Fahrenheit	inch, inches	pound	weather
difference	in front of	prediction	week
digit	kilogram	prism	weight
dime	left	product	yard
divide	length	pyramid	year

Step Up to Writing in Math   Vocabulary   Math Tool—P-1-1a

Math Tool P-1-1a

Math Words

Use this page to add more helpful words to your list.

_____   _____

_____   _____

_____   _____

_____   _____

_____   _____

_____   _____

_____   _____

_____   _____

_____   _____

_____   _____

_____   _____

_____   _____

_____   _____

Step Up to Writing in Math   Vocabulary   Math Tool—P-1-1b

Math Tool P-1-1b

Math Words

_____   _____

_____   _____

_____   _____

_____   _____

_____   _____

_____   _____

_____   _____

_____   _____

_____   _____

_____   _____

Step Up to Writing in Math   Vocabulary   Math Tool—P-1-1c

Math Tool P-1-1c

Breaking Down Definitions

Name: _____   Date: _____

Word	Definition	Example

Word	Definition	Example

Step Up to Writing in Math   Vocabulary   Math Tool—P-1-3a

Math Tool P-1-3a

Math Tools: Primary *(continued)*

Breaking Down Definitions

sum: the number that is the answer when you solve an addition problem

Word	Definition	Example
sum	– number • answer • in addition	4 + 4 ——→ 8

minus sign: the symbol that means subtract in a math problem

Word	Definition	Example
minus sign	– symbol • means subtract	12 ——→ – 10 2

week: a unit of measurement for time; the part of the month that is seven days in a row

Word	Definition	Example
week	– unit of measure • of time • part of a month • 7 days in a row	S M T W Th F S

Math Tool P-1-3b

Breaking Down Definitions

place value: the value of where a particular digit is in a number, such as units, tens, hundreds

Word	Definition	Example
place value	– value • of where digit is in a number • units, tens, hundreds	In the number 352, the place value of 5 is "tens." 5 x 10 = 50

square: a four–sided shape where all sides are straight and have equal length

Word	Definition	Example
square	– shape • 4 straight sides • all sides have equal length	□

volume: the amount of space an object takes up; capacity

Word	Definition	Example
volume	– amount • of space an object takes up • capacity	

Math Tool P-1-3c

Words That Look and/or Sound Alike

Name: _____ Date: _____

Word	How might you use this word in everyday life?	How might you use this word in math?
1. yard	Last Saturday I helped my grandfather plant flowers in his yard.	My partner and I used a yardstick to measure the height of the bookshelves and our teacher's desk. The shelves were exactly a yard, or three feet, high. The desk was four feet high. This is one foot more than a yard.
2. cup	When I pushed my grandma's china cup off the table, it broke into many pieces.	The chef needed a cup of flour for his recipe.
3.		

Math Tool P-1-4

Concept Map

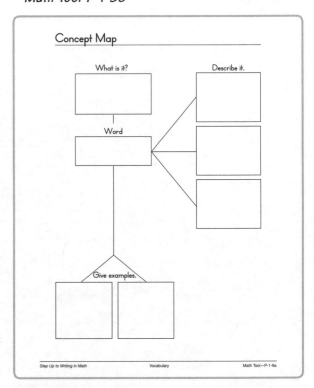

Math Tool P-1-6a

Math Tools: Primary *(continued)*

Concept Map

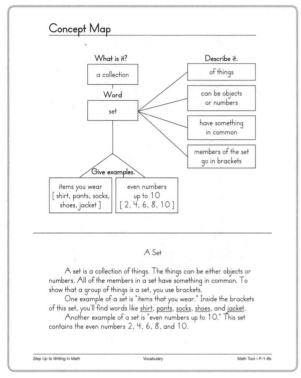

What is it?

a collection

Word

set

Describe it.

of things

can be objects or numbers

have something in common

members of the set go in brackets

Give examples.

items you wear
[shirt, pants, socks, shoes, jacket]

even numbers up to 10
[2, 4, 6, 8, 10]

A Set

A set is a collection of things. The things can be either objects or numbers. All of the members in a set have something in common. To show that a group of things is a set, you use brackets.

One example of a set is "items that you wear." Inside the brackets of this set, you'll find words like <u>shirt</u>, <u>pants</u>, <u>socks</u>, <u>shoes</u>, and <u>jacket</u>.

Another example of a set is "even numbers up to 10." This set contains the even numbers 2, 4, 6, 8, and 10.

Math Tool P-1-6b

Word Bank

Name: _____ Date: _____

Directions: _____
_____

Word Bank

_____
_____
_____
_____
_____
_____

Directions: _____

Word Bank

_____
_____
_____
_____
_____
_____

Math Tool P-1-7a

Word Bank

Directions: Use the words from the word bank to explain how to tell time on a clock.

Word Bank

o'clock
minute hand
hour hand
half hour

When the hour hand and minute hand are both on the 12, then it is 12 o'clock. When the hour hand is on the 12 and the minute hand is on the 6, then a half hour has passed and it is half past 12.

Directions: Use the words from the word bank to explain how to combine coins to equal 50 cents.

Word Bank

nickel
quarter
dime
equals

I could make 50 cents in a few ways using nickels, dimes, and quarters. Two quarters equals 50 cents. Five dimes equals 50 cents. Ten nickels equals 50 cents. Finally, I could mix different coins to make 50 cents.

Math Tool P-1-7b

Word Bank

Directions: Use the words in the word bank to describe how to make a pattern.

Word Bank

arrange
rule
shapes
objects

To make a pattern, you first have to make a rule for the pattern. For example, the rule might be ABBABBABB. Then you need to pick the shapes or objects you are going to use to make the pattern. After that, you arrange the shapes or objects using the rule.

Directions: Use the words in the word bank to define "symmetry."

Word Bank

shape
characteristic
mirror image
line

Symmetry is a characteristic of a shape. A shape is symmetrical if the left half is a mirror image of the right half. To test whether a shape is symmetrical, you can draw a line down the center of it and fold it in half. If both sides are the same, it is symmetrical.

Math Tool P-1-7c

Math Tools: Primary (continued)

Math Tool P-1-8a

Meaningful Sentences

Name: _____ Date: _____

Word: _____

Pointless Sentence	
Replace (substitution) Sentence	
Dictionary Sentence	
Meaningful Sentence	

Math Tool P-1-8b

Meaningful Sentences

Word: even number

Pointless Sentence	Our teacher taught us about even numbers.
Replace (substitution) Sentence	Even numbers.
Dictionary Sentence	Even numbers are numbers like 2, 4, 6, and 8.
Meaningful Sentence	When we lined up and counted ourselves at recess, the even numbers went in first. I was an odd number, so I went in second.

Word: difference

Pointless Sentence	There are differences in math.
Replace (substitution) Sentence	The difference is between two numbers.
Dictionary Sentence	The difference is what you get when you subtract one number from another.
Meaningful Sentence	When you have 8 pieces of gum and you give 2 away, you have 6 left. That is called the difference.

Math Tool P-1-8c

Meaningful Sentences

Word: odd number

Pointless Sentence	Odd numbers are fun.
Replace (substitution) Sentence	I can count using only odd numbers.
Dictionary Sentence	Odd numbers include 1, 3, 5, 7, and so on.
Meaningful Sentence	We have an odd number of students in our class. When we divide up into pairs, there is always one student left over.

Word: weight

Pointless Sentence	Weight is an interesting word.
Replace (substitution) Sentence	His weight is just right.
Dictionary Sentence	Weight is a type of measurement used to tell how heavy items are.
Meaningful Sentence	I checked my weight on the bathroom scale, and I weigh 50 pounds.

Math Tool P-1-8d

Meaningful Sentences With Definitions in Context

Directions: "Definitions in Context" show the definition in the text (the sentences you write). Use these five steps as you write this kind of sentence.

1. Choose a vocabulary word.
2. Read the definition of the word, and learn about the word.
3. Write a sentence that uses the vocabulary word and shows the meaning of the word.
4. When you are finished, circle the vocabulary word.
5. Underline words and phrases in your sentence that help show the meaning of the word.

Word: quarter
Mom cut my sandwich into four smaller parts so that I could eat a quarter of the sandwich at a time.

Word: rulers
In class, my friend and I measured all of the book covers with our rulers to see how many inches wide each book was.

Word: half
The page had ten problems, but I finished only five which was half of the problems.

Word: o'clock
At four o'clock the big hand is on twelve and the little hand is on four.

Math Tools: Primary (continued)

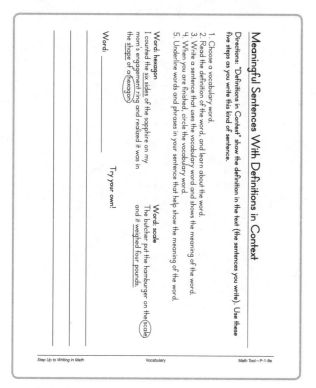

Meaningful Sentences With Definitions in Context

Directions: "Definitions in Context" show the definition in the text (the sentences you write). Use these five steps as you write this kind of sentence.

1. Choose a vocabulary word.
2. Read the definition of the word, and learn about the word.
3. Write a sentence that uses the vocabulary word and shows the meaning of the word.
4. When you are finished, circle the vocabulary word.
5. Underline words and phrases in your sentence that help show the meaning of the word.

Word: scale
The butcher put the hamburger on the (scale) and it weighed four pounds.

Word: hexagon
I counted the six sides of the sapphire on my mom's engagement ring and realized it was in the shape of a (hexagon).

Word: _____

Try your own!

Word: _____

Step Up to Writing in Math　　Vocabulary　　Math Tool—P-1-8e

Math Tool P-1-8e

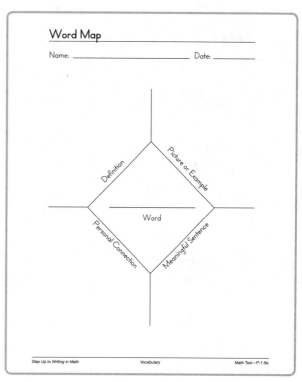

Step Up to Writing in Math　　Vocabulary　　Math Tool—P-1-9a

Math Tool P-1-9a

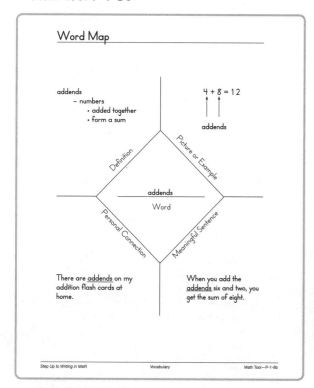

Step Up to Writing in Math　　Vocabulary　　Math Tool—P-1-9b

Math Tool P-1-9b

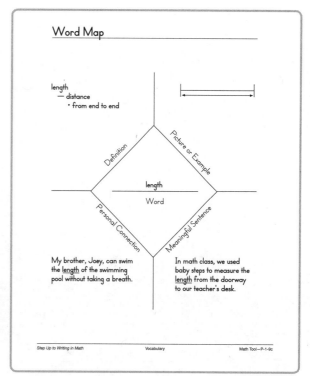

Step Up to Writing in Math　　Vocabulary　　Math Tool—P-1-9c

Math Tool P-1-9c

Math Tools: Primary–Intermediate

Riddles

Examples	Try your own!
1. I am what you try to figure out when you add two numbers. I rhyme with thumb. I usually sit right next to Mr. Equal Sign. Who am I? _____	_____ _____ _____ Who am I? _____
2. I am a unit of measurement. There are 12 of me in a foot. I have a worm named after me. Who am I? _____	_____ _____ _____ Who am I? _____
3. Like an octopus has eight legs, I have eight sides. I am a polygon. All my sides connect. Who am I? _____	_____ _____ _____ Who am I? _____

Math Tool P-1-10a

Riddles

Examples	Try your own!
4. I help you to measure things. I am smaller than an inch. You'll find me at the top of a ruler. Who am I? _____	_____ _____ _____ Who am I? _____
5. I am an answer. I can't live without subtraction. You can find me by taking one number from another. Who am I? _____	_____ _____ _____ Who am I? _____
6. I am a machine. I can help you with your math. I love to play with numbers. Who am I? _____	_____ _____ _____ Who am I? _____

Math Tool P-1-10b

Math Vocabulary List

above	cylinder	feet	mean
acute	data	fewer	measure
add	decimal	figure	meter
addend	decimal point	foot	metric
addition	degree	fourths	mile
after	degrees Celsius	fraction	millimeter
a.m.	degrees Fahrenheit	geometry	minus
amount	denominator	gram	minute
angle	difference	graph	minute hand
area	digit	half-dollar	missing
arithmetic	dime	half hour	money
around	distance	halves	month
average	divide	height	more
bar graph	dividend	hexagon	more than >
before	division	high	multiplication
between	divisor	hour	multiply
blocks	dollar	hour hand	negative
calendar	dollar sign	hundred	next
cardinal	doubles	hundreds	nickel
centimeter	edge	inch	number
cents	eighths	infinity	numeral
certain	ellipse	in front of	obtuse
chart	endpoint	kilometer	o'clock
circle	equal =	left	odd
clock	equals	length	ones
close to	equivalent	less than <	order
coins	estimate	line	ordinal
compare	even	line graph	ounce
cone	example	liter	part
count	face	mark	patterns
cube	factor	math	penny
cup	facts	maybe	percent

Math Tool I-1-1a

Math Vocabulary List

perimeter	quarter	side	thermometer
perpendicular	quarter hour	sixths	thirds
pictograph	quotient	size	triangle
pint	radius	solve	twelfths
p.m.	ray	sphere	under
positive	reasonable	square	value
pound	rectangle	subtract	volume
prediction	regroup	subtraction	weather
prism	remainder	sum	week
problem	right	survey	wide
product	seconds	symmetry	width
proportion	segment	table	yard
pyramid	set	temperature	year
quart	shape	tens	zero

Use these blank lines to add more helpful words to your list.

_____ _____ _____
_____ _____ _____
_____ _____ _____
_____ _____ _____
_____ _____ _____
_____ _____ _____
_____ _____ _____
_____ _____ _____

Math Tool I-1-1b

Math Tools: Intermediate *(continued)*

Math Vocabulary List

Math Tool I-1-1c

Breaking Down Definitions

Name: _____   Date: _____

Word	Definition Outline	Example, Illustration, Chart, or Table

Word	Definition Outline	Example, Illustration, Chart, or Table

Word	Definition Outline	Example, Illustration, Chart, or Table

Math Tool I-1-3a

Breaking Down Definitions

angle: the figure formed by two rays that meet at one point

Word	Definition Outline	Example, Illustration, Chart, or Table
angle	– figure • two rays • meet at one point	

denominator: the number below the line in a fraction, which represents the number of parts in the whole

Word	Definition Outline	Example, Illustration, Chart, or Table
denominator	– number • below line in fraction • represents the # of parts in whole	$\frac{1}{4}$ ←

line graph: a type of graph in which points are connected in a line to represent data

Word	Definition Outline	Example, Illustration, Chart, or Table
line graph	– type of graph • points connected • in a line – shows, represents • data • facts	cats found

Math Tool I-1-3b

Breaking Down Definitions

cardinal number: a number that shows a specific quantity — such as 10, 15, 22, or 42 — unlike ordinal numbers, which show ranking (like second, third, eighth)

Word	Definition Outline	Example, Illustration, Chart, or Table
cardinal number	– number • shows quantity • examples: 10, 15, 22, 42 • not an ordinal number ($2^{nd}, 3^{rd}, 8^{th}$)	2 birds 18 cookies 5 friends

data: information that is collected for a purpose but has not yet been interpreted. Data can be analyzed to show facts, trends, averages, etc.

Word	Definition Outline	Example, Illustration, Chart, or Table
data	– information • collected for a purpose • not interpreted • can show facts, trends, averages	832 kids like blue 407 kids like red 201 kids like orange 555 kids like pink

degree: a unit used for measuring; a unit on the temperature scale; a unit for measuring longitude or latitude – 360 degrees in a circle

Word	Definition Outline	Example, Illustration, Chart, or Table
degree	– unit for measuring • temperature – unit for showing • longitude • latitude	–10° C 88° F

Math Tool I-1-3c

Math Tools: Intermediate *(continued)*

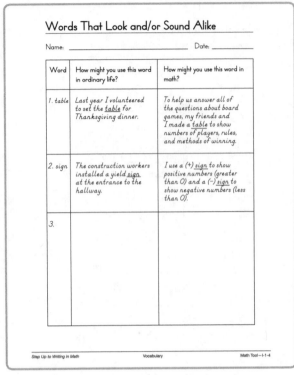

Math Tool *I-1-4*

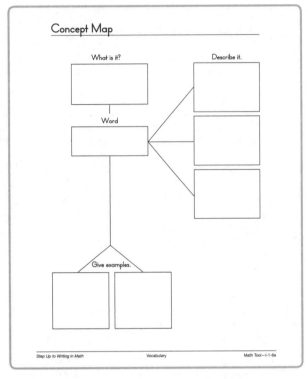

Math Tool *I-1-6a*

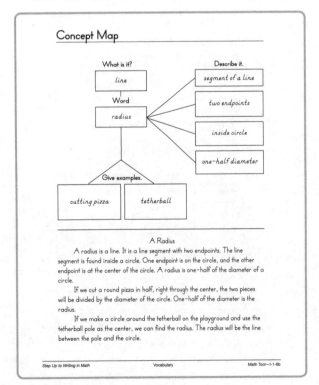

Math Tool *I-1-6b*

Word Bank

Name: _____ Date: _____

Directions: _____

Word Bank _____
_____
_____
_____
_____
_____
_____
_____

Directions: _____

Word Bank _____
_____
_____
_____
_____
_____
_____

Math Tool *I-1-7a*

Math Tools: Intermediate (continued)

Math Tool I-1-7b

Word Bank

Directions: Use some (or all) of the words in the word bank to define and describe what it means to "estimate" when solving a word problem.

Word Bank
- facts
- round up
- guess

When I solve a word problem, the first thing I do is underline the numbers and facts in the problem. Next, I round up the numbers to the nearest 5 or 10. Finally, I do the math. The estimate helps me check whether my real answer is right. If my estimate is close to my actual answer, then I am probably right.

Directions: Use some (or all) of the words in the word bank to describe the meaning of the word "perimeter."

Word Bank
- length
- around
- add
- sides

The perimeter is the sum of all four sides of shapes like squares or rectangles. To find the perimeter, you measure each side and add the numbers. You can also find the perimeter of a triangle by adding up the length of all three sides.

Math Tool I-1-7c

Word Bank

Directions: Use the terms in the following word bank to explain the term "infinity" as it is used in math class.

Word Bank
- numbers
- forever
- set

We use the word "infinity" when we are talking about a set of numbers that never ends. If I counted by 2s forever, I could make a set of numbers (2, 4, 6, 8, 10, 12, 14, and so on) that was infinite. In reality, I can't count forever, so I could never count to infinity.

Directions: Explain "negative numbers" using the words in the word bank.

Word Bank
- zero
- minus sign
- less than
- number

Negative numbers are numbers less than zero. They are written with minus signs. Some examples are −11, −7, and −1. One place we use negative numbers is when we talk about the temperature. If it is cold, it can be −4 or −6, which means 4 or 6 degrees below zero.

Math Tool I-1-8a

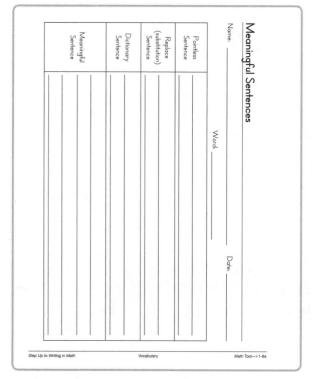

Meaningful Sentences

Name: _____ Word: _____ Date: _____

Pointless Sentence	
Replace (substitution) Sentence	
Dictionary Sentence	
Meaningful Sentence	

Math Tool I-1-8b

Meaningful Sentences

Word: area

Pointless Sentence	*Area is a word we use in math.*
Replace (substitution) Sentence	*In Chapter 5, the book talks a lot about area.*
Dictionary Sentence	*The area of the floor in a room is the length of the room times the width of the room.*
Meaningful Sentence	*"Grab the end of the tape measure," yelled Grandpa as he pulled the tape so he could measure the length and width of the floor. He wanted to buy tile to fit the whole area.*

Word: estimate

Pointless Sentence	*I love to estimate.*
Replace (substitution) Sentence	*Last week in math class we had to estimate.*
Dictionary Sentence	*To estimate means to give a close, but not exact, answer to a problem.*
Meaningful Sentence	*When I saw that my reading book had 56 pages, I estimated that I'd need to read about 12 pages each night if I wanted to finish it in 5 days.*

Math Tools: Intermediate *(continued)*

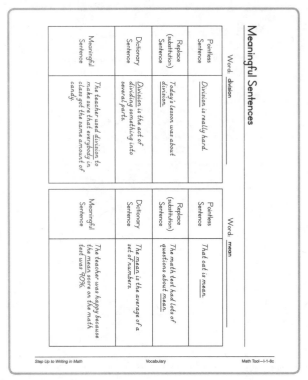

Math Tool I-1-8c

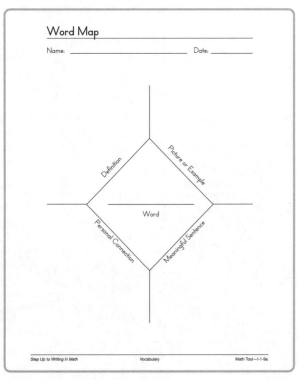

Math Tool I-1-8d

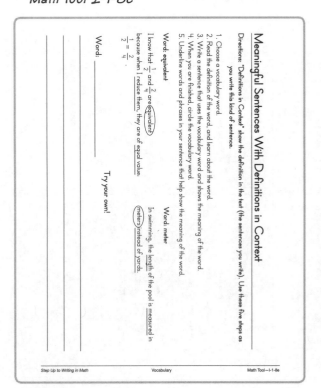

Math Tool I-1-8e

Word Map

Name: _____ Date: _____

Math Tool I-1-9a

Math Tools: Intermediate *(continued)*

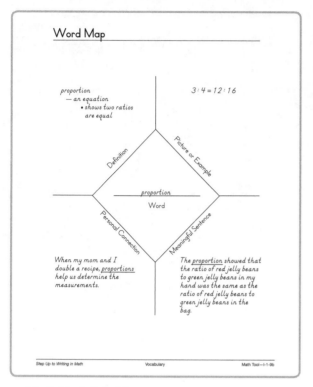

Math Tool I-1-9b

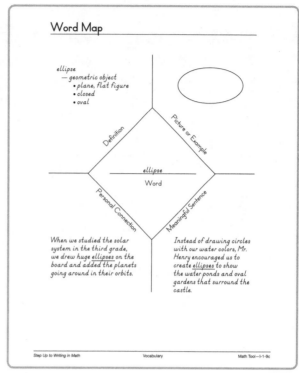

Math Tool I-1-9c

Riddles

Examples	Try your own!
1. People call me "sir" for short. I like pie. I hang around circles. Who am I? _____	_____ _____ _____ _____ Who am I? _____
2. I am a symbol. I am two very short, horizontal, parallel lines. You will find me in almost every chapter of your math book. I am always on your math test. Who am I? _____	_____ _____ _____ _____ Who am I? _____
3. I am a dot. I like to separate numbers. I can make dollars and cents, depending on where you put me. Who am I? _____	_____ _____ _____ _____ Who am I? _____
4. I can make a simple shape or a funny, strange shape. I am made up of line segments that all connect. My lines do not cross. I do not have any doors that open to the inside. Who am I? _____	_____ _____ _____ _____ Who am I? _____

Math Tool I-1-10a

Riddles

Examples	Try your own!
5. I am part of a shape. I am a line you cannot cross. I like to be on the outside. Who am I? _____	_____ _____ _____ _____ Who am I? _____
6. I have two friends named Ray. The protractor likes to hang out with me. You can't have an angle without me. Who am I? _____	_____ _____ _____ _____ Who am I? _____
7. I'm a unit of measure. You see me with angles. I'm not just about temperature. Who am I? _____	_____ _____ _____ _____ Who am I? _____
8. I am something you're looking for. I show up when you multiply. I am the answer man. Who am I? _____	_____ _____ _____ _____ Who am I? _____

Math Tool I-1-10b

Math Tools: Secondary

Math Vocabulary List

absolute value	concave	divisor	height
acre	cone	dollar	hexagon
actual	congruent	double	horizontal
acute	connect	dozen	hundredth
add	constant	duplicate	hypotenuse
addition	contain	edge	identify
adjacent	convert	elements	improper fraction
amount	convex	equal	inch
angle	coordinates	equality	increase
approximately	cost	equation	inequality
area	count	equivalent	infinite
average	cube	estimate	integers
bar graph	cubic foot	evaluate	interpret
base	cubic inch	even number	intersect
billion	cubic meter	exact	join
calculate	curve	expression	kilogram
capacity	cylinder	face	kilometer
Celsius	data	factor	label
center	decimal	factor tree	least
centimeter	decimal point	Fahrenheit	length
cents	decrease	fewer	less than
change	degree	figure	linear
circle	denominator	finite	liter
circle graph	depth	foot	lowest terms
circumference	determine	formula	mass
closed figure	diagonal	fraction	match
coin	diagram	frequency	mathematics
column	diameter	gallon	matrices
combination	difference	given	matrix
combine	digit	gram	maximum
common denominator	dime	graph	mean
common factor	dimensions	greater than	measure
common multiple	distance	greatest	median
compare	distributive	grid	member
comparison	divide	group	meter
compass	dividend	grouping	middle
computation	divisible	half	midpoint

Step Up to Writing in Math Vocabulary Math Tool—S-1-1a

Math Tool S-1-1a

Math Vocabulary List (continued)

mile	perimeter	rectangular	statistics
millimeter	perpendicular	reduce	straight
million	pint	regroup	subtract
minimum	placeholder	related facts	sum
minus	place value	remainder	surface
missing	plane	rhombus	surface area
mixed number	plot	rotation	symbol
most	plus	rounded number	symmetric
multiple	polygon	row	symmetrical
multiplier	polyhedron	scale	symmetry
multiply	positive	score	table
negative	pound	segment	temperature
nickel	prime number	semicircle	thousand
number	prism	sequence	times
number line	probability	set	total
numeral	problem	shaded	transformation
numerator	procedure	sharing	trapezoid
obtuse	product	sign	triangle
octagon	proper fraction	similar	unequal
odd number	proportion	simplest form	unit
odds	proportional	simplest terms	unknown
opposite	pyramid	simplify	unlimited
order	quadratic equation	single	value
ounce	quadrilateral	size	variable
outcome	quantity	slope	vertex
overestimate	quart	solid	vertical
pair	quarter	solution	vertices
parallel	quotient	solve	volume
parallelogram	radius	space	weight
parentheses	random	sphere	whole number
pattern	range	square	width
penny	ratio	square foot	x–axis
pentagon	ray	square inch	x–coordinate
per	reasonable	square meter	y–axis
percent	reciprocal	square number	y–coordinate
perfect square	rectangle	square root	zero

Step Up to Writing in Math Vocabulary Math Tool—S-1-1b

Math Tool S-1-1b

Math Vocabulary List

Use these blank lines to add more helpful words to your list.

Step Up to Writing in Math Vocabulary Math Tool—S-1-1c

Math Tool S-1-1c

Breaking Down Definitions

Name: _____   Date: _____

Term	Definition Outline	Example, Illustration, Chart, or Table

Step Up to Writing in Math Vocabulary Math Tool—S-1-3a

Math Tool S-1-3a

Math Tools: Secondary *(continued)*

Breaking Down Definitions

absolute value: a number's distance from zero on a number line

Term	Definition Outline	Example, Illustration, Chart, or Table
absolute value	– distance • on a number line • from zero to the number	⊢ 3 ⊣ –3 0

integers: the set of numbers consisting of the counting numbers, their opposites, and zero

Term	Definition Outline	Example, Illustration, Chart, or Table
integers	– set of numbers • counting numbers • their opposites • zero	[...–3, –2, –1, 0, 1, 2, 3...]

permutations: all possible arrangements of a given number of items in which the order of the items matters

Term	Definition Outline	Example, Illustration, Chart, or Table
permutations	– arrangements • all possible • of given # of items • order matters	

transformation: the process of changing one configuration into another according to a rule

Term	Definition Outline	Example, Illustration, Chart, or Table
transformation	– process • change one configuration to another • following a rule	

Step Up to Writing in Math   Vocabulary   Math Tool—S-1-3b

Math Tool S-1-3b

Breaking Down Definitions

vector: a quantity with both magnitude and direction

Term	Definition Outline	Example, Illustration, Chart, or Table
vector	– quantity • magnitude • direction	8 mph NE

square root: a number that, when multiplied by itself, equals a given number

Term	Definition Outline	Example, Illustration, Chart, or Table
square root	– number • when multiplied by itself • equals a given number	$5 \times 5 = 25$ square root of 25 = 5

parallelogram: a four-sided figure with opposite sides parallel

Term	Definition Outline	Example, Illustration, Chart, or Table
parallelogram	– figure • four-sided • opposite sides parallel	

angle bisector: a ray that divides an angle into two congruent angles

Term	Definition Outline	Example, Illustration, Chart, or Table
angle bisector	– ray • divides an angle • two congruent angles	

Step Up to Writing in Math   Vocabulary   Math Tool—S-1-3c

Math Tool S-1-3c

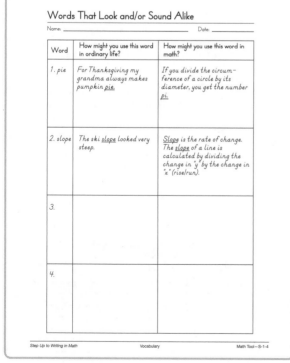

Math Tool S-1-4

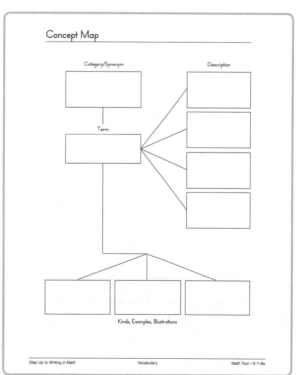

Math Tool S-1-6a

Math Tools: Secondary *(continued)*

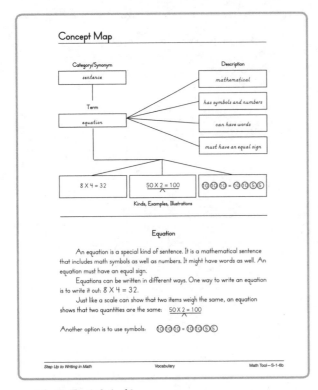

Concept Map

Category/Synonym
sentence

Term
equation

Description
mathematical

has symbols and numbers

can have words

must have an equal sign

8 X 4 = 32   50 X 2 = 100

Kinds, Examples, Illustrations

Equation

An equation is a special kind of sentence. It is a mathematical sentence that includes math symbols as well as numbers. It might have words as well. An equation must have an equal sign.

Equations can be written in different ways. One way to write an equation is to write it out: 8 X 4 = 32.

Just like a scale can show that two items weigh the same, an equation shows that two quantities are the same: 50 X 2 = 100

Another option is to use symbols:

Math Tool S-1-6b

Word Bank

Name: _____ Date: _____

Directions: _____

Word Bank

Directions: _____

Word Bank

Math Tool S-1-7a

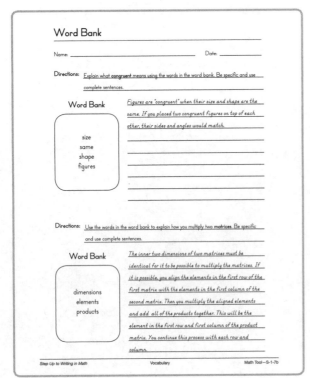

Word Bank

Name: _____ Date: _____

Directions: Explain what **congruent** means using the words in the word bank. Be specific and use complete sentences.

Word Bank

size
same
shape
figures

Figures are "congruent" when their size and shape are the same. If you placed two congruent figures on top of each other, their sides and angles would match.

Directions: Use the words in the word bank to explain how you multiply two **matrices**. Be specific and use complete sentences.

Word Bank

dimensions
elements
products

The inner two dimensions of two matrices must be identical for it to be possible to multiply the matrices. If it is possible, you align the elements in the first row of the first matrix with the elements in the first column of the second matrix. Then you multiply the aligned elements and add all of the products together. This will be the element in the first row and first column of the product matrix. You continue this process with each row and column.

Math Tool S-1-7b

Word Bank

Name: _____ Date: _____

Directions: Explain what a **factor** is by using the words in the word bank. Use complete sentences. Be specific.

Word Bank

expression
multiply
product

The factors of an expression are what you multiply together to get the original expression. In other words, the original expression is the product of its factors.

Directions: Using the words in the word bank, explain the **distributive property**. Be specific and use complete sentences.

Word Bank

multiply
sum
term

The distributive property states that adding terms together and then multiplying the sum by a number is the same as multiplying each term by that number and then finding the sum.

Math Tool S-1-7c

Math Tools: Secondary (continued)

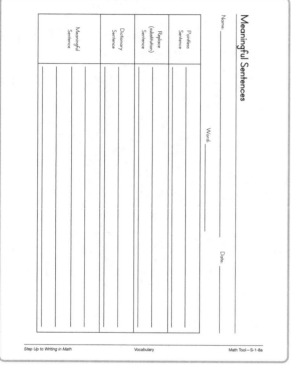

Math Tool S-1-8a

Meaningful Sentences

Name: _____ Date: _____

	Word: _____	Word: _____
Pointless Sentence		
Replace (substitution) Sentence		
Dictionary Sentence		
Meaningful Sentence		

Meaningful Sentences

	Word: liter	Word: cylinder
Pointless Sentence	You can use a *liter* jar to measure stuff.	My *cylinder* is nice.
Replace (substitution) Sentence	The *liter* of water sat on the kitchen counter.	I used a *cylinder* to hold my food.
Dictionary Sentence	A *liter* is a metric unit used to measure liquid; it is a little larger than a quart.	A *cylinder* is a three-dimensional shape consisting of the space between two parallel, equal-sized circles.
Meaningful Sentence	Margaret carefully picked up the *liter* of soda to pour it into the glass quart pitcher but quickly realized that not all of it would fit.	Jane reached into her bag for her lipstick, a small *cylinder* labeled "Rosy Diva."

Math Tool S-1-8b

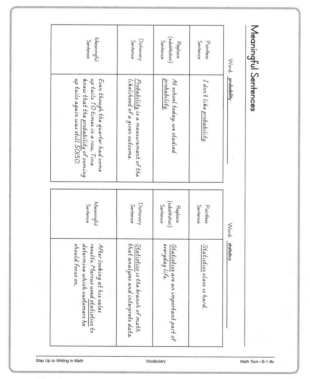

Math Tool S-1-8c

Meaningful Sentences

	Word: probability	Word: statistics
Pointless Sentence	I don't like *probability*.	*Statistics* class is hard.
Replace (substitution) Sentence	At school today, we studied *probability*.	*Statistics* are an important part of everyday life.
Dictionary Sentence	*Probability* is a measurement of the likelihood of a given outcome.	*Statistics* is the branch of math that analyzes and interprets data.
Meaningful Sentence	Even though the quarter had come up tails 10 times in a row, Tina knew that the *probability* of coming up tails again was still 50/50.	After looking at his sales results, Marcus used *statistics* to determine which customers he should focus on.

Math Tool S-1-8d

Meaningful Sentences With Definitions in Context

Directions: "Definitions in Context" show the definition in the text (the sentences you write). Use these five steps as you write this kind of sentence.

1. Choose a vocabulary word.
2. Read the definition of the word, and learn about the word.
3. Write a sentence that uses the vocabulary word and shows the meaning of the word.
4. When you are finished, circle the vocabulary word.
5. Underline words and phrases in your sentence that help show the meaning of the word.

Word: face

The group of tourists visiting the pyramids in Egypt stared at the (face) of the huge structure wondering how the ancient architects had designed the slope and configuration of blocks.

Word: congruent

In order to complete the picture's frame, I cut four (congruent) pieces of pine and glued them around the four equal sides of the poster.

Word: pound

Uncle Eli picked up a package of ground beef marked 1.6 ounces. He wondered if that (pound) of meat would be enough for Aunt Martha's meatloaf recipe.

Math Tools: Secondary (continued)

Meaningful Sentences With Definitions in Context

Directions: "Definitions in Context" show the definition in the text (the sentences you write). Use these five steps as you write this kind of sentence.

1. Choose a vocabulary word.
2. Read the definition of the word, and learn about the word.
3. Write a sentence that uses the vocabulary word and shows the meaning of the word.
4. When you are finished, circle the vocabulary word.
5. Underline words and phrases in your sentence that help show the meaning of the word.

Word: rotation

As I watched my little brother walk around the circle during the cakewalk, I realized he was moving just like the (rotations) we learned about in math. His body was always the same distance from the center of the circle, but his position changed by a certain angle.

Word: asymptote

When we drove across the desert, we could see the mountains in the distance. After driving for hours, I thought the mountains looked like (asymptotes) that we would keep approaching but never reach.

Word: _____

Try your own!

Step Up to Writing in Math • Vocabulary • Math Tool—S-1-8e

Math Tool S-1-8e

Word Map

Name: _____   Date: _____

Definition

Picture or Example

Word

Personal Connection

Meaningful Sentence

Step Up to Writing in Math • Vocabulary • Math Tool—S-1-9a

Math Tool S-1-9a

Word Map

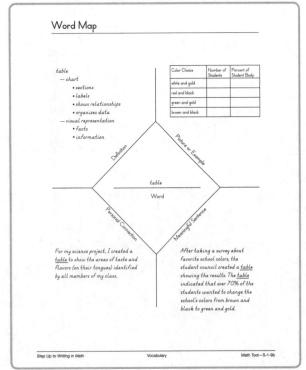

table
— chart
  • sections
  • labels
  • shows relationships
  • organizes data
— visual representation
  • facts
  • information

Color Choice	Number of Students	Percent of Student Body
white and gold		
red and black		
green and gold		
brown and black		

Definition

Picture or Example

table
Word

Personal Connection

Meaningful Sentence

For my science project, I created a table to show the areas of taste and flavors (on their tongues) identified by all members of my class.

After taking a survey about favorite school colors, the student council created a table showing the results. The table indicated that over 70% of the students wanted to change the school's colors from brown and black to green and gold.

Step Up to Writing in Math • Vocabulary • Math Tool—S-1-9b

Math Tool S-1-9b

Word Map

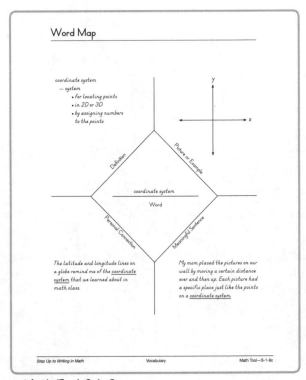

coordinate system
— system
  • for locating points
  • in 2D or 3D
  • by assigning numbers
    to the points

Definition

Picture or Example

coordinate system
Word

Personal Connection

Meaningful Sentence

The latitude and longitude lines on a globe remind me of the coordinate system that we learned about in math class.

My mom placed the pictures on our wall by moving a certain distance over and then up. Each picture had a specific place just like the points on a coordinate system.

Step Up to Writing in Math • Vocabulary • Math Tool—S-1-9c

Math Tool S-1-9c

Math Tools: Secondary *(continued)*

Riddles

Examples	Try your own!
1. I have the power to multiply. If you trace my path, I never go straight. You'll find me whispering in the ear of my base buddy. Who am I? _____	Who am I? _____
2. I don't exist. But when I square dance, I do. You all hate to think of me. Who am I? _____	Who am I? _____
3. I am straight. In the morning I rise and then go for a run. You can ski on me. Who am I? _____	Who am I? _____
4. I don't have to be at the center of things. I'm not mean. I'm the most popular. Who am I? _____	Who am I? _____

Math Tool S-1-10a

Riddles

Examples	Try your own!
5. You like me when you're shopping. Or at a restaurant. You can pick me out of a hundred. Who am I? _____	Who am I? _____
6. I keep going and going and going. I'm a product. I'm not always the least common. Who am I? _____	Who am I? _____
7. I like to go around things. Measuring me is easy. You know my cousin, circumference. Who am I? _____	Who am I? _____
8. I like it when arcs and radii are the same. I work at any degree. I often eat two pies. Who am I? _____	Who am I? _____

Math Tool S-1-10b

*W*hen students read or listen to lectures in math, they have an explicit purpose: to learn and understand content. In math textbooks, on math assessments, and in math discussions, students must comprehend directions, word problems, definitions, explanations, and other technical content.

In order to be successful readers, they must be active readers. Active readers set a purpose for reading and read for meaning. They develop strategies for interacting with the text so that they can remember and use the information. Interacting with text includes activities like marking the text, making symbols or sketches, taking notes, and asking and answering questions.

Section 2 of *Step Up to Writing in Math* offers strategies that help students actively engage in, think about, and make meaning from what they are reading. The strategies are visual, hands-on, and easy to learn.

This section includes two- and three-column methods for taking notes based on text or on class lectures. These note-taking strategies help students organize information effectively, which makes them better able to learn, to study, to discuss, to ask and answer questions, and to apply what they have learned. In addition, when note-taking tools are practical and useful, students are more likely to take notes and make the note taking their own, which helps establish good study skills. When notes are visual, clear, detailed, and accurate, students feel confident as they study and when they take exams.

The two- and three-column note-taking method is easy to use and works for students of all ages and abilities. Teachers can use this strategy to differentiate and scaffold instruction, to save time, to empower students, and to meet curriculum goals.

Families and others who support students in their studies appreciate work done using a two- or three-column format. These types of notes show what students know and do not know. They identify key concepts that teachers expect students to master, and they provide space for making math concepts visual with sketches and/or examples.

Section 2 also includes strategies for understanding word problems and for using the two- and three-column note-taking methods to explain how a word problem was solved.

Using these methods, students learn to identify and give detailed explanations for each step in their problem-solving process. And when students take notes carefully, they can use the notes to write short and long paragraph responses explaining how they solved a problem. (These types of paragraph responses are described and explained in Section 5.)

Learning to read strategically and take effective notes enables students to identify and organize the information that they can use to answer questions, understand new ideas, follow directions, and become more successful problem solvers.

Objectives

- Improve students' listening and reading comprehension skills

- Empower students to be active readers; increase confidence

- Teach important study skills; expect independent application

- Give students strategies for reading word problems

- Teach students how to analyze and use information to solve a word problem

- Use note taking to help students write about their problem-solving processes

SECTION **2** CONTENTS

2-1 Reading Notations

Encourage students to make notations when they are reading. Doing so can help them think about what they are reading and show comprehension. Their comments may include fragments or complete sentences.

Reading notations are helpful during class discussions and for reviewing important content. For example, a notation in the margin of the following text:

> **To add or subtract fractions with different denominators, find the least common multiple (LCM) of each denominator. This becomes the lowest common denominator (LCD).**

might look like:

> LCM and LCD look alike. Least common multiple/lowest common denominator!

The margins of the textbook are the most convenient place for students to make notations. When they are not allowed to write in the textbook, provide small self-stick notes. Later, have students add the self-stick notes to their note taking.

2-2 Marking the Text

Teach students to use highlighting or underlining to find and mark the main ideas and supporting information in a text.

You'll have to model this strategy to help them learn to select the most important information, or they may mark everything on the page. Tell students:

- It is better to mark too little than to mark too much.

- Read a paragraph first, then reread and mark key information the second time through.

- Mark words and phrases only, not complete sentences.

- Mark the text to show comprehension. For example:

> <u>Estimation</u> is just <u>smart guessing</u>. When people estimate, they are <u>doing math without relying on paper, pen, calculators, charts, or computers</u>. As they estimate, they <u>round numbers</u>. For example, they might <u>round 456</u> orders for candy <u>to 460</u> orders. In this case, they <u>would be rounding up</u> to the <u>nearest tens' place</u>.

Students usually need several demonstrations to see how to select only key information. They learn this skill by observing how others make decisions about what to underline or highlight.

(See **2-7 Marking Word Problems to Improve Understanding** and **2-8 Highlighting or Underlining Word Problems** for specific suggestions for marking and highlighting math word problems.)

Note: When students cannot mark on their text, consider making copies, modeling by using overhead transparencies, or giving students overhead transparencies to place over the text.

2-3 Two- and Three-Column Notes for General Text

Notes become more valuable as a study guide when students organize information on a page so it is easy to see and to use.

Two-column notes are easy to read and understand because they provide space for both key ideas and supporting information. Three-column notes build on the two-column model by adding space for examples and/or illustrations. Students can learn to take quality notes through these simple steps:

1. Fold or write lines that divide a sheet of notebook paper into either two or three parts. The visual dividers on the page make it easier to remember and use the notes later.

2. Label the top of the note page with name, date, subject, and a topic for the notes. The topic can be written in the form of a question that guides students' note taking.

3. Take notes one paragraph at a time. Read a paragraph, then reread for note taking.

4. Use words and phrases—not complete sentences—to make notes easier to write, read, and review for an exam.

5. List big ideas/major details in the left column. Add subtopics, examples, minor details, etc., in the second column. Use dashes and dots in the second column to show the hierarchy of details.

6. Reserve the third column (if you use three-column notes) for comments, connections, illustrations, insights, sketches, etc.

7. Make notes neat and complete.

8. Later, consider adding color to the notes as a way to carefully review for exams and class assignments.

Here is an example of good three-column notes based on the general text below:

Roman Numerals

When people work with Roman numerals, they must learn a code that is based on addition and subtraction. The ancient Romans used I for the number one. Three in a row—III— meant the number three. The number four, however, was written as IV. This is because V stood for five. To get the number four, they simply placed the I—the one—in front of the V. Writing the number three meant adding three ones—I—together; writing the number four meant subtracting the one—I—from the five—V.

The letter X stood for 10. If someone meant 20, he or she wrote XX—two tens. If people meant nine, they wrote IX. This showed that they were subtracting one—I—from 10—X.

The letter L was used for the number 50, and the letter C was used for 100. Writing the number 150 meant putting the two letters together: CL. The Romans also used D for 500 and M for 1,000. That is why the year 1987 would look like this: MCMLXXXVII.

Topic = Roman Numerals

Key/Star Idea	Subtopics/Details	Example/ Illustration/ Connection/ Insight
Code	- based on addition and subtraction - uses capital letters I, V, X, L, C, D, M	3 = III 4 = IV 9 = IX
Working with Roman numerals	- add and subtract - look for pattern - subtract for 9	2 tens = XX IX
Larger numbers	- 50 - 100 - 500 - 1,000	L C D M

Reading comprehension improves when students take notes. Students take more effective notes—and require less time to do so—when they can follow a note-taking format that their teacher has modeled and explained.

Before a Lesson

- Select several short informational pieces (like "Roman Numerals") to use for demonstration. If possible, use text from books students are or will be reading.

- Make overhead transparencies and student copies of the selected text, as needed.

- Take notes from the selected text as practice. Use the eight steps for two- or three-column note taking as you prepare your notes. Note especially the one idea per paragraph rule for taking notes on short pieces.

During a Lesson

- Clarify the purpose for note taking.

- With student input, take notes on the text you have chosen. Guide students through each of the steps of two- or three-column note taking. If you are taking notes on a unit or whole chapter, show them how to use the section headings for the big ideas that you will record on the left. The right side (or second column) lists subtopics, details, and so on. If you are taking notes on a small amount of text, show them how to pull out one main idea per paragraph.

- Build the notes on chart paper or the overhead. Have students copy your notes onto their own two- or three-column note paper.

- During this process, share your thoughts aloud and ask students to share theirs. Explain each step you take. Ask for input from your students to make the lesson interactive. Always take time to review how and why you are taking notes in this way. Ask students to explain why they think this method helps with organizing notes.

- After the class has finished taking notes, ask students to refer back to the purpose for note taking and evaluate whether they have met that goal.

- Ask students to orally answer questions using their notes as a guide. Encourage them to speak in complete thoughts, modeling and demonstrating as needed.

- Discuss whether (and why or why not) students found it easy to answer questions using their notes. Ask for suggestions for improving the notes.

- Collect students' notes to monitor their progress. When you return the notes, emphasize the value of keeping them to study for assessments.

Additional Ideas

- If students maintain vocabulary notebooks, decide whether you want them to record terms and definitions separately or with the chapter notes (or in both places).

- Combine the strategy **1-3 Breaking Down Definitions** with note taking from articles or math textbooks.

- Use abbreviations and symbols when appropriate. Use standard abbreviations or abbreviations that the class develops.

- When you ask students to use two- or three-column note taking during a lecture, provide them with the big ideas before or during the lecture. This will enable them to focus on taking the relevant notes on the right side of the paper.

- Provide students with an outline of your lecture in the two-column note format. Tell them to use the notes as a guide while you are speaking, and encourage them to add any notes that they think are relevant.

- Ask students to refer to their notes when writing responses to questions from the text or questions you have created.

- When students answer questions, have them use the two-column fold format. If they write questions in the left column and answers in the right column, they will create a handy tool for studying. The page can be folded so that only the questions or the answers can be seen. Another benefit: Questions and answers written this way take less time to review and grade.

- Have students share their notes. Once they have practiced the two- and three-column note-taking strategies, they will feel confident about taking notes independently. Their individual notes will begin to vary somewhat and, as a result, will be more interesting to share. When students share their notes with the class or in pairs, they have the opportunity to learn from one another.

- Review for quizzes and exams by asking students to read their notes aloud to a neighbor or by selecting a few students to share their notes with the whole group.

- Involve the whole class in a notes-based discussion, eliciting bits and pieces of the content from different students. Students will feel more comfortable participating since they have their notes in front of them.

- Use two-column notes marked Quotation/Response. On the left students quote from the text; on the right they respond, analyze, and/or make corrections.

- Students can use their notes to write summaries. Summary writing, like note taking, holds students accountable for comprehension. Both summaries and note taking are powerful tools for promoting good reading; both should be encouraged and expected on a regular basis. If students know that they will be asked to take notes and summarize, they almost always read more carefully. (See **Section 3: Summarizing Text and Writing About Graphs** for details on teaching students how to write summaries.)

2-4 Creating Textbook Study Guides

Textbooks are the basic resource for information and learning in many math classrooms. Reading from a textbook, however, is a challenge for many students. They may not know where to begin or how to deal with a textbook's large quantity of information.

Students need direct instruction in order to learn to use textbooks fully and effectively. One way to help them read textbooks better is to teach them to create **chapter and/or unit study guides** using two- and three-column notes.

A study guide organizes all of the information in a chapter or unit so that it is easy to read, easy to use, and easy to study for daily assignments and for high-stakes assessments.

Students create the basic two-column frame for study guides before actually reading a chapter or unit. Good study guides improve reading comprehension by helping students set a purpose for their reading. Study guides are also useful because students access and use background knowledge when they create one. They begin to make connections between new information and what they already know.

Building a study guide is a way of front-loading students to help them feel successful as they read. Study guides organized in the two-column format give students confidence because they are useful for remembering lessons learned.

Creating a Study Guide

Keep study guides simple by applying the two- or three-column note-taking strategy and these guidelines:

1. Quickly review and scan the pages of a chapter or unit. In particular, look for:
   - headings and subheadings;
   - charts, tables, and graphs;
   - special articles;
   - captions to pictures or illustrations; and
   - questions to match subheadings.

2. Start actual note taking at the end of the chapter or unit—sections that publishers often call "Review," "Chapter Quiz," or "Overview."

   Use all of the information provided in these last pages to organize the first part of the study guide. Final pages of a chapter or unit in a textbook contain information like: a summary, questions, key facts, terms to remember, and challenges for application of content.

3. Take notes listing big ideas, chapter vocabulary, questions, and so on in the left column. Add details, subtopics, examples, etc., to the second column. (In some cases the second column will be blank until the study guide is completed while reading or during class lessons.)

   Use paper folded into two or three columns. In either case, leave blank space on the right side of the page for adding more information during lectures, discussions, or reading. Use the left column to list big ideas from:

   – Any summary or list of facts provided.

   – Any questions provided. (Copy questions as they are, or turn them into subtopics for note taking; add answers later as you complete the study guide.)

   – Any key concepts or math terms. (Add subtopics and details as you read.)

   – Any ideas/activities that call for higher-level thinking and/or application.

4. Work through the chapter, listing the textbook's boldface subtopics on the left—leaving room for notes and details in the second column.

5. Read captions, charts, and tables that present key information and concepts. Turn this information into notes. Reviewing and/or introducing these important elements again sets a purpose for reading.

6. Record any important terms; add definitions in the right column during the lecture or when carefully reading the text.

Note: Study guides do not have to include all of this information. The idea is to help students create a framework for notes they will take as they read, leaving space for more notes and examples that you give during class presentation.

A study guide would look like this after the details are filled in during careful reading of the text and/or during lectures.

Topic = Review of Fractions

fraction	– number made of two numbers
	  • numerator
	    (number of equal parts talked about)
	  • denominator
	    (total number of equal parts)
	– example
	  • $2/3$
	    2 = numerator and 3 = denominator
	– equal parts
	  • 2 equal parts = halves
	  • 3 equal parts = thirds
	  • 8 equal parts = eighths
	– ratios
	  • comparison of two numbers
	  • 3 : 4 is a ratio
	    compares 3 to 4

equivalent fractions	– do not look alike
	– represent the same number
	  • $1/2$ same as $2/4$
	  • $2/3$ same as $4/6$ or $8/12$
	– represent the same amount
	– make equivalent fractions
	  • multiply the numerator and
	    the denominator by the
	    same number
	      $2/4 \times 4 = 8/16$

simplifying fractions	– –

Before a Lesson

- Read and review the example study guide "Review of Fractions."

- Create an example to show during the lesson. Large poster paper or overhead transparencies work well. They are visual and can be used over and over again.

- Select a chapter to use for demonstration and practice. Using the next chapter the students will be reading works best.

During a Lesson

- Explain the purpose of a study guide. Show students the example you have created.

- Using chart paper or a projector, help students create a chapter study guide. In the beginning, this will be time-consuming, but students will catch on quickly. Keep in mind that time spent creating a study guide with the class is time saved when students actually read the chapter.

- Model each step of the process. As students work with you, they are learning the math content (and remembering what they know). They will appreciate all of the information you share as they write and make plans to read.

- As you model note taking, remind students to leave space between notes. The empty "white space" makes the notes easier to read and refer back to later.

2-5 Framed Responses

Teachers can use this strategy to gauge students' understanding of material they have read.

A framed response is a short paragraph that the teacher creates with blank spaces. Students fill in the blanks with phrases and clauses to show their comprehension of text or a lecture. For example, if a teacher assigns students this framed paragraph:

Division Problems

Division problems have three parts. The dividend is the _____

_____, and the divisor is the _____

_____. To solve a division problem, you must _____.

_____. The answer to the division problem

is called the _____.

---

the completed paragraph would look something like this:

> **Division Problems**
>
> **Division problems have three parts. The dividend is the** <u>total before it is divided</u> <u>into parts</u> **, and the divisor is the** <u>number of equal parts that the dividend will</u> <u>be divided into.</u> **To solve a division problem, you must** <u>divide the dividend by the</u> <u>divisor. An example of this is 32 divided by 4</u> **. The answer to the division problem is called the** <u>quotient. The quotient in the example problem is 8</u> .

Use the framed responses on **Math Tool 2–5** as they are or as models for framed responses that you design. (See **3-5 Framed Paragraphs for Writing About Graphs**, **5-4 Using Framed Paragraphs to Practice for Writing in Math Assessments**, and **6-4 Framed Paragraphs** for ideas of other uses for framed responses.)

Keep in mind that you do not need to present framed responses in the form of a handout. Often, the best way to present a framed response is to write it on the board or chart paper, having students copy the frame and then add their response pieces.

Evaluating framed responses should not be time-consuming. Use index cards instead of full sheets of paper. They are easy to read and return. Giving a letter grade is optional.

Tool S-2-5

When reviewing students' responses, circle interesting points they make. Share some of the responses as a part of a class discussion. Use students' responses to determine what they understand and do not understand.

2-6 Other Strategies for Improving Reading Comprehension

Two additional strategies for improving students' reading skills are explained in greater detail in subsequent sections of *Step Up to Writing in Math*: Summarizing Text and Accordion Races.

After students understand how to take good notes, they can learn to use those notes to write summaries. Summary writing, like note taking, holds students accountable for comprehension by showing whether students have understood what they have read. Both summaries and note taking are powerful tools for promoting good reading; both should be encouraged and expected on a regular basis across the curriculum. The strategy presented in **3-1 Four-Step Summary Paragraph** explains a quick and easy strategy for good, clear summary writing.

Using a proven and practical summarizing strategy like this one will make students more confident when they write. Reading and scoring the summaries will go quickly because the students' writing will be clear and organized.

The strategy presented in **6-1 Accordion Paragraphs** can help students learn how to organize their ideas in expository/informational writing, recognize transitions, sequence information, write paragraphs and reports, and develop topic sentences and conclusions. The strategy **6-3 Accordion Races** extends the accordion approach to writing to help students improve their reading comprehension and their practical reading skills.

In an accordion race, teams of students receive a set of sentences written on strips of paper. The students must arrange the strips to create a clear, coherent paragraph. As they read the strips, they must find the topic sentence, then arrange all the other sentences so that the paragraph makes sense. This activity requires students to read actively, looking for details and sorting information. Consider using the accordion race examples on **Math Tools 6-3a, 6-3b,** and **6-3c** (and those you create) to promote good reading skills.

2-7 Marking Word Problems to Improve Understanding

Use this strategy to teach students about the structure of word problems and to slow them down as they read.

Many students, especially those who struggle with reading, need extra time and instruction on reading word problems. This strategy pushes students to recognize and think about the parts of a word problem:

1. Read the problem.

   > Last week during the Tuesday practice, the middle school biking team pedaled $12\frac{3}{4}$ miles. On Wednesday they increased their distance by $1\frac{1}{8}$ miles. How many miles did they pedal over both days?

2. Reread the problem, and underline all of the numbers in context and the math-related terms.

   > Last week during the Tuesday practice, the middle school biking team pedaled <u>$12\frac{3}{4}$</u> <u>miles</u>. On Wednesday they <u>increased</u> their <u>distance</u> by <u>$1\frac{1}{8}$ miles</u>. <u>How many miles</u> did they pedal over <u>both days</u>?

3. Put a *W* above the "who" or "what" in the word problem.

> Last week during the Tuesday practice, the middle school biking $\overset{W}{\text{team}}$ pedaled $12\frac{3}{4}$
>
> $\overset{W}{\text{miles}}$. On Wednesday they <u>increased</u> their <u>distance</u> by $1\frac{1}{8}$ <u>miles</u>. <u>How many miles</u> did
>
> they pedal over <u>both days</u>?

4. Circle the situation/issue/circumstance. Possible items students can circle include the clauses or phrases with specific action verbs like gave, lost, found, added, sold, and used.

> Last week during the Tuesday practice, the middle school biking $\overset{W}{\text{team}}$ pedaled $12\frac{3}{4}$
>
> miles. On Wednesday they increased their distance by $1\frac{1}{8}$ miles. How many miles did
>
> they pedal over both days?

5. Box the question that needs to be answered.

> Last week during the Tuesday practice, the middle school biking $\overset{W}{\text{team}}$ pedaled $12\frac{3}{4}$
>
> miles. On Wednesday they increased their distance by $1\frac{1}{8}$ miles. How many miles did
>
> they pedal over both days?

As students mark and analyze word problems, they assess their own reading skills. This activity also provides an opportunity for teachers to learn about students' reading strengths and weaknesses.

Using this strategy (or your variation on the strategy) several times early in the year, and then whenever students seem to be struggling with word problems, will open the door for dialogue and questions. Often students do not know how to explain what it is that they do not understand. With a slight push they may be able to ask for help and find clarification.

Before a Lesson

- Choose word problems to use for demonstration.

- Make an overhead transparency and student copies of Math Tool 2-7 as needed.

- Make student copies of practice problems.

During a Lesson

- Display **Math Tool 2-7**.

- Explain to students that this activity is a chance to look carefully at word problems, learn more about how they are written, think about how easy (or difficult) they are to understand, and ask questions about challenges they have with reading word problems.

- Read through the problem on **Math Tool 2-7** and the suggestions for marking the word problems. Discuss and ask questions about each step.

- Give students copies of the practice problems you have selected. Take students through the five steps for analyzing word problems. Stop to add steps or change steps as needed to fit your methods for helping students with word problems.

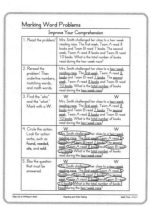

Tool P-2-7

It is possible that some students have never stopped to think about word problems as the unique form of writing that they are—a form that has its own purpose and structure. When students have finished the activity, ask them to write a paragraph describing and defining a word problem. This will help you see what they have learned or know about word problems. Consider making a concept map for word problems (see **1-6 Concept Maps**).

Note: See **7-2 Creating Word Problems** for information about helping students write their own word problems.

2-8 Highlighting or Underlining Word Problems

This strategy shows students a different method for marking word problems; it helps them focus on more than just the numbers.

In addition to asking students to highlight the numbers and the context for those numbers, this strategy asks them to analyze and justify what they've highlighted or underlined in a word problem. This strategy involves five steps:

1. Read the question in the word problem before reading the entire problem. (Reading the question first focuses thinking. It also helps guarantee that the question will be read at least three times.)

2. Read the entire word problem without highlighting or underlining it. It is important to understand the whole problem before dissecting it.

3. Highlight/underline the question.

4. Using the question as a guide, highlight/underline only the information necessary to answer it. All numbers needed to answer the question must be highlighted or underlined in context. In addition, highlight/underline the clue words that reveal what operations should be used to come up with the answer.

5. In writing, explain the purpose of each item that is highlighted or underlined. This analysis requires mathematical thinking. Place these notes near or next to the word problems.

For example, for the word problem:

> **It takes Josie 7 minutes to ride her bike 1 mile. She is going to ride 6 miles.**
>
> **How long will it take her to ride 6 miles?**

The highlighted version would look something like:

> This tells me how long it takes to go 1 mile. This number will be a factor in this multiplication problem.
>
> This is the distance Josie can go in 7 minutes.
>
> It takes Josie 7 minutes to ride her bike 1 mile. She is going to ride 6 miles.
>
> **How long will it take her to ride 6 miles?**
>
> This is what I need to find out.
>
> This is the number I need to multiply by 7. It's a factor.

From this, a student could determine:

> 7 minutes per mile
>
> x 6 miles
>
> ————————————————————————
>
> It will take Josie 42 minutes to ride her bike 6 miles.

For another example, consider this word problem:

> In 1976, Grace bought 8 antique bowls. It's now 2006, and she still has them.
>
> If the bowls were 65 years old when she bought them, how old are they now?

Highlighted, it might look like:

This is the number I'll subtract from 2006 to determine how many years have passed.

This just gives me a context for my answer.

In 1976, Grace bought 8 antique bowls. It's now 2006, and she still has them.

If the bowls were 65 years old when she bought them, how old are they now?

This is the number that I need to add to the number of years that have passed.

This tells me what I am trying to find.

"Now" refers to 2006.

$$
\begin{array}{r}
2006 \ (\text{now}) \\
- \ 1976 \ (\text{then}) \\
\hline
30 \ \text{years have passed.}
\end{array}
$$

$$
\begin{array}{r}
65 \ (\text{years old when bought}) \\
+ \ 30 \ (\text{years that have passed}) \\
\hline
\end{array}
$$

The 8 antique bowls are 95 years old now.

Before a Lesson

- Select several word problems for practice. Start with easier problems so students can focus on learning the strategy rather than grappling to solve the word problem.

- Provide copies of the word problems you have selected and highlighters/pencils as needed.

During a Lesson

- Engage students in a discussion about why reading and solving word problems can be difficult. Use the following points (and others that you add) to encourage discussion:

  - Some problems are poorly written.

  - Students often focus on the numbers in a problem and ignore the context for those numbers.

  - Students may be overwhelmed by the amount of information in word problems.

  - Students may be poor readers or lack confidence as readers.

  - Students may have problems with vocabulary.

  - Students might be unable to distinguish between important and unimportant information.

  - Students may lack the math knowledge that is required to interpret or solve the problem.

- Model the five-step highlighting/underlining strategy. Make changes to this process as needed to fit your style and class goals. The purpose is to show students how to read and identify the most important pieces of information in context.

- Explain that this systematic approach helps isolate necessary information in a word problem. Note that some students are natural problem solvers and have their own systems for dissecting word problems. As with other strategies in this book, you may require that every student try the strategy, then ask students to share their own methods for problem solving.

- As you model the strategy, share your thought processes aloud. Explain your interpretations of key words, important phrases, and mathematical symbols. Students learn to read word problems by hearing you explain your thinking.

- Repeat this process with several word problems. Students will need multiple practice opportunities to learn the strategy. Once you have modeled several problems, ask for student volunteers. Give students time to practice individually and with peers.

After students feel comfortable independently justifying what they have highlighted or underlined in text that they're reading, most can move directly from highlighting/underlining to setting up and solving word problems. They should always be prepared, though, to orally explain why the information they have highlighted or underlined is important.

For students with special needs, highlighting or underlining word problems on a regular basis can help them move toward independence, but with guidance from the teacher.

2-9 Using Two-Column Notes to Read and Solve Word Problems

Use this strategy (Math Tools 2-9a, 2-9b, 2-9c) to help students carefully read word problems, sort and use information from the problems, and practice making illustrations for them.

The two-column format gives students a step-by-step structure that makes reading and solving word problems more manageable. In the left column, students should record the seven steps involved in solving a word problem using this strategy; in the right column, they should include their response to each step.

The seven steps are:

1. **Restate the problem.** Write the question that needs to be answered using your own words. Restating the question shows that you know the directions and you comprehend the word problem.

2. **List the facts.** Writing the facts is a reading strategy; it shows that you are ready to solve the problem and can identify important information.

3. **List the clue words.** Writing down the clue words or phrases may help you identify and think about concepts or operations you will have to use to solve the problem. Often it helps to put the symbol for the corresponding operation or concept next to each clue word or phrase.

4. **Estimate or predict.** Use mental math; write your prediction or estimate for the answer.

   A prediction uses words—for example:

He will not have enough marbles.	They will get fewer rides than Group B.

   An estimate uses numbers—such as:

25 square yards	390 miles	$200.00

5. **Illustrate the problem.** Create a chart, a drawing, or a graph to show your understanding of the problem. Illustrating when solving word problems means showing steps that let others understand your math thinking. Always use an equal sign (=) and math symbols (- or +, for example) along with your illustrations to guarantee success. (See **2-10 Hints for Illustrating Word Problems** for tips that help students show their math thinking as they illustrate word problems.)

6. **Solve the problem.** Show all of the computations (steps) that you use to solve the problem. Number the steps as a way to help those who are reading and scoring your work.

7. **Write the final answer in a complete sentence.** Use part of the question in your sentence to create a context for the answer and demonstrate your understanding of the problem and your confidence in your answer. Always remember to label your answer and to be specific ($0.50, 10 pounds, 150 acres, 1,000 miles).

For example, if students were given the word problem:

Farmer Hall's Pumpkins

Farmer Hall planted 88 rows of pumpkins. Each row produced 34 pumpkins. Farmer Hall sold one-half of the pumpkins to local supermarket owners. He left the other half in his pumpkin patch for the town's schoolchildren to pick and take home. How many pumpkins were left in Farmer Hall's pumpkin patch?

They would create two-column notes that looked like:

Farmer Hall's Pumpkins

Restate the problem.	How many pumpkins were left in Farmer Hall's pumpkin patch?
List the facts.	– 88 rows - 34 pumpkins per row - half left in patch - half to supermarkets
List the clue words.	- each (x) - half left for kids (÷)
Estimate or predict.	1500
Illustrate the problem.	88 34 [ ] = total pumpkins Total pumpkins ÷ 2 = _____
Solve the problem.	88 rows × 34 pumpkins ———— 2992 1496 2)2992 2800 192 180 12
Write the final answer in a complete sentence.	There were 1496 pumpkins left in Farmer Hall's pumpkin patch.

Before a Lesson

- Make overhead transparencies and student copies (as needed) of **Math Tools 2-9a** through **2-9g**.

- Choose word problems to use to practice this strategy with the class. Solve the problems using the two-column guide as preparation for demonstration and modeling. Anticipate where students might have difficulties or questions.

- Make overhead transparencies and student copies of practice problems.

During a Lesson

- Display **Math Tool 2-9a**, and describe the steps used in this strategy for solving word problems.

- Display **Math Tool 2-9b**. Present the word problem to the students.

- Display **Math Tool 2-9c**. Take students through each step used to solve the word problem. Explain the answers and information listed in the right column. Explain your expectations for each step, especially for illustrations. (See **2-10 Hints for Illustrating Word Problems** for ideas and examples.)

- Stop to ask questions, and give students time to ask for clarification.

- Use problems that you have selected for practice in a second guided lesson.

- Give students a chance to try the strategy independently or with a partner.

- Repeat the process with **Math Tools 2-9e** through **2-9g**.

Tool I-2-9a

Tool I-2-9e

Tool I-2-9b

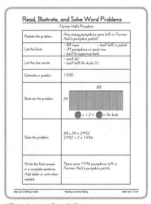

Tool I-2-9f

Tool I-2-9c

Tool I-2-9g

Tool I-2-9d

Additional Ideas

- Instead of using Math Tool 2-9a, have students fold notebook paper into the two-column note format. Ask them to add the directions from Math Tool 2-9a on the left, leaving space to complete their work on the right. Display a copy of Math Tool 2-9a to help students set up their pages.

- Explain that this strategy is just one way to read and solve a word problem. Discuss the strengths and weaknesses of this strategy.

- Take time to ask how using the steps can help with reading comprehension.

- Have students explain and display their responses when they use the two-column method. Make several overhead transparencies using Math Tool 2-9a. Have students work in pairs, using overhead markers to demonstrate how they solve a word problem. Let them display their work. Support students as they present, adding explanation and clarification as needed.

- Have students explain their steps orally or in a paragraph format using Math Tool 2-9d as a model.

- Teach students how to use their notes to explain their problem-solving process. The strategy **5-1 Explaining Steps Taken to Solve a Word Problem** gives specific details and more examples. When you teach the two-column notes strategy for solving word problems, you can introduce students to this simple method for writing about steps they take to solve the problems:

  - Display the paragraph in Math Tool 2-9d and/or give students copies of the paragraph.

  - Remind students that the first sentence in the paragraph is called the topic sentence. It is the controlling statement that lets readers know what the paragraph will explain.

  - Point out the connector words—also called transitions—that make it easy for everyone to see the steps (for example, *first*, *next*, and *finally*).

  - Most important, make sure students hear and see the examples and explanations in the paragraph. Tell them that those phrases are what they need to include so that people understand how they solved the problem.

Note: This strategy asks students to illustrate their math thinking. Students are expected to show with drawings, sketches, graphs, charts, etc., how they plan to solve a word problem. The goal is to have students visualize the problem and its solution before they begin their computations. (See **2-10 Hints for Illustrating Word Problems** for ways to help students with this task.)

2-10 Hints for Illustrating Word Problems

Students need guidance, examples, and time to learn how to make illustrations that demonstrate their math thinking.

Share the following tips to help students develop the skills to work quickly and still produce quality work.

- Your illustration can be a chart, graph, table, or series of sketches.

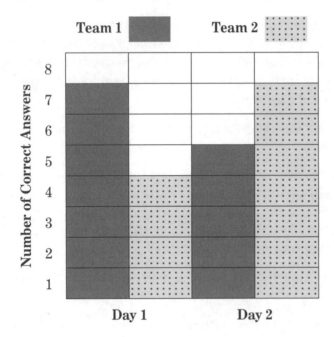

- When you use a series of sketches, you are creating a math sentence—an equation that will need math symbols (- or +, for example) and an equal sign (=).

☐ ☐ ☐ + ☐ ☐ =

△ △ x △ △ =

☐ + 20 = Total

- Make illustrations simple. Do not add details to drawings; instead, keep them plain and easy to re-create.

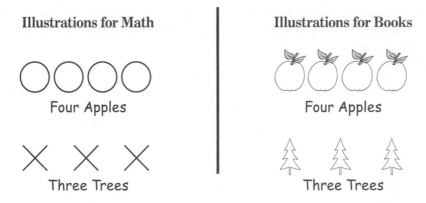

Illustrations for Math	**Illustrations for Books**
Four Apples	Four Apples
Three Trees	Three Trees

- Keep in mind that illustrations in math are different from illustrations for other writing assignments. For a math assignment, illustrations mean "show your math thinking," or show the steps you plan to use as you solve the problem.

Problem 1:   Collecting Seashells

Courtney went to the beach with her aunt. They collected seashells. When they returned home, they sorted the shells by their shapes into five groups. Two groups had four shells. Three groups had five shells. How many shells did Courtney and her aunt collect in all?

Just an Illustration   **A Math Illustration**

Problem 2:   Buying Gas

Jerry pulls into his local gas station. He has $14.00 in his pocket. He buys 5 gallons of gas and pays $1.74 a gallon. How much change did Jerry have in his pocket after he paid for the gas?

Just an Illustration   **A Math Illustration**

5 × $1.74 = [price of gas]

$14.00 − [price of gas] = Change

2-11 Using Three-Column Notes With Illustrations to Solve a Word Problem

This strategy (Math Tools 2—11a through 2—11f) uses a series of repeated illustrations to help students visualize and find the answer to a problem. Students move from concrete statements to pictures in order to learn abstract concepts.

The model-drawing approach (Hogan, 22) breaks a problem into manageable chunks in order to find the correct answer.

In this strategy, teachers ask students to divide their page into three columns. In the left column, teachers and students work together to explain the facts and steps that they have to work with in the word problem. In the middle column, they illustrate each fact or step as they work the problem. In the right column, they include the calculations related to each fact or step. For example, if students were given this word problem:

What time is 4 hours before 2:15 P.M.?

they would create three-column notes that look like:

Facts	Illustration	Math Computation
1. The time of day is 2:15 P.M.	(clock showing 2:15)	2:15 P.M.
2. When I subtract 2 hours, the time is 12:15 P.M.	(clock showing 1:15 P.M.) 1:15 P.M. (clock showing 12:15 P.M.) 12:15 P.M.	2:15 P.M. – 1 hour = 1:15 P.M. 1:15 P.M. – 1 hour = 12:15 P.M.
3. When I subtract 2 more hours, the time is 10:15 A.M.	(clock showing 11:15 A.M.) 11:15 A.M. (clock showing 10:15 A.M.) 10:15 A.M.	12:15 P.M. – 1 hour = 11:15 A.M. 11:15 A.M. – 1 hour = 10:15 A.M.

Final answer/complete sentence: The time 4 hours before 2:15 P.M. is 10:15 A.M.

Before a Lesson

- Make overhead transparencies and student copies of **Math Tools 2-11a** through **2-11c** as needed.

- Select problems for students to use as they learn this strategy. Choose easy problems at first, and slowly move students on to more challenging problems.

- Practice the strategy with your selected problems using chart paper. The chart paper examples will be helpful later for modeling and answering questions.

During a Lesson

- Display **Math Tool 2-11a**. Read the problem with the class.

- Give students copies of **Math Tool 2-11b**. Display a copy, and walk students through the steps. Explain each step. Ask students to rephrase your explanations.

- After you have explained all steps, review the steps and process again. Ask and answer questions.

- Using a problem you have selected, guide students as they work to solve the problem.

- Draw illustrations; ask students to imitate your work.

- After the lesson is complete and the class has solved your problem, discuss the process. Ask students for suggestions about using or improving the strategy.

- Give students time to work with a partner or small group to solve other problems you have selected. Using chart paper makes this activity a bit more fun. Students can use the charts as they explain their steps to classmates, and they can share illustrations.

- Repeat the process using **Math Tools 2-11d** through **2-11f**.

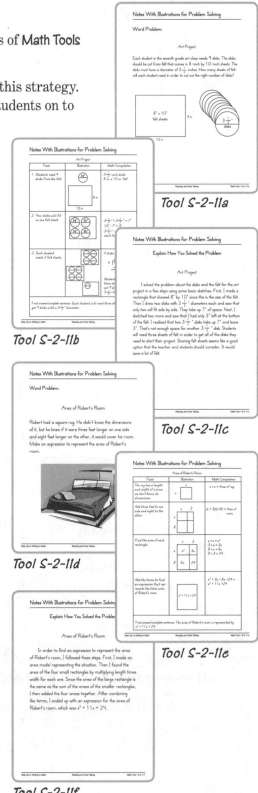

Tool S-2-11a

Tool S-2-11b

Tool S-2-11c

Tool S-2-11d

Tool S-2-11e

Tool S-2-11f

Additional Ideas

Just as with strategy **2-9 Using Two-Column Notes to Read and Solve Word Problems**, students can use their three-column notes to write full paragraphs that explain the steps they took to solve a word problem. The strategy **5-1 Explaining Steps Taken to Solve a Word Problem** gives details and more examples.

When you teach the three-column strategy for illustrating and solving word problems, teach students to explain their problem-solving process in a paragraph or short report.

– Display **Math Tool 2-11c**. Have students match the report to the actual problem-solving steps described on **Math Tool 2-11b**.

– Ask students to explain the organization in the report in **Math Tool 2-11c**. Help them locate the topic sentence, the transitions, and the elaboration—the sentences that give evidence and explanation.

– Let students know that they will learn and will eventually be responsible for writing paragraphs or short reports that explain how they solved a word problem.

2-12 Using Three-Column Notes to Explain a Problem-Solving Process

Use this strategy (Math Tools 2-12a to 2-12d) to give students a way to think about what they are doing as they solve math problems. It will also help them think about why they are taking each step in their problem-solving process. It can be used as a vehicle to show problem-solving methods or as a tool to solidify understanding of a math concept.

In this strategy, students are given a grid in which to make notes as they solve problems. The grid includes three columns with these headings: *Steps* (tell what to do); *Reasons* (explain why); and *Work* (solve the problem). The number of rows varies depending on the problem students are solving, but the first row should always be "list the facts," and the last row should always be "check the answer."

Note: Writing these steps over and over may seem redundant, but it can really help struggling students remember to include these crucial steps. It also gives them confidence, as they always know where to begin and end.

Here are the steps (Math Tool 2-12a) to take in this strategy:

1. At the top of the page, write the question or a summary of the problem in your own words.

2. In the left-hand column labeled "Steps," write the steps you take to solve the problem. Write the steps as if you were giving directions to a student over the phone (or as if you were coaching yourself). Start each direction or command with a math verb. For example:

List the facts . . .	Subtract the amount . . .
Add the money . . .	Check your answer . . .

3. In the middle column labeled "Reasons," explain why you are taking each step. Start with words like *to, so, in order to,* or *because.*

. . . because I need to know what information I'm working with	. . . in order to figure out how much more they need
. . . to find out the total amount they already have	. . . so that I can make sure my calculations are correct

4. In the right-hand column labeled "Work," show your work. Read the first and second columns, and follow your own directions.

Note: Students should start in the left column and work toward the right for each step.

5. At the bottom of the page, write your final answer in a complete sentence. Make sure the final answer includes units of measure and labels. Look back to the question or problem summary at the top of the page, and use its language to create your final answer sentence. Then read the sentence you have created, and check your answer for reasonableness.

Before a Lesson

- Make overhead transparencies and student copies of **Math Tools 2-12a** through **2-12d**, as needed.

- Review and practice the strategy using problems you have selected. Choose problems that require different skills to solve. In the beginning, it is best to select problems that are very easy to solve. This gives students time to learn the strategy. Later they will be able to use the strategy for more challenging problems.

During a Lesson

- Display **Math Tool 2-12a**. Point out the *Word Problem* space at the top of the page and the *Question* space below it. Explain these and the rest of the labels on the form. Tell students that even though the examples have spaces for four or five steps to show how to solve the problem, other problems may require fewer or more spaces.

- Show students that they will be asked to give their final answer in a complete sentence.

- Display **Math Tool 2-12b**. Read the problem, then explain how the problem was solved. Stop to ask and answer questions.

- Repeat the process with **Math Tool 2-12c**. Point out that explanations for problem solving may differ because students use different approaches.

- Use **Math Tool 2-12a** (or notebook paper folded into thirds) and problems you have selected to guide lessons to help students learn this strategy. Follow the same steps as those on **Math Tools 2-12b** and **2-12c**. Explain your thinking and decision making at each step.

- Guide students as they practice this strategy independently or with peers.

Tool P-2-12a

Tool P-2-12b

Tool P-2-12c

Tool P-2-12d

Additional Ideas

- Just as with the strategies from **2-9 Using Two-Column Notes to Read and Solve a Word Problem** and **2-11 Using Three-Column Notes With Illustrations to Solve a Word Problem**, students can use their notes developed in this strategy to write full paragraphs that explain the steps they took to solve a math problem. You can introduce students to this simple method for writing about steps in problem solving using **Math Tool 2-12d**. Display the examples. Read through each paragraph. Guide a discussion about the similarities and differences between the two explanations for problem solving. (See also **5-1 Explaining Steps Taken to Solve a Word Problem** and **5-2 Turning an Explanation Into a Formal Paragraph**.)

- Suggest that students use their three-column notes to study for assessments.

- Give students options for homework—for example, "Do problems 15 to 20," or ask them to "choose one problem and solve it using the three-column format."

- Include a problem on an assessment that students are required to solve using the three-column format.

- Use paragraphs on **Math Tool 2-12d** to guide a discussion about how problems can be solved correctly in a number of different ways. Give students time to compare the steps they used to solve a problem with the steps that other classmates used.

- Experiment. The three-column strategy is a powerful teaching tool. Look for more uses. For example, the three-column strategy works well when teaching students a specific procedure or algorithm. You can also use it to build fluency with a particular process. Each time students use the three-column format, they are reteaching themselves the process.

2-13 Avoiding Common Stumbling Blocks With Word Problems

When students read math word problems, they sometimes encounter difficulties that do not relate at all to the math concepts, math computation, or math question in the problem.

Consider the following examples as you work with struggling readers and typical students who encounter problems as they read.

Unusual or Higher-Level Verbs

The following word problem uses the verbs *contribute* and *donate*. These verbs, not common to some readers, can cause a problem. Students who do not recognize the verbs may feel that they cannot solve the problem.

> **Joe, Julian, Juan, and Jared are hungry for pizza. At the pizza parlor, a large pizza with two toppings is $9.45. Juan has $3.50 that he is willing to <u>contribute</u>. Julian and Joe each have $2.00. How much money does Jared need to <u>donate</u> in order for the boys to be able to buy the pizza?**

Help students by:

- Pointing out the fact that most words like these are synonyms for the verbs that are commonly used in math problems. Show students that *donate* and *contribute* can be replaced by verbs like *have*, *share*, and *give*. Watch for challenging verbs, and start a synonym list on chart paper. Keep the list visible; add new verbs as you or your students encounter them.

- Teaching them to use context clues to understand the meanings of the words.

Names or Proper Nouns That Students Cannot Pronounce

Occasionally students come upon a proper noun that they cannot pronounce. It might be the name of a product, a city, or even a person. These words, of course, are insignificant when it comes to solving the problem. But take nothing for granted. Create problems with unusual names for people, products, and places. Ask students how to handle problems like these. Give them your advice and reassurance.

> The <u>Kirplani</u> family spent $138.00 a week on groceries and $32.50 a week on gasoline for their truck and car. How much money did the family need to budget for a year's worth of food and gasoline?

Help students by:

- Assuring them that they are not the only ones who have encountered the pronunciation problem.

- Giving them an easy method for dealing with the problem:

  - Tell students to replace the unfamiliar name with their own first or last name.

  - Tell them to replace names with the letter N and read as "the N family" (n for name).

- Reviewing the important (and unimportant) facts in word problems.

Unfamiliar Objects or Expressions

Even students who use English as their first and only language encounter terms they do not know. Words *camper*, *tortilla*, *soufflé*, *toll road*, *jumper*, or *recliner* might throw some.

> Stan and his brother drove their <u>camper</u> an average of 175 miles a day for 2 weeks as they vacationed in Montana and Idaho. How many miles did they travel in those two weeks?

Help students by:

- Showing them how to discover meaning in context. The words *drove* and *miles* give a hint that a *camper* is some sort of vehicle.

- Reminding them that a letter or symbol can replace nouns. Doing this will not change the outcome of the problem. Have them repeat, "Stan and his brother drove their ■ an average of 175 miles. . . ."

- Asking them to work in pairs and write word problems that refer to unfamiliar objects or expressions. Give them time to solve their problems and share what they have learned with classmates.

Math Terms That Students Do Not Know or Have Forgotten

"I know it, but I just can't remember!" is a familiar cry from students who are stumped by even familiar math terms when reading word problems. Helping students during math assessments isn't possible, of course, but addressing the problem on a daily basis will help.

> Meg uses an <u>average</u> of 14 pieces of notebook paper each day in school. How many packages of notebook paper with 150 pages in each would Meg need to make it through a month with 20 school days?

Help students by:

- Stopping to check for knowledge of math terms when students are ready to solve word problems. Have a student volunteer to list all math terms in the problem on the board. Call on students to define each term. Call on other students to rephrase the definitions and give examples.

- Requiring a math term definition on a "ticket out" at the end of class once or twice a week. A "ticket out" is a small piece of paper or index card used as an exit slip at the end of class or on the way to lunch. On the paper, ask students to define a math term you have selected. A stack of "tickets" are easy to review, and they provide powerful insight into who knows and who does not know the meaning of even ordinary math terms. (Keep index cards handy. They work well for "tickets out" and other short writing assignments.)

- Establishing a formal way of collecting math terms and their definitions. (See **Section 1: Vocabulary** for several practical ideas.)

Clue Words and Phrases

Check to find out whether all students realize that those who write word problems usually include clues for solving the problem. Help students learn to look for clue words and phrases. Show them how to use the clue to decide how to solve the problem.

Students who are learning English as a second language can probably find the clue words in problems written in their first language; however, they will need your help to point them out in problems written in English.

> Last year, the librarian bought 192 new books. If the librarian buys the <u>same number</u> of books each year, <u>about how many</u> books will she buy in the next 3 years?

Help students by:

- Discussing the concept of context clue words.

- Making a chart with a list of clue words and phrases the class mentions.

- Adding definitions to the clue words and phrases. For example, the phrase *about how many* indicates that the answer to the problem should be an estimate or approximation.

- Telling students to be detectives and to offer advice to other students about the clue words or phrases they have found.

- Checking knowledge of clue words and phrases by using the "ticket out" strategy.

- Warning students that some clue words have different meanings when taken out of context. Remind students to read the whole problem—not just look for numbers and clue words.

Math Tools: Primary

Framed Responses

What I Learned

When I read _____ , I

learned two facts. First, I _____

_____ . Next, I _____

_____

_____ .

- -

What I Learned

I read pages _____ in our math book and

learned two new math words. First, I learned the word_____

_____ , which means

_____ .

After that I learned _____ . It means

_____

_____ .

Math Tool P-2-5

Marking Word Problems
Improve Your Comprehension

1. Read the problem!	Mrs. Smith challenged her class to a two-week reading race. The first week, Team A read 8 books and Team B read 7 books. The second week, Team A read 8 books and Team B read 10 books. What is the total number of books read during the two-week race?
2. Reread the problem! Then underline numbers, matching words, and math words.	Mrs. Smith challenged her class to a <u>two-week reading race</u>. The <u>first week</u>, Team A read <u>8 books</u> and Team B read <u>7 books</u>. The <u>second week</u>, Team A read <u>8 books</u> and Team B read <u>10 books</u>. What is the <u>total number</u> of books read during the <u>two-week race</u>?
3. Find the "who" and the "what." Mark with a W.	W W Mrs. Smith challenged her class to a <u>two-week reading race</u>. The <u>first week</u>, Team A read <u>8 books</u> and Team B read <u>7 books</u>. The <u>second week</u>, Team A read <u>8 books</u> and Team B read <u>10 books</u>. What is the <u>total number</u> of books read during the <u>two-week race</u>?
4. Circle the action. Look for action verbs, such as **found, needed, ate,** and **sold.**	W W Mrs. Smith challenged her class to a <u>two-week reading race</u>. The <u>first week</u>, Team A read <u>8 books</u> and Team B read <u>7 books</u>. The <u>second week</u>, Team A read <u>8 books</u> and Team B read <u>10 books</u>. What is the <u>total number</u> of books read during the <u>two-week race</u>?
5. Box the question that must be answered.	W W Mrs. Smith challenged her class to a <u>two-week reading race</u>. The <u>first week</u>, Team A read <u>8 books</u> and Team B read <u>7 books</u>. The <u>second week</u>, Team A read <u>8 books</u> and Team B read <u>10 books</u>. What is the <u>total number</u> of books read during the <u>two-week race</u>?

Math Tool P-2-7

Read, Illustrate, and Solve Word Problems

Write the question.	
List the facts.	
Write the clue words.	
Make a guess (estimate or predict).	
Illustrate the problem.	
Solve the problem.	
Write the final answer in a complete sentence. Add labels or units when needed.	

Math Tool P-2-9a

Read, Illustrate, and Solve Word Problems

Word Problem:

Friends Coming to a Party
Louis is having a party. He invited 1 3 friends, and 7 have already arrived. If everyone who was invited comes to the party, how many more friends are coming to the party?

Math Tool P-2-9b

Math Tools: Primary *(continued)*

Read, Illustrate, and Solve Word Problems

Friends Coming to a Party

Write the question.	How many more friends are coming to Louis' party?
List the facts.	– 13 friends are coming – 7 arrived
Write the clue words.	–how many more? –everyone
Make a guess (estimate or predict).	6
Illustrate the problem.	○○○○○○○○○○○○○ 13 - [4 circles + 3 circles] = ○○○ ○○○
Solve the problem.	13 – 7 = 6
Write the final answer in a complete sentence. Add labels or units when needed.	Six more friends are on their way to Louis' party.

Step Up to Writing in Math   Reading and Note Taking   Math Tool—P-2-9c

Math Tool P-2-9c

Read, Illustrate, and Solve Word Problems

Friends Coming to a Party
To find the answer to the problem about how many more kids are coming to the party, I used these steps. First, I read carefully and listed the facts. Louis invited 13 kids to the party. I knew that 7 friends were already there. Next, I looked for clues. The words "how many more" told me I would need to subtract. Then I guessed that there were 6 more kids coming. After that, I drew pictures to show how I would solve the problem. Finally, I solved the problem. I subtracted 7 from 13. I saw that 6 more friends were coming to Louis' party.

Step Up to Writing in Math   Reading and Note Taking   Math Tool—P-2-9d

Math Tool P-2-9d

Read, Illustrate, and Solve Word Problems

Word Problem:

Cat Food
The Adler family is going on vacation, and the neighbors are taking care of their cat, Tito. Tito eats one-half of a can of cat food each day. The Adlers will be gone for six days. How many whole cans of cat food will Tito eat?

Step Up to Writing in Math   Reading and Note Taking   Math Tool—P-2-9e

Math Tool P-2-9e

Read, Illustrate, and Solve Word Problems

Cat Food

Write the question.	How many whole cans of cat food will Tito eat?
List the facts.	– eats one-half a can a day – gone for six days
Write the clue words.	– one-half can – each day – how many whole
Make a guess (estimate or predict).	3
Illustrate the problem.	DDDDDD = half cans ⊃⊂ ⊃⊂ ⊃⊂ = full cans
Solve the problem.	1 + 1 + 1 = 3
Write the final answer in a complete sentence. Add labels or units when needed.	Tito will eat three whole cans of cat food in six days.

Step Up to Writing in Math   Reading and Note Taking   Math Tool—P-2-9f

Math Tool P-2-9f

Math Tools: Primary *(continued)*

<u>Read, Illustrate, and Solve Word Problems</u>

Cat Food

To figure out how many whole cans of cat food Tito will eat, I followed a couple of steps. First, I read the problem and wrote down the important parts. I wrote the question, how much Tito eats, and how long the Adlers will be gone. Next, I listed the clue words. The words <u>half</u>, <u>each day</u>, and <u>how many whole</u> told me I would need to add. Then I guessed three cans by counting on my fingers. After that I solved the problem by drawing the six halves and turning them into three whole cans. My estimate was right! Tito will eat three whole cans of cat food while the Adlers are away.

Math Tool P-2-9g

Notes With Illustrations for Problem Solving

Word Problem:

Snowman Project

The children in Ms. Berry's class are making snowmen with string and paste. Each student is given two strings that are 8 feet long. The students each cut 2 feet from the first string to make the head for the snowman. They then cut 3 feet to use for the body. If the students want to make a second, matching snowman, how much of the second 8–foot string will they need?

| 1' | 2' | 3' | 4' | 5' | 6' | 7' | 8' |

| 1' | 2' | 3' | 4' | 5' | 6' | 7' | 8' |

Math Tool P-2-11a

Notes With Illustrations for Problem Solving

Snowman Project

Facts	Illustration	Math Computation
1. Children have 8' of string for first snowman.	1'|2'|3'|4'|5'|6'|7'|8'	8 feet
2. Children use 2' of string for head.	2' 6'	8 feet – 2 feet used ——— 6 feet left over
3. Children use 3 more feet for body.	2' 3' 3'	6 feet – 3 feet used ——— 3 feet left over
4. Second snowman project also needs 5' of string.	2' 3'	2 feet for second head + 3 feet for second body ——— 5 feet needed for second snowman
5. How much more string needed for a second snowman?	2'	5 feet needed – 3 feet left over ——— 2 more feet needed from second string

Final answer/complete sentence: The children will need two feet from the second eight–foot string to make another snowman.

Math Tool P-2-11b

Notes With Illustrations for Problem Solving

Snowman Project

I answered the question about the string and the snowman project in just a few steps. To start, I drew a picture to show the 8–foot string. Then I drew the string again to show that the kids cut 2 feet from the string to make the head of the snowman. This meant they had 6 feet left. In my next picture, I showed that they used 3 feet for the body. I also showed that they had 3 feet of string left over. Next, I showed a string with 5 feet to show how much the kids needed for another snowman. They have 3 feet from the first string left over. This means the kids in Ms. Berry's class will need just 2 feet from the second string.

Math Tool P-2-11c

Math Tools: Primary (continued)

Notes With Illustrations for Problem Solving

Word Problem:

Wheels on the Buses

Pete is playing with his toy buses. He has three buses. Each bus has four wheels. How many total wheels are on the buses?

Step Up to Writing in Math   Reading and Note Taking   Math Tool—P-2-11d

Math Tool P-2-11d

Notes With Illustrations for Problem Solving

Wheels on the Buses

Facts	Illustration	Math Computation
1. Each bus has four wheels.		4 wheels
2. There are three buses.		4 wheels + 4 wheels ——— 8 wheels 8 wheels + 4 wheels ——— 12 wheels

Final answer/complete sentence:
The three buses have a total of twelve wheels.

Step Up to Writing in Math   Reading and Note Taking   Math Tool—P-2-11e

Math Tool P-2-11e

Notes With Illustrations for Problem Solving

Wheels on the Buses

To figure out how many wheels were on the buses, I did several things. First, I drew a picture of a bus to show that a bus has 4 wheels. Then I drew 3 buses to show all the buses Pete is playing with. Next, I added 4 plus 4, which is 8. Then I added 8 plus 4, which is 12. This showed me the sum of all the wheels. There are 12 wheels on Pete's buses.

Step Up to Writing in Math   Reading and Note Taking   Math Tool—P-2-11f

Math Tool P-2-11f

Three-Column Notes for Problem Solving

Word Problem:

Question:

Steps (Tell what to do.)	Reasons (Explain why.)	Work (Solve the problem.)

Final answer in a complete sentence:

Step Up to Writing in Math   Reading and Note Taking   Math Tool—P-2-12a

Math Tool P-2-12a

Math Tools: Primary–Intermediate

Three–Column Notes for Problem Solving

Word Problem: Josie had 13 cents in her piggy bank. Then she earned 20 cents for taking out the recycling and 50 cents for cleaning the cat box. How much more money does she need to earn to have $1.00?

Question: How much more money does Josie need to earn to have $1.00?

Steps (Tell what to do.)	Reasons (Explain why.)	Work (Solve the problem.)
1. List the facts.	– so I know what information I'm working with	– 13 cents in piggy bank to start – earned 20 cents and 50 cents
2. Add 13 cents, 20 cents, and 50 cents.	– to find out how much Josie has	13 20 + 50 ── 83
3. Subtract 83 cents from $1.00.	– to find out how much more money Josie needs to earn to have $1.00	$1 = 100 cents 100 – 83 ── 17
4. Check the answer.	– to make sure it is correct	13 20 50 + 17 ── 100

Final answer in a complete sentence: Josie needs to earn 17 more cents to have $1.00.

Math Tool P-2-12b

Three–Column Notes for Problem Solving

Word Problem: Josie had 13 cents in her piggy bank. Then she earned 20 cents for taking out the recycling and 50 cents for cleaning the cat box. How much more money does she need to earn to have $1.00?

Question: How much more money does Josie need to earn to have $1.00?

Steps (Tell what to do.)	Reasons (Explain why.)	Work (Solve the problem.)
1. List the facts.	– to know what numbers I need	– Josie had 13 cents – she earned 20 cents for recycling – she earned 50 cents for cat box
2. Change $1.00 to 100 cents.	– so I can subtract the other cents from it	$1.00 = 100 cents
3. Subtract 20 cents and 50 cents (70 cents) from 100 cents.	– because she earned that much money from doing her chores	20 100 +50 –70 ── ── 70 30
4. Subtract 13 cents from 30 cents.	– because she already had 13 cents in her piggy bank	30 – 13 ── 17
5. Check the answer.	– to be sure it's right	17 13 20 + 50 ── 100

Final answer in a complete sentence: Josie needs to earn 17 more cents to have $1.00.

Math Tool P-2-12c

Three–Column Notes for Problem Solving

Directions: Write a paragraph about your problem solving.

Example 1:

Earning Money

To find out how much more money Josie needs to earn to have $1.00, follow these steps: First, list the facts so that you know what information you're working with. Then, add 13 cents, 20 cents, and 50 cents to find out how much Josie already has (83 cents). After that, subtract 83 cents from $1.00 to find out how much more money Josie needs to earn to have $1.00. Finally, check your answer to make sure it's correct. If you follow these steps, you'll find out that Josie only needs 17 cents to have $1.00.

Example 2:

Earning Money

To figure out how much more money Josie needs to earn to have $1.00, I followed a couple of steps: First, I listed the facts to know what numbers I needed. Then I changed $1.00 to 100 cents so that I could subtract the other cents from it. Next, I subtracted 70 cents from the 100 cents because that's what Josie earned from doing her chores. I also subtracted 13 cents from the 30 cents that was left because she already had that 13 cents in her piggy bank. Finally, I checked my answer to be sure it was right. I found out I was right that Josie only needs to earn 17 cents more to add up to $1.00.

Math Tool P-2-12d

Framed Responses

Title: _____

After reading _____

_____ in class today, I realized I had learned two important facts. First,

_____. Next, I learned _____

_____

_____

_____.

- -

Title: _____

Pages _____ in Chapter _____ explain how to

_____. First, you start by

_____. Then _____

_____. Finally, _____

_____.

- -

Title: _____

As I read _____, I learned about

_____. First of all, I _____

_____. I also

_____

_____.

Math Tool I-2-5

Math Tools: Intermediate *(continued)*

Math Tool I-2-7

Marking Word Problems
Improve Your Comprehension

1. Read the problem!	Julio and his father want to build a fence in their yard. They need four nails for each board on the fence. If the fence has 50 boards, how many nails should Julio's father buy if he wants 20 extra nails in case some get bent or dropped?
2. Reread the problem! Then underline all numbers and math–related terms.	Julio and his father want to build a fence in their yard. They need <u>four</u> nails for <u>each board</u> on the fence. If the fence has <u>50 boards</u>, <u>how many</u> nails should Julio's father buy if he wants <u>20 extra nails</u> in case some get bent or dropped?
3. Find the "who" and the "what." Mark them with a W.	[W] Julio and his father want to build a fence in their yard. They need <u>four</u> nails for <u>each board</u> on the [W] fence. If the fence has <u>50 boards</u>, <u>how many</u> nails should Julio's father buy if he wants <u>20 extra nails</u> in case some get bent or dropped?
4. Circle the situation, issue, or circumstance. Look for action verbs.	[W] Julio and his father want to (build a fence) in their yard. They (need four nails) for each board on the fence. If the (fence has 50 boards,) how many nails should Julio's father buy if he (wants 20 extra nails) in case some get bent or dropped?
5. Box the question that needs to be answered.	[W] Julio and his father want to (build a fence) in their yard. They (need four nails) for each board on the fence. If the (fence has 50 boards,) [how many nails should Julio's father buy] if he (wants 20 extra nails) in case some get bent or dropped?

Step Up to Writing in Math · Reading and Note Taking · Math Tool—I-2-7

Math Tool I-2-9a

Read, Illustrate, and Solve Word Problems

Restate the problem.	
List the facts.	
List the clue words.	
Estimate or predict.	
Illustrate the problem.	
Solve the problem.	
Write the final answer in a complete sentence. Add labels or units when needed.	

Step Up to Writing in Math · Reading and Note Taking · Math Tool—I-2-9a

Math Tool I-2-9b

Read, Illustrate, and Solve Word Problems

Word Problem:

Buying a Stereo

A stereo plus two speakers sold as a set costs $285.50. Sold separately, the two speakers cost $155 and the stereo costs $160. How much does Chano save by buying the set?

Step Up to Writing in Math · Reading and Note Taking · Math Tool—I-2-9b

Math Tool I-2-9c

Read, Illustrate, and Solve Word Problems
Buying a Stereo

Restate the problem.	How much will Chano save if he buys the stereo and speakers as a set?
List the facts.	– speakers = $155 – stereo = $160 – set = $285.50
List the clue words.	– separately – how much – set – save – cost
Estimate or predict.	$20
Illustrate the problem.	(each) (set) [$155] +[$160] – [ ][ ] = savings Total – cost of the set = savings
Solve the problem.	$155.00 $315.00 + 160.00 – 285.50 ———— ———— $315.00 $29.50 cost if bought saved if bought separately as a set
Write the final answer in a complete sentence. Add labels or units when needed.	Chano will save $29.50 if he buys the stereo and speakers as a set.

Step Up to Writing in Math · Reading and Note Taking · Math Tool—I-2-9c

Math Tools: Intermediate *(continued)*

Read, Illustrate, and Solve Word Problems

Buying a Stereo

    To figure out how much Chano would save, I used these steps. First, I took time to list the facts so I could compare the prices alone and as a set. Then I looked for clue words. The word "save" told me that I would be subtracting, since people save money when they buy something for less money. Next, I estimated that Chano could save $20. I did this by rounding off the sum of $155 and $160 in my head and comparing it with the $285.50. After that, I drew a sketch to make my comparison. I could quickly see that the set was the best buy. Finally, I solved the problem. The set costs $285.50, and the parts sold separately cost $315. Chano will save $29.50 if he buys the set and not the separate parts.

Math Tool *I-2-9d*

Read, Illustrate, and Solve Word Problems

Word Problem:

Farmer Hall's Pumpkins

Farmer Hall planted 88 rows of pumpkins. Each row produced 34 pumpkins. Farmer Hall sold one-half of the pumpkins to the local supermarket owners. He left the other half in his pumpkin patch for the town's school children to pick and take home. How many pumpkins were left in Farmer Hall's pumpkin patch?

Math Tool *I-2-9e*

Read, Illustrate, and Solve Word Problems

Farmer Hall's Pumpkins

Restate the problem.	How many pumpkins were left in Farmer Hall's pumpkin patch?
List the facts.	– 88 rows – half left in patch – 34 pumpkins in each row – half to supermarkets
List the clue words.	– each (x) – half left for kids (÷)
Estimate or predict.	1500
Illustrate the problem.	88 34 [diagram] s ÷ 2 = s for kids
Solve the problem.	88 x 34 = 2992 2992 ÷ 2 = 1496
Write the final answer in a complete sentence. Add labels or units when needed.	There were 1496 pumpkins left in Farmer Hall's pumpkin patch.

Math Tool *I-2-9f*

Read, Illustrate, and Solve Word Problems

Farmer Hall's Pumpkins

    To find out how many pumpkins were left in the pumpkin patch, I completed a few math steps. First, I listed all of the facts. Farmer Hall had 88 rows of pumpkins with 34 pumpkins in each. He sold half of them to the supermarkets and kept the rest for kids to pick. Then I estimated that there might be about 3000 total pumpkins because I rounded 88 to 100 and 34 to 30 and multiplied 100 by 30. Half of that would be 1500 pumpkins. Next, I made a quick sketch with lines to show the farm with 88 rows being divided by 2. Finally, I multiplied 88 by 34 to get the total number of pumpkins that Farmer Hall had. He had 2992 pumpkins. Then I divided 2992 by 2 since one-half of the pumpkins went to the stores and one-half were left for picking. I learned that there were 1496 pumpkins in the patch for any students who came to take a pumpkin home.

Math Tool *I-2-9g*

Math Tools: Intermediate *(continued)*

Notes With Illustrations for Problem Solving

Word Problem:

Enough Cake for Grandma?

Logan has four people in his family: himself, his mom, his dad, and his sister. Logan's family baked a cake for their Sunday picnic. At the picnic, they divided the cake into 10 equal pieces and then ate 40% of the cake. That night, Logan's dad ate another piece for a snack. On Monday morning, Logan put a piece in his lunch. Mom put the rest away for dinner that night. Since the cake was cut into equal-size pieces and all of the pieces that the family ate were the same size, will there be enough pieces for all the members of Logan's family, plus Logan's grandma when she comes for dinner on Monday night?

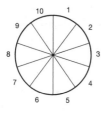

Math Tool I-2-11a

Notes With Illustrations for Problem Solving

Enough Cake for Grandma?

Facts	Illustration	Math Computation
1. The family ate 40% of the cake.		100% - 40% eaten 60% left
2. Dad ate an extra piece as a snack.		60% - 10% eaten 50% left
3. Logan put another piece in his lunch.		50% - 10% eaten 40% left
4. Grandma comes to dinner.		4 + 1 5 total people
5. There will not be enough cake left.		40% family + 10% Grandma 50% needed for 5 people

Final answer/complete sentence: *There will not be enough pieces because only 40% (4 pieces) of the cake is left. The family plus Grandma will need 5 pieces, or 50%.*

Math Tool I-2-11b

Notes With Illustrations for Problem Solving

Enough Cake for Grandma?

I solved the question about the cake in a few easy steps. First, I drew a cake with 4 pieces gone. I made all of the cut pieces the same size. The missing pieces are the 40% that the family ate at the picnic.

Then I drew the cake with 5 pieces gone. When Dad ate a piece, it left only 50% of the cake. I did this again when Logan took a piece for lunch. This left 4 pieces, or 40% of the cake.

After that I drew 4 people to show the family and 1 person to show Grandma. This meant that 5 people needed 50% of the cake. Since there was only 40% left, there were not enough pieces for each person to have a piece.

The family, of course, can cut up the 40% in a different way and share it. I think they will!

Math Tool I-2-11c

Notes With Illustrations for Problem Solving

Word Problem:

Dinner With Francis

Francis invited Sally over for dinner. Francis had two-thirds of a small ten-inch pizza left over and Sally brought three-fourths of a small ten-inch pizza she had left over. How much total pizza did they have?

Math Tool I-2-11d

Math Tools: Intermediate *(continued)*

Notes With Illustrations for Problem Solving

Dinner With Francis

Facts	Illustration	Math Computation
Francis has two-thirds. Sally has three-fourths.		$\frac{2}{3} + \frac{3}{4}$
The common denominator is 12.	$\frac{2}{3} + \frac{3}{4}$	$3 \times 4 = 12$
Francis' pizza is equivalent to $\frac{8}{12}$ of a whole pizza.		$\frac{2}{3} \times \frac{4}{4} = \frac{8}{12}$
Sally's pizza is equivalent to $\frac{9}{12}$ of a whole pizza.		$\frac{3}{4} \times \frac{3}{3} = \frac{9}{12}$
Combine the pizzas.		$\frac{8}{12} + \frac{9}{12} = \frac{17}{12}$
Reduce the fraction.		$17 - 12 = 5$ $\frac{17}{12} = 1\frac{5}{12}$
Final answer/complete sentence: *Francis and Sally have $1\frac{5}{12}$ pizzas.*		

Math Tool I-2-11e

Notes With Illustrations for Problem Solving

Dinner With Francis

   To solve the pizza problem I performed these steps. First, I found the common denominator. Multiplying the denominators together gives a common denominator of 12.

   Next, I drew a circle and split it into thirds. I shaded two of the parts. I multiplied $\frac{2}{3}$ by $\frac{4}{4}$ to get $\frac{8}{12}$. I drew lines on Francis' circle to show that it was divided into 12 parts. I multiplied $\frac{3}{4}$ by $\frac{3}{3}$ to get $\frac{9}{12}$ and drew lines on Sally's circle to show it was divided into 12 parts.

   Then, I added the fractions $\frac{8}{12}$ and $\frac{9}{12}$ to get $\frac{17}{12}$. I can check this by counting all of the new shaded pieces of pizza.

   Finally, I wrote a mixed number by subtracting 12 from 17. This means that there is one whole pizza and $\frac{5}{12}$ of another pizza.

   Francis and Sally have $1\frac{5}{12}$ pizzas to eat.

Math Tool I-2-11f

Three-Column Notes for Problem Solving

Word Problem:

Question:

Steps (Tell what to do.)	Reasoning (Explain why.)	Work (Solve the problem.)

Final answer in a complete sentence:

Math Tool I-2-12a

Three-Column Notes for Problem Solving

Word Problem: Mrs. Jones' social studies class received the following scores on their chapter test: 77, 90, 88, 50, 85, 75, 98, 90, 84, and 89. What is the median score?

Question: *Find the median score on Mrs. Jones' social studies test.*

Steps (Tell what to do.)	Reasoning (Explain why.)	Work (Solve the problem.)
1. List the facts.	so I know what information I'm working with	test scores = 77, 90, 88, 50, 85, 75, 98, 90, 84, 89
2. Arrange the scores in order.	so that I can "count in" to find the middle score	50, 75, 77, 84, 85, 88, 89, 90, 90, 98
3. Starting from each end count inwards to find the number in the middle.	this is how you find the median	the middle numbers are 85 and 88
4. Average the two middle numbers.	since there are two numbers in the middle of the data set, you need to average them to find the median	$85 + 88 = 173$ $173 \div 2 = 86.5$

Final answer in a complete sentence: *The median score on Mrs. Jones' social studies test was an 86.5.*

Math Tool I-2-12b

Math Tools: Intermediate–Secondary

Three–Column Notes for Problem Solving

Word Problem: Mrs. Jones' social studies class received the following scores on their chapter test: 77, 90, 88, 50, 85, 75, 98, 90, 84, and 89. What is the median score?

Question: *Find the median score on Mrs. Jones' social studies test.*

Steps (Tell what to do.)	Reasoning (Explain why.)	Work (Solve the problem.)
1. List the facts.	*so I know what information I'm working with*	*test scores = 77, 90, 88, 50, 85, 75, 98, 90, 84, 89*
2. Arrange the scores in order.	*so that I can "count in" to find the middle score*	*50, 75, 77, 84, 85, 88, 89, 90, 90, 98*
3. Count the total number of scores.	*so that I can figure out how many scores to "count in" to find the median*	*there are 10 test scores*
4. Divide the number of scores by 2.	*this tells me how many scores I need to "count in" to find the median*	*10 ÷ 2 = 5*
5. "Count in" five test scores and average the fifth and sixth scores.	*since there is an even number of scores, you need to average the two in the middle to find the median*	*85 + 88 = 173* *173 ÷ 2 = 86.5*

Final answer in a complete sentence: *The median score on Mrs. Jones' social studies test was an 86.5.*

Math Tool I-2-12c

Three–Column Notes for Problem Solving

Directions: Write a paragraph about your problem solving.

Example 1:

The Median Score

To find the median score on Mrs. Jones' social studies test, follow these steps. First, list the facts so that you know what information you're working with. Then, arrange the scores in order, so that you can "count in" to find the middle score. Starting from each end, count inwards to find the middle. Since there are two numbers in the middle of the data, you need to average them to find the median. The median score on Mrs. Jones' social studies test is an 86.5.

Example 2:

The Median Score

To figure out the median score on Mrs. Jones' social studies test, I followed a couple of steps. First, I listed the facts to know what information I was working with. Then, I arranged the scores in order so that I could count in to find the middle score. Next, I counted the total number of scores. After that, I divided the number of scores by 2 to find out how many scores I needed to count in to find the median. Finally, I counted in 5 test scores and averaged the fifth and sixth scores. Since the number of scores is an even number, I had to average the two in the middle to find the median. I figured out that the median score on Mrs. Jones' social studies test was an 86.5.

Math Tool I-2-12d

Framed Responses

Title: _____

Today as I read _____, I learned two facts about _____

First, _____

_____. I also learned that _____

_____

_____

Title: _____

Section _____ in our math textbook describes _____

_____. First, it _____

_____. Then _____

Finally, it _____

_____

Title: _____

During class today, as we read and discussed _____

I learned something new. To begin, _____

_____. This also _____

Most important, it _____

_____

Math Tool S-2-5

Marking Word Problems

Improve Your Comprehension

1. Read the problem!	During the summer before starting high school, Hayden earned money mowing lawns. He deposited $800 in a savings account for college. His bank offered Hayden a 6% simple interest annual rate. If Hayden doesn't withdraw any money from the account and the interest rate stays the same, how much will he have at the end of five years?
2. Reread the problem! Then underline all numbers and math–related terms.	During the summer before starting high school, Hayden earned money mowing lawns. He deposited $800 in a savings account for college. His bank offered Hayden a 6% simple interest annual rate. If Hayden doesn't withdraw any money from the account and the interest rate stays the same, how much will he have at the end of five years?
3. Find the "who" and the "what." Mark them with a W.	During the summer before starting high school, Hayden earned money mowing lawns. He deposited $800 in a savings account for college. His bank offered Hayden a 6% simple interest annual rate. If Hayden doesn't withdraw any money from the account and the interest rate stays the same, how much will he have at the end of five years?
4. Circle the situation, issue, or circumstance. Look for action verbs.	During the summer before starting high school, Hayden earned money mowing lawns. He deposited $800 in a savings account for college. His bank offered Hayden a 6% simple interest annual rate. If Hayden doesn't withdraw any money from the account and the interest rate stays the same, how much will he have at the end of five years?
5. Box the question that needs to be answered.	During the summer before starting high school, Hayden earned money mowing lawns. He deposited $800 in a savings account for college. His bank offered Hayden a 6% simple interest annual rate. If Hayden doesn't withdraw any money from the account and the interest rate stays the same, how much will he have at the end of five years?

Math Tool S-2-7

Math Tools: Secondary (continued)

Read, Illustrate, and Solve Word Problems

Restate the problem.	
List the facts.	
List the clue words.	
Estimate or predict.	
Illustrate the problem.	
Solve the problem.	
Write the final answer in a complete sentence. Include labels or units when needed.	

Math Tool S-2-9a

Read, Illustrate, and Solve Word Problems

Word Problem:

Ordering Carpet

Mary has a room that is 21 feet long and 18 feet wide. How much carpet (sold by the yard) will she need if she carpets half of the room?

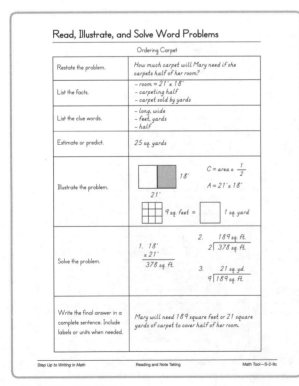

Math Tool S-2-9b

Read, Illustrate, and Solve Word Problems

Ordering Carpet

Restate the problem.	*How much carpet will Mary need if she carpets half of her room?*
List the facts.	*– room = 21' x 18'* *– carpeting half* *– carpet sold by yards*
List the clue words.	*– long, wide* *– feet, yards* *– half*
Estimate or predict.	*25 sq. yards*
Illustrate the problem.	$C = area \times \frac{1}{2}$ $18'$ $A = 21' \times 18'$ $21'$ *9 sq. feet = 1 sq. yard*

Solve the problem.	1. $18'$
	   $\times 21'$
	   $\overline{378 \text{ sq. ft.}}$
	
	2. $\frac{189 \text{ sq. ft.}}{2 \overline{) 378 \text{ sq. ft.}}}$
	
	3. $\frac{21 \text{ sq. yd.}}{9 \overline{) 189 \text{ sq. ft.}}}$

Write the final answer in a complete sentence. Include labels or units when needed.	*Mary will need 189 square feet or 21 square yards of carpet to cover half of her room.*

Math Tool S-2-9c

Read, Illustrate, and Solve Word Problems

Explain How You Solved the Problem

Carpet for Mary's Room

    I solved the problem about ordering carpet by following these steps. First, I listed the facts about the length and width of the room. I noted that Mary was carpeting only half of the room. I listed clue words, especially the fact that carpet is sold by the yard. It told me that I would need to convert feet into yards. At a glance, I estimated that Mary would need about 25 square yards of carpet. Next, I sketched a picture of the room and jotted down the formula for finding the area of a room. Mary's room is 21 feet by 18 feet. That means the room is 378 square feet in area. Then I divided the 378 by 2, since only half of the room gets carpet. The room needs 189 square feet of carpet. Finally, I divided the 189 by 9 to change the square feet to square yards. There are 9 square feet in 1 square yard. Mary will want to buy 21 square yards of carpet for her room. I was a bit off in my estimate.

Math Tool S-2-9d

Math Tools: Secondary *(continued)*

Read, Illustrate, and Solve Word Problems

Word Problem:

Number of Deer in the National Park

Mark is a biologist studying the deer population in a national park. He captures and tags 154 deer and then lets them go back in the park. Several weeks later he captures 50 deer. Six out of the 50 have tags. How many deer can Mark assume are in the park?

Math Tool S-2-9e

Read, Illustrate, and Solve Word Problems

Number of Deer in the National Park

Restate the problem.	*Approximately how many deer are in the park?*
List the facts.	*– 154 deer were tagged* *– 50 deer were captured* *– 6 of the 50 had tags*
List the clue words.	*"Six out of the 50" tells me I will use ratios.*
Estimate or predict.	*1500 deer*
Illustrate the problem.	*6 tagged 154 tagged* *50 = x*
Solve the problem.	$\frac{6}{50}$ $\frac{154}{x}$ $6x = 50*154$ $x = 1283.3$ $6x = 7700$ $\frac{6x}{6}$ $\frac{7700}{6}$
Write the final answer in a complete sentence. Include labels or units when needed.	*Mark can assume there are about 1283 deer in the park.*

Math Tool S-2-9f

Read, Illustrate, and Solve Word Problems

Explain How You Solved the Problem

Number of Deer in the National Park

In order to solve the deer in the park problem, I followed these steps. First, I wrote down the important facts. Mark originally tagged 154 deer and released them back into the park. Fifty deer were then captured, with only six having tags. "Six out of 50" led me to believe that I would need ratios and proportions to solve this problem. Next, I made an educated guess of the number of deer in the park and came up with 1500. I then made a drawing to help me visualize the situation. Finally, I set up the proportions and solved for x by using cross-multiplication. I figured out that Mark can assume that there are approximately 1283 deer in the park.

Math Tool S-2-9g

Notes With Illustrations for Problem Solving

Word Problem:

Art Project

Each student in the seventh grade art class needs 9 disks. The disks should be cut from felt that comes in 8-inch by 10-inch sheets. The disks must have a diameter of $3\frac{1}{2}$ inches. How many sheets of felt will each student need in order to cut out the right number of disks?

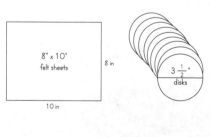

8" x 10" felt sheets — 8 in — 10 in — $3\frac{1}{2}$" disks

Math Tool S-2-11a

Math Tools: Secondary *(continued)*

Notes With Illustrations for Problem Solving

Art Project

Facts	Illustration	Math Computation
1. Students need 9 disks from the felt.	(circle $3\frac{1}{2}$") rectangle 8 in by 10 in	$3\frac{1}{2}$ inch disks 8 in. x 10 in. felt
2. Four disks will fit on one felt sheet.	four circles $3\frac{1}{2}$" each	$3\frac{1}{2}$" + $3\frac{1}{2}$" = 7" 10" - 7" = 3" $3\frac{1}{2}$" - 3" = $\frac{1}{2}$" too short for a third disk
3. Each student needs 3 felt sheets.	illustrations of disks	4 disks to a sheet $4\overline{)9}$ $\frac{2r1}{-8}$ 1 Students will need three sheets of felt to cut 9 disks with a $3\frac{1}{2}$" diameter.

Final answer/complete sentence: *Each student will need three sheets of felt to get 9 disks with a $3\frac{1}{2}$" diameter.*

Step Up to Writing in Math   Reading and Note Taking   Math Tool—S-2-11b

Math Tool S-2-11b

Notes With Illustrations for Problem Solving

Explain How You Solved the Problem

Art Project

I solved the problem about the disks and the felt for the art project in a few steps using some basic sketches. First, I made a rectangle that showed 8" by 10" since this is the size of the felt. Then I drew two disks with $3\frac{1}{2}$" diameters each and saw that only two will fit side by side. They take up 7" of space. Next, I sketched two more and saw that I had only 3" left at the bottom of the felt. I realized that two $3\frac{1}{2}$" disks take up 7" and leave 3". That's not enough space for another $3\frac{1}{2}$" disk. Students will need three sheets of felt in order to get all of the disks they need to start their project. Sharing felt sheets seems like a good option that the teacher and students should consider. It would save a lot of felt.

Step Up to Writing in Math   Reading and Note Taking   Math Tool—S-2-11c

Math Tool S-2-11c

Notes With Illustrations for Problem Solving

Word Problem:

Area of Robert's Room

Robert had a square rug. He didn't know the dimensions of it, but he knew if it were three feet longer on one side and eight feet longer on the other, it would cover his room. Make an expression to represent the area of Robert's room.

Step Up to Writing in Math   Reading and Note Taking   Math Tool—S-2-11d

Math Tool S-2-11d

Notes With Illustrations for Problem Solving

Area of Robert's Room

Facts	Illustration	Math Computation
The rug has a length and width of x since we don't know its dimensions.	x by x square	$x \cdot x$ = Area of rug
Add three feet to one side and eight to the other.	grid with x, 3 and x, 8	$(x + 3)(x + 8)$ = Area of room
Find the area of each rectangle.	grid x^2, $3x$, $8x$, 24	$x \cdot x = x^2$ $3 \cdot x = 3x$ $8 \cdot x = 8x$ $8 \cdot 3 = 24$
Add the terms to find an expression that represents the total area of Robert's room.	$x^2 + 11x + 24$	$x^2 + 3x + 8x + 24 = x^2 + 11x + 24$

Final answer/complete sentence: *The area of Robert's room is represented by $x^2 + 11x + 24$.*

Step Up to Writing in Math   Reading and Note Taking   Math Tool—S-2-11e

Math Tool S-2-11e

Math Tools: Secondary *(continued)*

Notes With Illustrations for Problem Solving

Explain How You Solved the Problem

Area of Robert's Room

In order to find an expression to represent the area of Robert's room, I followed these steps. First, I made an area model representing the situation. Then I found the area of the four small rectangles by multiplying length times width for each one. Since the area of the large rectangle is the same as the sum of the areas of the smaller rectangles, I then added the four areas together. After combining like terms, I ended up with an expression for the area of Robert's room, which was $x^2 + 11x + 24$.

Step Up to Writing in Math   Reading and Note Taking   Math Tool—S-2-11f

Math Tool S-2-11f

Three-Column Notes for Problem Solving

Word Problem:

Problem Summary:

Steps	Rationale	Work

Final answer in a complete sentence:

Step Up to Writing in Math   Reading and Note Taking   Math Tool—S-2-12a

Math Tool S-2-12a

Three-Column Notes for Problem Solving

Word Problem: Pop King popcorn comes in 12 oz. packages. Due to the machine that puts the popcorn in the package, the weight of each package varies slightly. The engineers at Pop King determined that each package has a mean weight of 12 oz. with a standard deviation of 0.3 oz. If a package weighs more than 12.5 oz. the machine rejects it. What is the probability that a package will get rejected?

Problem Summary: *In a population with a mean of 12 and standard deviation of 0.3, what is the probability of a data point being greater than 12.5?*

Steps	Rationale	Work
1. Draw, label, and shade a normal curve.	this will help me to decide what to do with the z-score probability	 12 12.5
2. Calculate the z-score.	this tells me how many standard deviations away from the mean the score is	$z = \dfrac{12.5 - 12}{0.3} = 1.67$
3. Look up the corresponding probability in the normal table.	this tells me the percentage area under the curve between the mean and the z-score	the probability is 0.4525
4. Add 0.4525 to 0.5.	this tells me the total area under the curve that is to the left of 12.5	$0.4525 + 0.5 = 0.9525$
5. Subtract 0.9525 from 1.0.	this tells me the area under the curve above 12.5, which is the probability of a number being greater than 12.5	$1.0 - 0.9525 = 0.0475$

Final answer in a complete sentence: *The probability of a package of popcorn being rejected is 0.0475, or 4.75%.*

Step Up to Writing in Math   Reading and Note Taking   Math Tool—S-2-12b

Math Tool S-2-12b

Three-Column Notes for Problem Solving

Word Problem: Pop King popcorn comes in 12 oz. packages. Due to the machine that puts the popcorn in the package, the weight of each package varies slightly. The engineers at Pop King determined that each package has a mean weight of 12 oz. with a standard deviation of 0.3 oz. If a package weighs more than 12.5 oz. the machine rejects it. What is the probability that a package will get rejected?

Problem Summary: *In a population with a mean of 12 and standard deviation of 0.3, what is the probability of a data point being greater than 12.5?*

Steps	Rationale	Work
1. Draw, label, and shade a normal curve.	this tells me whether I need to add or subtract the probability found from the z-score	 12 12.5
2. Calculate the z-score.	so that I can look up the probability in the table	$z = \dfrac{12.5 - 12}{0.3} = 1.67$
3. Look up the corresponding probability in the normal table.	this tells me the probability of getting that z-score	the probability is 0.4525
4. Subtract 0.4525 from 0.5.	I do this because I want to find the probability greater than 1.67	$0.5 - 0.4525 = 0.0475$

Final answer in a complete sentence: *The probability of a package of popcorn being rejected is 0.0475, or 4.75%.*

Step Up to Writing in Math   Reading and Note Taking   Math Tool—S-2-12c

Math Tool S-2-12c

Math Tools: Secondary *(continued)*

Three-Column Notes for Problem Solving

Directions: Write a paragraph about your problem solving.

Example 1:

Data Point

To find the probability of a data point being greater than 12.5, you need to follow a couple of steps. First, draw, label, and shade a normal curve to help you decide what to do with the z-score probability. Then, calculate the z-score to find out how many standard deviations away from the mean the score is. Look up the corresponding probability in the normal table. This will tell you the percentage area under the curve between the mean and the z-score. Add the probability, 0.4525, to 0.5 to find the total area under the curve that is to the left of 12.5. Subtract that number from 1.0 to find the area under the curve above 12.5. This is the probability of being greater than 12.5. By following these steps, you will find that the probability of a package of popcorn being rejected by the machine is 0.0475, or 4.75%.

Example 2:

Data Point

In order to find the probability of a data point being greater than 12.5, I followed a couple of steps. First, I drew, labeled, and shaded a normal curve to figure out whether I needed to add or subtract the probability found from the z-score. Then, I calculated the z-score so that I could look up the probability in the table. Next, I looked up the corresponding probability in the normal table to find out the probability of getting that z-score. Finally, I subtracted that probability from 0.5 to find the probability greater than 1.67. I found out that the probability of a package of popcorn being rejected by the machine is 0.0475, or 4.75%.

| *Step Up to Writing in Math* | Reading and Note Taking | Math Tool—S-2-12d |

Math Tool S-2-12d

SUMMARIZING TEXT AND WRITING ABOUT GRAPHS

*S*tudents who can create a clear, concise summary of articles, lectures and lessons, videos and films, or textbook chapters—either orally or in writing—show that they understand the content and meaning of the piece they are summarizing. Knowing how to write summaries quickly and accurately is an important academic skill.

Section 3 presents an easy-to-learn and easy-to-teach strategy for writing a summary. It includes four predictable steps, which students can follow whenever they are asked to summarize. Even nonreaders, like prekindergarten and kindergarten students, can master this strategy; they can learn to summarize what they learn during read-aloud activities. They will echo their teachers, who present a topic sentence for the summary, and then—using small cards, paper strips, or their hands—quickly and accurately give the summary facts that support the topic sentence.

The four-step summary method can easily be put to use in other types of writing, including writing about graphs.

Students read, explain, analyze, interpret, and critique graphs, charts, and tables every day in most math classrooms. Even primary students learn to collect and display information so that it is easy to understand. In addition, students work with graphs, charts, and tables in other classes, including social studies, science, geography, and history.

According to *Curriculum Focal Points for Prekindergarten Through Grade 8 Mathematics*, new standards at state and national levels demand that students not only create and interpret graphs, charts, and tables, but also communicate through speech and writing what they know about graphs, charts, and tables. They must be able to "communicate, interpret, answer, and/or use the results of data collection." (NCTM, 2006.)* Data analysis is a necessary and important component of math instruction at every grade level.

The *Step Up to Writing in Math* strategy **3-1 "Four-Step" Summary Paragraph** (also referred to as the I-V-F method) offers a practical approach to teaching students to communicate about data represented in graphical form. Students apply what they learn about summary writing to a system for explaining their interpretations of graphs, charts, and tables. They can also use this system to describe graphs.

In math, students must represent data in numerous ways: pictographs, frequency tables, horizontal and vertical bar graphs, Venn diagrams, dot plots, line plots, charts, tables, line graphs, circle graphs, scatter plots, histograms, etc. Analyzing data in all of these formats is simpler when students use the *Step Up to Writing in Math* strategies.

Objectives

- Teach students a practical summary-writing process

- Improve reading comprehension

- Help students remember and share what they have learned

- Give students the opportunity to demonstrate comprehension of key ideas and to synthesize information

- Improve students' ability to communicate about what they learn in math texts and/or articles.

- Provide strategies for reporting about graphs, tables, charts, and data in other graphical formats

- Prepare students for informal and formal assessments

---

* Standards are listed with the permission of the National Council of Teachers of Mathematics (NCTM). NCTM does not endorse the content or validity of these alignments.

SECTION **3** CONTENTS

3-1 Four-Step Summary Paragraph

A summary is a short text that includes the key ideas of a unit, chapter, article, lecture, and so on. Summaries keep the same tone as the original piece; they do not contain opinion and do not require a formal conclusion.

When students summarize, they process information and are more likely to retain it. This strategy teaches students how to summarize a unit, a chapter, a single page of text, an article, or a lecture quickly and concisely.

The *Step Up to Writing* four-step approach to summary writing is often called the I-V-F strategy.

The letters I, V, and F stand for: identify the item, select a verb, and finish your thought. The steps for writing a summary using this strategy are quite simple:

1. Create a topic sentence using paper folded into three columns with the labels I, V, and F. The verb should be a summary verb, such as *tells*, *explains*, or *describes*. For example:

I Identify the item.	V Select a verb.	F Finish your thought.
The article "The Numbers Game: Why Math Books Are Hot"	explains	why math books meant for reading pleasure are popular.

2. Rewrite the sentence in a standard format, without the dividing lines.

> The article "The Numbers Game: Why Math Books Are Hot" explains why math books meant for reading pleasure are popular with kids and adults.

3. Create the fact outline by listing key facts that you will use to write the summary. Use a dash for each fact or key idea provided in the text. The facts should reflect the entire piece and should be sequenced to match the story, article, movie, etc. In our example, the fact outline might look like:

- lots of books
- movies
- feelings of confidence
- explain mysteries
- people more sophisticated
- high-tech world
- appreciate math and connection to world
- understand abstract concepts
- solve mysteries

4. Finally, use the topic sentence and fact outline to write the summary. Each fact should become a sentence or a part of a sentence. No formal conclusion is necessary. (As students progress with this strategy, they begin to understand that although they should use the fact outline as a guide, they can make changes and additions as needed when they actually write the paragraph. However, when students first learn the strategy, following the fact outline helps guarantee success.)

Reading About Math

The article "The Numbers Game: Why Math Books Are Hot" explains why math books meant for reading pleasure are popular with kids and adults. Today readers of all ages have a number of books about math to enjoy, and math-oriented movies like *Good Will Hunting* are available. Some experts believe that perhaps citizens are more comfortable with math on the whole because our society is so high-tech. Others suggest that the interest comes from a desire to appreciate the connection that math has to the world. People are also drawn to understand abstract concepts and to solve mysteries. At least one college is offering a reward for solving some famous math mysteries.

Here is another example of the I-V-F strategy in action:

1. Create the topic sentence in three columns.

I Identify the item.	**V** Select a verb.	**F** Finish your thought.
Page 11 in our math workbook	explains	how to read a calendar.

2. Rewrite the sentence in the normal way without the lines.

> Page 11 in our math workbook explains how to read a calendar.

3. Make a list of facts—a fact outline.

> - name of month
> - days of week
> - numbers in different places
> - some have more days
> - count weeks
> - count Mondays

4. Write the paragraph. Use your summary topic sentence and your fact outline.

> ### Learning About Calendars
>
> Page 11 in our math workbook explains how to read a calendar. On each page of the calendar, the name of the month is at the top. The days of the week are printed above the squares in each column. Sunday is on the left side, and Saturday is the last one on the right. Each page in the calendar has the number 1 in a different place. That is because the first day for each month is different. Each calendar page has different numbers because the months have different numbers of days. A calendar can help us count the number of weeks in a month.

Before a Lesson

- Select short articles or subsections from the math textbook to use for demonstration and practice.

- Practice writing summaries, imitating the examples above.

- Create examples to share with students using chart paper or overhead transparencies.

- Set expectations for what you want students to include in their summaries.

- Keep in mind that summaries are often meant to be short; good summaries use about two-thirds to three-fourths of a page. This is a good rule for beginning writers and for advanced, proficient writers. Writers of all skill levels use the same steps and the same strategies for summary writing. As they become proficient writers, only the content and the sophistication of the writing changes.

Note: Two-, three-, or four-page summaries are rare. These are more like retells or reports that include major and minor details.

During a Lesson

- Start by sharing examples and explaining the purpose and importance of summary writing.

- Explain how and why you will be asking for summaries. Share your expectations for quality work.

- Using the examples you have created, take students through the steps for writing a summary paragraph.

- Create a summary or two with students in guided lessons.

- Give students time to write summaries individually or with their peers.

- Discuss the results. Give students time to ask and answer questions, as well as to make suggestions for using or improving the summary-writing strategy.

Additional Ideas

- Make summarizing a regular part of class instruction. It is not always necessary to have students write out the paragraph version of the summary. Save time by having students complete only the topic sentence and fact outline. Then have students share their summaries orally, in a small- or whole-group setting.

- Whole-group summaries are effective. When students know that they are expected to summarize information that they read or hear, they have a purpose and incentive to stay focused. More important, summarizing (alone or with others) gives students an opportunity to internalize what they have learned.

- Use summaries as a warm-up for the next day's lesson. Students will welcome the chance to show off what they remember, and the review will set the tone for learning more about the same topic.

Examples:

1. The math lesson yesterday helped us review the rules for multiplication.

2. Section 5 that we started yesterday gives information about using scales to measure distance.

3-2 Practicing I-V-F Summary Topic Sentences

To be successful at summary writing, students must be able to write a solid summary topic sentence. The topic sentence serves as the controlling statement in the summary. It lets readers know what the paragraph will summarize. When students write clear topic sentences, they establish a sense of focus for the summary. This leaves them free to think about content.

Core to the I-V-F strategy is selecting the right verb for the topic sentence. Three verbs that usually work well in summary topic sentences are *tells*, *explains*, and *describes* (the "TED" verbs).

The I-V-F summary strategy is easy to learn, but students must practice it in order to develop the skills they need to select the main idea of an article or chapter. They also need help forming clear topic sentences that summarize a lesson, a lecture, a video, or a film. Help students master this skill by using the I-V-F strategy frequently. You can adapt it for a variety of tasks. Use the I-V-F topic sentence strategy:

- When students have finished viewing a video or film.

The video "Saving for a Goal"	explains	how interest works and savings accounts grow.

- When students have read a news article.

The article in Sunday's paper	describes	three serious problems with our city's budget for road and sidewalk repairs.

- When students read books.

The book *Harry Measures the World*	tells	about a small boy who uses his new ruler and tape measure on everything he sees.

- When students start a new unit or chapter.

The chapter 17 overview	describes	important math concepts that we will cover in this section.

- When students read special feature articles in their textbooks.

The article about the Statue of Liberty	explains	how to create scale drawings.

You can have students practice topic sentences in a variety of ways:

- by writing on the back of handouts,

- by writing on index cards or small slips of paper as a "ticket out" at the end of class,

- by dedicating pages in their math notebooks, and/or

- by writing them on self-stick notes and attaching them to pages in their textbooks.

3-3 Writing to Explain a Graph

The process for explaining, analyzing, critiquing, or interpreting graphs in a paragraph form is the same process used to write a summary (**3-1 Four-Step Summary Paragraph**).

- The verb choice and the purpose for the paragraph are different, but the paragraph structure is the same.

- One other difference to note is that in describing a graph or other visual representation of data, students should use complete sentences in their fact outline, rather than just words and phrases.

The four steps to write about graphs are:

1. Write an I-V-F topic sentence with a strong action verb that shows the purpose for the paragraph.

2. Rewrite the sentence in the standard way—not broken into three parts.

3. Make a fact outline with complete sentences to support the topic sentence. The sentences will be facts or observations about the graph.

4. Combine the topic sentence and the sentences from the fact outline to write the paragraph.

For example, suppose that students were asked to analyze this graph:

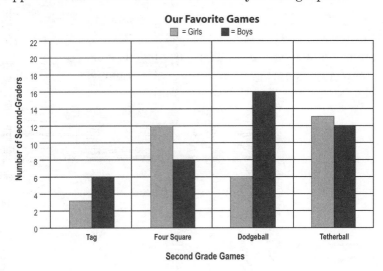

First, they would write the topic sentence in the I-V-F three-column format.

I	V	F
Identify the item.	Select a verb.	Finish your thought.
The graph that we made today	shows	which games all of the second-grade boys and girls in our school like the best and the least.

Next, they would rewrite the summary topic sentence in the standard sentence form.

> The graph that we made today shows which games all of the second-grade boys and girls in our school like the best and the least.

Then they would support the topic sentence with a list of facts or observations about the graph.

> - Boys like dodgeball the best.
> - Girls like tetherball the best.
> - Boys and girls like tetherball almost the same.
> - Tag is the game that second-graders like the least.
> - Only 9 students say that tag is their favorite game.

Finally, they would write a paragraph using the summary topic sentence and the sentences from their fact outline.

> ### Our Favorite Games
>
> The graph that we made today shows which games all of the second-grade boys and girls in our school like the best and the least. Boys like dodgeball the best. Sixteen boys voted for dodgeball. Girls like tetherball the best. Thirteen girls voted for tetherball. Boys and girls like tetherball almost the same. Twelve boys and thirteen girls marked tetherball as their favorite. Tag is the game that second-graders like the least. Only three girls and six boys voted for tag.

Before a Lesson

- Review Math Tools 3-3a and 3-3b. Read the matching paragraphs on Math Tool 3-3c.

- Make overhead transparencies and student copies, as needed, for Math Tools 3-3a, 3-3b, and 3-3c.

- Practice the strategy with graphs that you will use for demonstration in class.

During a Lesson

- Explain to students that you will be using the summary-writing strategy (**3-1 Four-Step Summary Paragraph**) for a slightly different purpose.

- Start by modeling several examples using an overhead projector. First, display Math Tools 3-3a and 3-3b. Explain how students can create an I-V-F topic sentence and an informal fact outline from looking at, and thinking about, a graph.

- Display Math Tool 3-3c, and explain how students can use their I-V-F topic sentence and their fact outline to write a paragraph describing or analyzing the graph.

- Display a graph that you have selected. Work through each step in the four-step summary writing process, explaining the steps and your thinking as you go. Ask and answer questions.

- Display a second graph. In a guided-lesson format, complete the steps with help from students. Discuss the steps. Ask students to explain the steps.

- Have students work in small groups using graphs from their textbooks or math materials. Give students time to share their work with classmates.

- Discuss the importance of being able to read and interpret graphs for class, for tests, and for real-world activities.

Tool I-3-3a

Tool I-3-3b

Tool I-3-3c

3-4 Analyzing, Interpreting, or Critiquing Graphs at Different Levels

Assignments for writing about graphs will vary. At times, students will be asked simply to explain what a graph shows. But at other times, they will have to explain what a graph can predict, how a graph is misleading, how effective a graph is, or how one graph is better than another.

The four-step strategy for explaining graphs presented in **3-3 Writing to Explain a Graph** can be adapted for these and similar assignments by using the proper verb or verb phrase. Here are some examples of appropriate verbs for different purposes:

- Verbs for describing a graph:

  - shows   - illustrates

  - presents   - shares

  - gives   - displays

  - provides   - demonstrates

- Verbs for making predictions or generalizations based on information in a graph:

  - shows   - explains

  - identifies   - reveals

  - predicts   - suggests

  - can be used to predict

- Verbs for analyzing a graph for errors or deceptiveness:

  - misleads   - fails to

  - misrepresents   - contains

  - neglects to   - can be used to mislead

Add verbs and verb phrases to these lists as you teach graphs, and create lists of your own to fit specific assignments. Share the verbs and verb phrases from each list with students, but do so a few at a time, depending on their age and ability level.

Demonstrate the different ways students might be asked to analyze the same graph. (Use guided lessons and group activities.)

For example, consider this scatter plot:

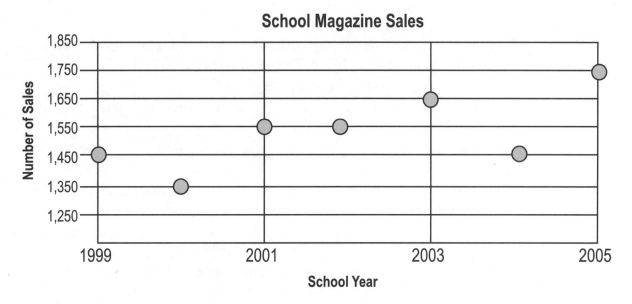

For one assignment, students might be asked to explain what this graph shows. Their work would look something like the examples in **3-3 Writing to Explain a Graph.**

Assignment 1: What does this graph show?

- Students would write the topic sentence in the I-V-F three-column format.

I	V	F
Identify the graph.	Select a verb.	Finish your thought.
The "School Magazine Sales" scatter plot	shows	the growth and decline in annual magazine sales at our local middle school.

- Then they would write the topic sentence in standard form.

> The "School Magazine Sales" scatter plot shows the growth and decline in annual magazine sales at our local middle school.

- Next, they would create a fact outline listing facts and observations that support the topic sentence.

> - With the exception of the 2000 school year, sales every year have been the same as or higher than they were in 1999.
> - The best year for sales was 2005.
> - The biggest drop in sales was between the 2003 and 2004 school years.
> - Sales dropped by 200 between 2003 and 2004.

- And finally, they would write a paragraph using the topic sentence and sentences from the fact outline.

> ### School Magazine Sales
>
> The "School Magazine Sales" scatter plot shows the growth and decline in annual magazine sales at our local middle school. With the exception of the 2000 school year, sales of magazine subscriptions every year have been the same as or higher than sales in 1999. The best year for sales was 2005. The biggest drop in sales was between the 2003 and 2004 school years. Sales dropped by 200 between 2003 and 2004.

A different assignment might ask students what they can predict based on the same graph. They would take the same steps to write their paragraph, but their answer would look very different.

Assignment 2: What does this graph help you predict?

- They would use the I-V-F three-column format to write a topic sentence.

I	V	F
Identify the graph.	Select a verb.	Finish your thought.
The "School Magazine Sales" scatter plot	can be used to predict	the growth in annual magazine sales at our local middle school.

- Then they would write the topic sentence in standard form.

> The "School Magazine Sales" scatter plot can be used to predict the growth in annual magazine sales at our local middle school.

- Next, they would create a fact outline listing facts and observations that support the topic sentence.

> - A "line of best fit" drawn through the points shows a gradual increase.
> - Extending this line allows us to see that about 1,750 magazines should be sold in 2006.
> - The slope of this line is approximately 57 magazines per year.
> - An equation for this line would be M = 57Y + 1350, where M is the number of magazines sold and Y is the number of years since 1999.
> - By using this equation, we can predict that 1,749 magazines will be sold in 2006.

- Finally, students would write a paragraph using the topic sentence and sentences from the fact outline.

> ### The Future of School Magazine Sales
>
> The "School Magazine Sales" scatter plot can be used to predict the growth in annual magazine sales at our local middle school. A line of best fit drawn through the points shows a gradual increase in sales. Extending this line allows us to see that about 1,750 magazines should be sold in 2006. The slope of this line is approximately 57 magazines per year. An equation for this line is M = 57Y + 1350, where M is the number of magazines sold and Y is the number of years since 1999. By using this equation, we can predict that 1,749 magazines will be sold in 2006.

A third assignment might take students even further from a straightforward explanation of the graph. Showing students examples of the different types of questions they might have to answer about a single graph helps them feel prepared when they are asked to analyze graphs in the future, whether in math class, on assessments, or in other classes that use data analysis.

Assignment 3: How does this graph mislead the reader?

- Again, the first step is to write the topic sentence.

I	V	F
Identify the graph.	Select a verb.	Finish your thought.
The "School Magazine Sales" scatter plot	misrepresents	the growth and decline in annual magazine sales at our local middle school.

- Then students can write their topic sentence in standard form.

> The "School Magazine Sales" scatter plot misrepresents the growth and decline in annual magazine sales at our local middle school.

- Next, students need to support the topic sentence by creating a fact outline.

> - The plots start in the lower left-hand corner of the graph and move to the upper right-hand corner.
>
> - This makes it appear that sales more than doubled.
>
> - The graph starts at 1,250, instead of 0.
>
> - This makes the increases and decreases appear bigger than they are.
>
> - The biggest drop in sales, between 2003 and 2004, is only approximately 12%.
>
> - The increase in sales from 1999 to 2005 is approximately 20%.

- Finally, as in the previous examples, students can write a paragraph using the topic sentence and supporting sentences from the fact outline.

> ### School Magazine Sales Are Pretty Stable
>
> The "School Magazine Sales" scatter plot misrepresents the growth and decline in annual magazine sales at our local middle school. The plots start in the lower left-hand corner of the graph and move to the upper right-hand corner. This makes it appear that sales more than doubled when they increased by only 300. Also, the graph starts at 1,250 instead of 0. This makes the increases and decreases appear bigger than they are. The biggest drop in sales, occurring between 2003 and 2004, is only approximately 12%. The increase in sales from 1999 to 2005 is only approximately 20%.

Before a Lesson

- Review the examples of different ways of interpreting the same graph.

- Create assignments to use for demonstration and practice.

During a Lesson

- Explain to students that you will be using the summary-writing strategy (**3-1 Four-Step Summary Paragraph**) for a slightly different purpose.

- Display and review summaries that students have written.

- Display graphs and paragraphs that you have created to explain, analyze, interpret, and/or critique those graphs. Walk students through the steps you took to complete the final paragraph.

- Use another graph in a guided lesson; with help from students, complete all steps leading to the final paragraph.

- Give students time to practice on their own or with classmates using graphs they have studied or will be studying.

Additional Ideas

- Collect paragraphs that explain or analyze graphs. Keep them in a notebook for students to review and use as examples.

- Give students one graph with several different assignments. Let them work in pairs or small groups to complete the work. Share and discuss the results.

- Have pairs of students create graphs in the computer lab and write assignments to match their graphs. Later, ask students to exchange the graphs and complete one another's assignments.

- Use graphs, charts, tables, etc., from science and/or social studies for these activities. Do this on your own or create an interdisciplinary activity.

- Have students (individually or with peers) create their own surveys and graph results. Then have them interpret their work and write paragraphs to share with the class.

- Use graphs from newspapers and magazines. Have students analyze their accuracy and effectiveness.

3-5 Framed Paragraphs for Writing About Graphs

A framed paragraph can help students (both typical students and those with limited writing skills) learn to explain or analyze a graph, chart, table, or other graphical representation. Framed paragraphs can also save time. Teachers can create frames, make copies, and have them handy for responses when only a few minutes are available for writing.

Framed paragraphs are an effective way to give students more practice writing about graphs. They also work well for homework assignments and when students work with substitute teachers.

However, they should be used along with the strategies and tools from **3-1 Four-Step Summary Paragraph** and **3-3 Writing to Explain a Graph**. Framed paragraphs are not a substitute for direct instruction and guided practice. It is important that students learn to work independently as they interpret and write about graphs.

Use **Math Tool 3-5** as an example. Make an overhead transparency and student copies as needed. In a guided lesson, complete the work with input from students.

Tool S-3-5

Use the following examples as guides when you create your own framed paragraphs:

Page 540 Line Graph

The line graph on page 540 shows _____

_____. First, _____

_____. It also

_____

_____. Finally, _____

_____.

The Dean Family Trip

The table showing the miles per gallon of gasoline that the Dean family

used on their car trip gives _____. First, _____

_____. Second, _____

_____.

Mrs. Kenny's Library Program

The chart about Mrs. Kenny's library program tells _____

_____. Weekly story time _____

_____. The puppet shows

_____

_____. Craft classes are _____

_____ .

Pie Chart

The large pie chart near the school's front office gives facts about _____

_____. First, it _____

_____. Next, it

_____ .

My _____

The _____ that I created shows three facts about _____

_____. First, _____

_____. Next, _____. It

also _____ .

Refer to **6-4 Framed Paragraphs** for additional examples and for ideas of other uses for framed paragraphs.

Note: Students improve their writing skills the most when they are asked to rewrite their paragraphs on notebook paper rather than just filling in the blanks.

Math Tools: Primary

Writing to Explain a Graph

Assignment: Explain what this pie graph shows.

Summer Activities

$\frac{1}{2}$ →   Swimming: 16 students

Playing baseball: 8 students ← $\frac{1}{4}$

Riding bikes: 8 students ← $\frac{1}{4}$

I	V	F
The pie graph	shows	what sports the students in my class enjoyed the most this summer.

Facts: –Half of our class enjoyed swimming the most.

–A quarter of the class liked playing baseball, and another quarter liked riding bikes.

–Adding 16 students, and 8 students, and 8 students gives the total number of students in our class.

Step Up to Writing in Math   Summarizing Text and Writing About Graphs   Math Tool—P-3-3a

Math Tool P-3-3a

Writing to Explain a Graph

Assignment: Explain what this bar graph tells us.

Farmer Dell Goes to Market

Number of Bushels (1–9)

carrots   onions   cucumbers   potatoes   tomatoes
Kinds of Vegetables

I	V	F
The "Farmer Dell" bar graph	shows	us the number of bushels of vegetables that were sold.

Facts: –Farmer Dell sold a total of 34 bushels of vegetables at the Farmer's Market.
–He sold the same number of bushels of onions and tomatoes.
–He sold fewer cucumbers than any other vegetable.

Step Up to Writing in Math   Summarizing Text and Writing About Graphs   Math Tool—P-3-3b

Math Tool P-3-3b

Writing to Explain a Graph

Example 1:
Summer Activities

The pie graph shows what sports the students in my class enjoyed the most this summer. Sixteen kids, or half of our class, enjoyed swimming the most. A quarter of the class liked playing baseball, and the other quarter liked riding bikes. If you add 16 students, and 8 students, and 8 students, you will find the total number of students in our class. We have 32 students in this class. They all like summertime, but they like different activities.

Example 2:
Farmer Dell Goes to Market

The graph about Farmer Dell and his vegetables shows the number of bushels of different vegetables he sold at the Farmer's Market. All together, he sold a total of 34 bushels of vegetables at the market. He sold the same number of bushels of onions and tomatoes. Shoppers bought 8 bushels of onions and 8 bushels of tomatoes. He sold fewer cucumbers than any other vegetable. Farmer Dell sold only 5 bushels of cucumbers.

Step Up to Writing in Math   Summarizing Text and Writing About Graphs   Math Tool—P-3-3c

Math Tool P-3-3c

Framed Paragraph for Writing About a Graph

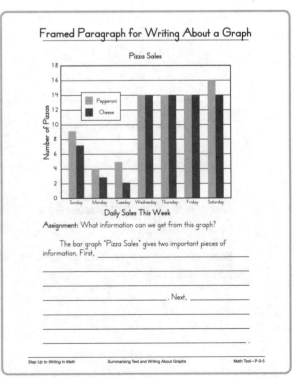

Pizza Sales

Number of Pizzas

Pepperoni
Cheese

Sunday Monday Tuesday Wednesday Thursday Friday Saturday
Daily Sales This Week

Assignment: What information can we get from this graph?

The bar graph "Pizza Sales" gives two important pieces of information. First, _____
_____
_____
_____. Next, _____
_____
_____
_____
_____.

Step Up to Writing in Math   Summarizing Text and Writing About Graphs   Math Tool—P-3-5

Math Tool P-3-5

Math Tools: Intermediate

Writing to Explain a Graph

Assignment: Explain what this pie chart shows us.

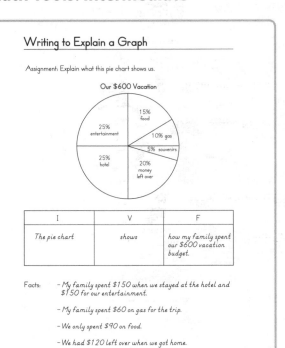

Our $600 Vacation

15% food
10% gas
5% souvenirs
20% money left over
25% hotel
25% entertainment

I	V	F
The pie chart	shows	how my family spent our $600 vacation budget.

Facts:
– My family spent $150 when we stayed at the hotel and $150 for our entertainment.
– My family spent $60 on gas for the trip.
– We only spent $90 on food.
– We had $120 left over when we got home.

Math Tool I-3-3a

Writing to Explain a Graph

Assignment: Explain what this bar graph shows.

Average Daily Sales at the School Store

Dollars Earned: $20, $18, $16, $14, $12, $10, $8, $6, $4, $2, 0

Kinds of Supplies: pencils, pens, paper, scissors, glue

I	V	F
The bar graph	describes	the daily sales in the school store.

Facts:
– The students make an average of $14 a day selling paper.
– Scissors bring in the least amount of money.
– On average, the students sell $42 worth of school supplies a day.
– In a week with 5 school days, students make about $210.

Math Tool I-3-3b

Writing to Explain a Graph

Example 1:

Our $600 Vacation

The pie chart shows how my family spent our $600 vacation budget. We spent 50% for the hotel and for our entertainment. The hotel charged $150, and the tickets for the animal park for 5 people were $30 each. So that was also a total of $150. My parents spent 10% of the $600 on gas for the trip. They spent $60. However, we only spent $90 on food. This was only 15% of our budget. The best part was buying souvenirs. We only spent $30, but we all had fun shopping. When we got home, we saw that we had $120 left. That was 20% of the money we left with. We are saving it for another trip in the fall.

Example 2:

Average Daily Sales at the School Store

The bar graph describes the average daily sales of supplies in the school store. The students make an average of $14 a day selling paper, which is their highest-selling school supply. They bring in the least amount of money selling scissors. They only make $4 a day on scissors. But they do sell a good amount of school supplies overall. On average, the students sell $42 worth of school supplies every day. In a week with five school days, they make about $210.

Math Tool I-3-3c

Framed Paragraph for Writing About a Graph

Assignment: What conclusions can you draw from these results?

Chapter Three Test Scores

64   72   77   86   100

Box-and-Whisker Plot
The box-and-whisker plot "Chapter Three Test Scores" gives information about how the class did on the Chapter Three test. First, _____
_____
_____.The graph also _____
_____
_____.
Finally, _____
_____
_____
_____.

Box-and-Whisker Plot
The box-and-whisker plot "Chapter Three Test Scores" gives information about how the class did on the Chapter Three test. First, *we can easily see that the highest score was a 100 and the lowest was a 64. The graph also shows that the median, or middle, score was a 77. This means that half the class scored above 77, and the other half of the class scored below 77.* Finally, *we can see that the first quartile was 72 and the third quartile was 86. This means that a fourth of the class scored below 72 and a fourth of the class scored above 86.*

Math Tool I-3-5

Math Tools: Secondary

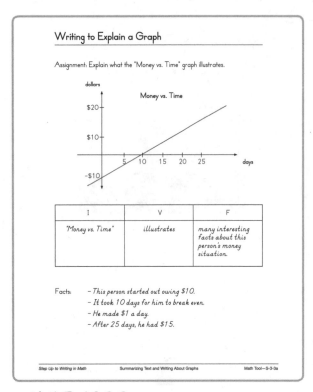

Math Tool S-3-3a

Writing to Explain a Graph

Assignment: Explain what the "Money vs. Time" graph illustrates.

I	V	F
"Money vs. Time"	illustrates	many interesting facts about this person's money situation.

Facts: – This person started out owing $10.
– It took 10 days for him to break even.
– He made $1 a day.
– After 25 days, he had $15.

Writing to Explain a Graph

Assignment: Explain what information you can get from the "Favorite Ice Cream Flavors" histogram.

I	V	F
"Favorite Ice Cream Flavors"	shows	what flavors of ice cream the students in our school like best.

Facts: – The favorite flavor of ice cream is cookie dough.
– Chocolate is second, and bubble gum is third.
– The least favorite flavors are mint chip and rocky road.
– Approximately 52 students like cookie dough best.
– Forty-four like chocolate best.
– 30, 21, and 12 students like bubble gum, mint chip, and rocky road, respectively.

Math Tool S-3-3b

Writing to Explain a Graph

Example 1:
Money vs. Time

The graph "Money vs. Time" illustrates many interesting things about this person's money situation. The y-intercept shows that the person started out owing $10. The x-intercept shows that this person broke even on the 10th day. The slope of the line indicates that this person made $1 a day. This person had $15 after 25 days.

Example 2:
Favorite Ice Cream Flavors

The histogram "Favorite Ice Cream Flavors" shows what flavors of ice cream the students in our school like best. The favorite flavor of ice cream is cookie dough. Chocolate is second, and bubble gum is third. The least favorite flavors are mint chip and rocky road. Approximately 52 students like cookie dough best. About 44 like chocolate best. Only 30, 20, and 12 students like bubble gum, mint chip, and rocky road, respectively.

Math Tool S-3-3c

Framed Paragraph for Writing About a Graph

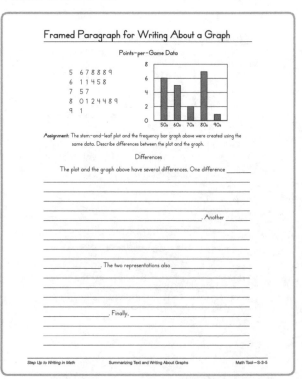

Math Tool S-3-5

SECTION 4 ASKING AND ANSWERING QUESTIONS

*T*he ability to answer questions quickly and accurately is an important skill for all students. They are expected to answer questions, both orally and in writing, each day in class, as well as on weekly and monthly exams and on formal district or state assessments.

The strategies in Section 4 help students master the skills of asking and answering questions. Asking questions can help redirect or clarify thinking and lead to deeper understanding. Answering questions allows students to demonstrate what they know and allows teachers to assess their understanding.

Students need to learn to answer questions at different levels of difficulty and questions created for different purposes. *Step Up to Writing in Math* strategies help teachers consciously craft questions of different types to meet the needs of all students. These strategies also make students aware of different types of questions so that they can better answer them. Many students need guidance on how to take control of their learning. This section includes lists of sample questions that students can ask in order to progress in their problem solving.

It also provides a simple strategy for training students to quickly, accurately, and completely answer oral and written questions. This strategy helps set a standard for answering questions in all classes. Using the strategy and keeping standards high helps improve performance on high-stakes assessments because giving great short answers becomes a habit for students.

Finally, this section provides instructions for helping students prepare for essay-type questions, sometimes called *extended responses*. The strategy includes teaching students how to effectively read prompts and questions and how to turn the questions into effective topic sentences that then guide the organization of the response.

Objectives

- Encourage math students and their teachers to ask a variety of questions

- Teach students to recognize and answer different types of questions

- Provide strategies that call for different levels of questioning

- Teach students how to answer questions quickly and successfully

- Prepare students for exam questions that require short, constructed responses and/or essay responses

- Empower students with questioning skills

4-1 Asking a Variety of Questions

Teachers can use the list of questions on the following pages for a variety of purposes: to assess student understanding, to inform instruction, to redirect student thinking, to get to know students, to encourage thinking and creativity, and to ensure that they are asking a variety of questions.

Before a Lesson

- Review the list of questions to determine which are appropriate for your lesson. Reword questions to more specifically address your topic and fit your style. Jot questions down for quick reference during the lesson.

During a Lesson

- Incorporate questions into your presentations and class discussion.

- Rephrase questions as needed to encourage participation.

- Pause after asking a question and after a student responds.

- Rephrase student responses to help other students with listening and to solicit more responses to the same question.

Additional Ideas

- Guide a discussion on the importance of asking and answering questions. Help students understand why "wrong answers" and "silly questions" are often very helpful.

- Share the list (or part of the list) of questions with students. Ask them which kinds of questions are most helpful to them. Ask for suggestions about improving the questions.

- Have students use the list to ask questions of their classmates.

- Use questions from the list as focus points during small-group discussions.

- Make notes about the effectiveness or ineffectiveness of a question.

- Add questions of your own or ones suggested by the students.

A Variety of Questions

- **Questions that tap into prior knowledge:**
  - What do you know about this topic?
  - How would you create a concept map or word web related to this topic?
  - Where have you seen this pattern before?
  - Have you seen this happen in other cases?
  - What previously existing knowledge are you using to solve this problem?

- **Questions that ask for clarification:**
  - Can you restate the problem in your own words?
  - Can you restate the directions in your own words?
  - What do you want to know?
  - Are you saying . . . ?
  - What do you mean?
  - Where are you stuck?
  - I'm not sure I understand what you are saying. Can you explain it to me again?
  - Why did you do that?
  - Why do you think that?
  - Can you draw a picture to illustrate the problem?
  - Is there anything that I (the teacher) didn't make clear?

- **Questions that inform instruction and/or help students' progress:**
  - What are you thinking? Can you tell me more?
  - Why did you take that step?
  - Is your answer reasonable? Why?
  - What would happen if . . . ?
  - What step will you take next?
  - Can you ask me a question about what you don't understand?
  - Are there any questions?
  - Where do you think the discrepancy occurred?
  - Can you solve the problem in any other way?
  - Where can you find the answer to that question?
  - Have you examined your reasoning?
  - Have you followed the directions?
  - Does that make sense?

- **Questions that ask for connections and/or relationships:**
    - How is this connected to other math ideas you have learned?
    - What do you know about this topic?
    - What would a concept map or word web related to this topic look like?
    - Where have you seen this pattern before?
    - How is this like . . . ?
    - Have you seen this happen in other cases?
    - Have you ever solved a problem like this one before?
    - What previously existing knowledge are you using to solve this problem?
    - What relationship(s) does your data fail to reveal?
    - What links can you make to other mathematical concepts?
    - What generalizations can you make from this math situation? How can you defend your answer?
    - What are some real-life applications of this math concept?
    - How might you use this application at home?
    - Why is . . . possible? What math concepts support your answer?
    - What patterns or relationships apply to this problem? Which ones have you found?
    - How can you use what you already know to solve this problem?

- **Questions that ask for explanations, justifications, and/or reasoning:**
    - How did you solve the problem?
    - What was your plan of attack for solving the problem?
    - What operations or key words did you use to solve the problem?
    - What tools are necessary to solve this problem? Why?
    - What steps did you take to solve the problem? Why?
    - What can you use to justify your answer?
    - What decisions did you make? Why?
    - How does this operation work?
    - Why is your answer reasonable? What evidence proves the reasonableness of your answer?
    - What can you draw to illustrate your thinking?

- **Questions that ask for comparisons or contrasts:**
  - How is this strategy more or less efficient than another?
  - Which strategy is more elegant or effective? Why?
  - How does your solution compare with other methods discussed in class?
  - How does your plan of attack differ from other students' plans of attack?
  - How are your results similar to and/or different from those of another group?
  - Do you agree or disagree with their results?

- **Questions that ask for analysis:**
  - What patterns or relationships apply to this problem?
  - What patterns do you see?
  - What would happen if . . . ?
  - Why do you think that will work?
  - How do you think they got the answer?
  - Why is this one different?
  - What do you think about that comment?
  - How could you prove that?
  - What decision do you think he should make?

- **Questions that ask for predictions and/or conclusions to be made:**
  - What conclusions can be drawn?
  - Can you predict the next . . . ?
  - If this is true, what conclusions can we make?
  - What assumptions are you making?
  - What would happen if . . . ?
  - Is that always true?

- **Questions that ask for illustrations:**
  - What makes a good "math" illustration?
  - How are math illustrations different from illustrations in a story?
  - What picture illustrates the problem?
  - How can you illustrate your thinking through pictures?
  - What picture or illustration can you use to help you remember this term?
  - What other terms can you use instead of illustration? (representation, picture, etc.)

- **Questions that ask for immediate usefulness:**
  - What is the usefulness of this mathematical process/concept in your other classes?
  - When might your science (or social studies, art, etc.) teacher ask you to use geometric shapes (or change decimals to fractions, or plot a graph, etc.) in class?
  - How does what you've learned support the information or skills being taught in your other classes?

- **Questions that ask for multiple solutions and/or stimulate creativity:**
  - What alternative strategies could you have used?
  - What alternative strategy can you develop for this procedure?
  - What are some other ways to represent this problem?
  - Can you do this any other way?
  - What other possible solutions are there?

- **Questions that ask for synthesizing and/or summarizing:**
  - What are the key ideas in this chapter?
  - What terms would you include in a concept map or word web that represents this unit?
  - What are the important words or concepts that you should remember for future units or other classes?
  - What are all of the concepts you applied in order to solve the problem?
  - What are all of the operations you used to solve the problem?
  - What are the concepts you need to know for the unit and/or semester test?

- **Questions that tap into affective aspects of learning:**
  - Have you ever felt successful in math class? When? Why?
  - How did you feel about today's activity?
  - How can you (or others) create a positive "can do" attitude about math?
  - What goals have you set for yourself to improve/add to your math skills?
  - What strengths do you bring to this math class?
  - What can we do in this math class to eliminate your weaknesses?
  - How do you learn best?
  - What feelings do you experience when you are solving a problem?

- **Questions that require teachers' self-reflection and/or self-evaluation:**
  - Will the tasks I am asking students to do lead to inquiry and justification?
  - Are the tasks I am asking students to do relevant to them?
  - What prior knowledge can I help them connect to what we are studying now?
  - Am I answering the students' questions?
  - Am I teaching for a variety of learning styles?
  - Am I giving males and females equal attention?
  - Am I giving students ample time to answer questions?
  - Am I asking all types of questions?
  - Am I asking students to engage in discourse with others?
  - Am I doing a good job orchestrating conversations in class?
  - Am I asking questions that elicit, extend, and challenge students' thinking?
  - Am I aware of students' comprehension levels?
  - Do my students understand the concept, or have they just memorized steps?
  - Am I asking questions that will help students become better problem solvers?
  - Am I asking questions that will help students succeed or progress?
  - What misconceptions do my students have about math or math concepts?
  - What have I learned?
  - How am I growing and changing as a math teacher?

4-2 Using the CROWD Strategy to Create Better Questions

The CROWD questioning strategy (Burns, Griffin, & Snow, 1999) is a tool for teachers and students. The acronym CROWD stands for:

C Completion	These questions are fill-in-the-blank.	Lines that never intersect are called _____ lines.
R Recall	These questions require students to retell key facts and/or events.	What do we call lines that intersect to form right angles?
O Opened-ended	These questions require students to use new information to critique and/or express opinions.	What instruments or tools are useful for drawing parallel or perpendicular lines? Explain.
W What? = Vocabulary	These questions require students to show their knowledge of vocabulary by explaining what a particular word means.	The text says that perpendicular lines intersect. What does it mean when lines intersect?
D Distancing/Making Connections	These questions require students to apply new information and knowledge.	Besides engineers and construction workers, what other people in various professions, jobs, or careers need to know about lines and how they work?

You can use this list of question types to create a variety of questions for class discussions and assessments. This strategy for developing questions can also help students develop two academic skills: understanding different types of questions and creating questions of their own.

Before a Lesson

- Review the meaning of the CROWD acronym.

- Make overhead transparencies and student copies, as needed, of **Math Tools 4-2a** and **4-2b**.

- Choose a topic, then create sample questions related to that topic. You should create one question that corresponds to each letter in the CROWD acronym. You will use these questions as you demonstrate the strategy.

Tool P-4-2a

Tool P-4-2b

During a Lesson

- Explain the importance of being able to ask and answer questions.

- Using **Math Tool 4-2a**, introduce students to the CROWD acronym and explain the types of questions included in the CROWD strategy.

- Display example questions from **Math Tool 4-2b**, or use example questions that you have created.

- Help students answer the questions. As they answer the questions, explain again the differences among the types of questions and the purpose for each kind. Also explain to students where they might find the answers.

- With students, create a list of CROWD questions based on content that students are studying or have studied. Use an overhead transparency of **Math Tool 4-2a** or chart paper.

- Discuss the types of questioning; explain why all types are important and necessary.

Additional Ideas

- Before reading an article or selection from a textbook, give students a set of CROWD questions to focus their thinking and to set a purpose for listening or reading.

- At the end of a lesson, ask students to create CROWD questions that they can use during a class discussion or review.

- Use CROWD questions to create a quiz or to help students review for an exam.

- Make CROWD questions a part of a study guide (see **2-4 Creating Textbook Study Guides**).

- Keep a laminated card with the CROWD acronym and its meanings handy. Use the card to inspire variety in student questions during class discussions.

- Use the CROWD strategy to create variety in test questions.

4-3 Teaching Concrete, Critical, and Creative Questions

The Concrete, Critical, and Creative strategy (Sparks, 1987) is similar to the CROWD strategy. Students and teachers can use this strategy to create and ask a variety of questions, focus a discussion, review for exams, or teach/learn how to find the answers to questions.

- **Concrete** questions involve:
  - reading the lines,
  - an answer that is in the text, and
  - everyone having the same answer.

  For example: *What are Arabic numerals? What are Roman numerals?*

- **Critical** questions involve:
  - reading between the lines,
  - sharing opinions,
  - explaining insights, and
  - analyzing.

  For example: *Why is it important for students to learn to read both Arabic and Roman numerals?*

- **Creative** questions involve:
  - reading beyond the lines,
  - applying knowledge,
  - helping others understand concepts, and
  - using knowledge to solve problems or complete tasks.

  For example: *Why would advertisers or publishers choose Roman numerals over Arabic numerals to share a message or provide information?*

Before a Lesson

- Make overhead transparencies and student copies of Math Tools 4-3a and 4-3b, as needed.

- Review the example Concrete, Critical, and Creative questions on Math Tool 4-3b.

- Prepare a list of content-appropriate questions for each category—concrete, critical, and creative—to use for demonstration and modeling.

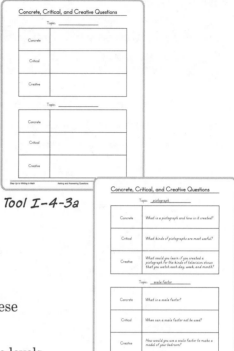

Tool I-4-3a

Tool I-4-3b

During a Lesson

- Explain to students the three levels of questions.

- Demonstrate the three levels of questions using Math Tools 4-3a and 4-3b, along with questions that you have created.

- Discuss where students would find the answers to these questions.

- With help from students, create questions on all three levels for the current unit of study.

Additional Ideas

- Orally share a list of content-relevant questions, and ask students to categorize each question as concrete, critical, or creative.

- Check for prior knowledge before asking higher-level questions.

- Review assessments you have created to ensure that you have included questions at each level.

- Use Concrete, Critical, and Creative questions written on index cards for a quick quiz.

- Ask students to identify Concrete, Critical, and Creative questions in their textbooks, handouts, and/or practice tests.

4-4 Encouraging Great Short Answers

Use this strategy to teach students how to quickly, accurately, and completely answer oral and written questions. This strategy helps students recognize the difference between acceptable and unacceptable answers by providing feedback in an easily recognizable format.

Use this strategy to label answers on students' homework and assessments to set standards for answers given in class and to empower students to show what they know.

 Sad face = not acceptable: The answer is not necessarily the wrong answer; it just does not meet the standards for a great short answer.

 Straight face = better, but not quite there: The answer has correct information but does not meet all the standards for a great short answer. It may not be a complete sentence or a complete answer.

 Happy face = the quality of work expected from all students. A happy face means the answer:
- is a complete sentence;
- is a complete, specific, and accurate answer;
- uses words from the question in the answer; and
- does not leave the reader guessing.

Note: When students write or give an oral answer to a question, they should not begin with a "question word." Question words include: Who? What? Where? When? Why? How? (Incorrect: "*How* I found the answer....")

Students at all grade levels catch on quickly to this strategy when they see the happy, sad, and straight (indifferent) faces. However, the strategy can also be taught using symbols as simple as plus and minus signs. Labeling answers to questions *not acceptable, acceptable at lower grade levels,* and *expected from secondary students* is another option.

The key to success is giving students a clear way to recognize each of three levels of answer quality, then setting expectations for the highest level—the happy face standard.

Before a Lesson

- Review and make overhead transparencies and student copies of Math Tools 4-4a, 4-4b, and 4-4c.

- Create practice questions to use for modeling and demonstration.

- Review the meanings of the sad face, the straight (indifferent) face, and the happy face symbols.

During a Lesson

- Display **Math Tool 4-4a**. Explain the meaning of each face.

- Use **Math Tools 4-4b** and **4-4c** to show students examples of the three types of responses, and ask them to determine which type is the strongest.

- Ask students to explain why the happy face answer is the strongest. Ask them when it might be appropriate to answer with only a word or a phrase. Ask them why being able to give a complete "great short answer" with details is an important academic skill.

- Set the expectation that the happy face answer is the standard for all short answers—oral and written—in your classroom. Using **Math Tool 4-4a** and a question that you have created, model the three kinds of answers. Practice two or three times until students can quickly give examples of each kind of answer.

- Have students practice happy face answers orally. Model for them how to put the question in the answer.

- Have students work in pairs; ask them to draw a sad, straight, and happy face on a large piece of paper. Give them a question, or have them create their own. Then ask them to write examples of sad face, straight face, and happy face answers.

- Remind students that you will always want and be looking for happy face answers.

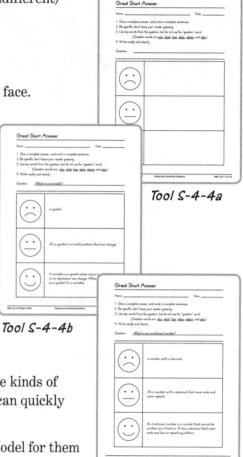

Tool S-4-4a

Tool S-4-4b

Tool S-4-4c

Additional Ideas

- Use this strategy to teach students how to write the answer to a math problem in a complete sentence. Explain how to use relevant words from the question to create the sentence. Explain that when the answer to a problem is in the context of a sentence, it is more meaningful and helps show why an answer is reasonable and makes sense.

- Ask students to rehearse their answers, oral and written, with their peers. Rehearsing answers gives students the opportunity to find careless mistakes they may have made.

4-5 Writing Clear, Concise, Organized Essay Answers

Students are increasingly being asked to write essay answers (extended responses) on state and national assessments. For students who are not used to developing math-related essays, this can be a challenge. Writing clear essay answers to math questions requires thought and practice.

The general rule for writing in math is to use several short paragraphs. In language arts, history, and social studies classes, students frequently learn to write longer and more detailed essays. Math writing is more like technical writing, which calls for short, clear paragraphs.

Students can learn to write solid math essays through three steps:

1. Turn the question or prompt into a topic sentence. For example, a student given the prompt:

   > **Explain what rounding numbers means in math class. Give examples of when you or someone else might round a number.**

   could turn it into the topic sentence (introduction):

   > Rounding numbers means changing a number that does not have to be exact. It means estimating to make it simpler. There are many ways each day that a person might need or want to round a number.

2. Make a quick outline of details or examples that support the topic sentence, such as:

   > Topic: rounding numbers
   > ★ concert
   > ★ school survey
   > ★ fabric

If time permits, students can add more detail to the outline, but in a testing situation where time (and sometimes writing space) is limited, the short outline will do. Just jotting down the key words for the examples will help with organization of the final answer.

3. Turn the topic sentence and outline into an essay. Transition words and phrases like *one*, *another*, and *next*—or *first*, *second*, *third*, and *finally*—help with the organization of ideas and can be especially helpful in writing short math essays that contain a lot of information. Encourage students to use a transition each time they introduce a key idea or important point. For example:

> ### Rounding Numbers
>
> Rounding a number means changing a number that does not have to be exact. It means estimating to make it simpler. There are many ways each day that a person might need or want to round a number.
>
> First, he might round a number when he attends a concert and wants to tell a friend how many people were there. Instead of telling the friend that 39,924 people attended, he would round the number and tell him that 40,000 people enjoyed the concert.
>
> <u>Another</u> example might be when he uses decimals or fractions. He would tell a friend that 55% of the students in the school survey said they prefer chocolate ice cream, even if the actual number was 55.154%.
>
> He could <u>also</u> round numbers if he purchased fabric for an art project. If the directions said that he would need three and three-fourths yards, he might want to round off. That would mean that 3.75 yards would become 4.0 yards.

Before a Lesson

- Create or choose a question or prompt that requires students to develop a formal paragraph or essay. Write the prompt or question on the board or on an overhead transparency.

- Make an overhead transparency of an essay response to the prompt or question that you have created or chosen.

Note: Practicing with two or three questions/prompts will help you anticipate problems students might have turning a question/prompt into a topic sentence. (See **Section 6: Writing for General Assignments** for instructions about teaching and writing topic sentences.)

During a Lesson

- Teach students how to turn a question into a topic sentence. Use this strategy and topic-sentence writing techniques from **5-2 Turning an Explanation Into a Formal Paragraph** and **6-1 Accordion Paragraphs** to help students master this skill.

- Show students that an essay answer (extended response) is like a paragraph. Explain that the topic sentence controls the rest of the paragraph or essay and can help them organize their ideas.

- Explain to students that jotting a quick, informal outline below the topic sentence is a great way to plan the paragraph or essay. (See **6-1 Accordion Paragraphs** about informal outlines.)

- Remind students to use transition words and phrases. (See **5-1 Explaining Steps Taken to Solve a Word Problem** and **6-1 Accordion Paragraphs** for more information about transitions.)

- Share the prompt or question that you want students to address. Help the class orally state the topic sentence. Write it on the board or chart paper once you have a final version. Create an informal outline and, together with the class, turn it into a formal response. Use transitions each time you introduce a key idea (a new reason, detail, or fact).

- Discuss the process with the class. Assure them that they will have many opportunities to practice this skill.

- Since there is a limited amount of time available for teaching writing in math class, have students practice creating essay responses in pairs or groups of three. Consider using overhead transparencies. Students like writing on them and sharing their work with classmates. As students read and share, you can assess their work and offer suggestions for improvement.

- Look for other ways students can practice this skill so that they feel prepared for extended-response type questions in class and on exams.

- Look for opportunities to practice this across subject areas and in interdisciplinary activities.

4-6 Empowering Students With Questioning Skills

Encourage students to take control of their own learning by helping them build the confidence and skills they need to ask questions and seek clarification.

Give students alternative statements that they can substitute for "I don't know," or give them a list of leading questions that can help them get unstuck when they aren't understanding a math concept. For example, some alternatives to "I don't know" are:

- Will you help me with this part?
- I am not sure that I understand. Could you explain this again?
- Can you please explain this in a different way?
- I wasn't listening, or I didn't hear. Will you please repeat the directions?
- What do you want us to do?
- Could you give me an example? Could you give me another example?
- I know this part, but I don't know what to do next.
- Will you help me read this problem?

- I don't understand in English. Will you help me with the words?
- Will you explain this word to me?
- Can you draw me a picture?
- Where am I? The last step I took was . . .
- I'm not sure what this problem is asking. Will you help me think about it?
- I don't know if I'm supposed to add, subtract, multiply, or divide. Will you help me decide?
- Are you saying . . . ?
- What do you mean when you say . . . ?
- Why is this important? When will we use it in "real life"?

Before a Lesson

- Determine which phrases you deem unacceptable, such as "I don't get it" or "I don't know."

- Determine what you will consider acceptable alternatives to the unacceptable responses.

- Decide on your rules and goals for students when they ask questions. For example: *Students will further their problem solving and understanding by asking themselves and their teachers more and better questions.* Or: *All students will participate by asking questions.*

- Have chart paper and markers available for students.

During a Lesson

- Explain your expectations for student questions. Give examples of the types of comments and questions you want to hear and don't want to hear.

- Divide students into small groups. Challenge them to come up with comments and questions that they could use in math class to solve problems or increase their understanding.

- Use your list of acceptable alternatives to guide and encourage the small groups. Share only a few suggestions at a time with students. Creating their own class list of questions and comments is a valuable exercise for students.

Additional Ideas

- Remind students on a regular basis about the importance of asking for help and clarification.

- Teach students how to talk themselves through a problem that they're stuck on. Provide a list of leading questions, such as:
  - Was I successful? Why or why not?
  - What tools, operations, or key words can I use to solve the problem?
  - Why am I stuck? What questions did I fail to ask?
  - What questions could I ask?
  - What is still puzzling me? What do I not understand?
  - How can I find the answer to my question?
  - Am I checking my thinking as I go along?
  - What information did I not monitor?
  - What is the next step I need to take?
  - What other possible methods could I have used?
  - What information am I still unsure about?
  - What is my plan of attack?

- Give students a script for explaining where their understanding has broken down. Allow specific questions only after they have given their explanation. For example:
  - The question is asking me to . . .
  - I know that . . .
  - The strategy that I tried (or am planning to try) is . . .
  - I got confused, or I don't understand . . .
  - My question is . . .

Note: See **7-4 Journal Entries** for more ideas about giving students time and space to share feelings, frustrations, successes, and needs in math class.

Math Tools: Primary

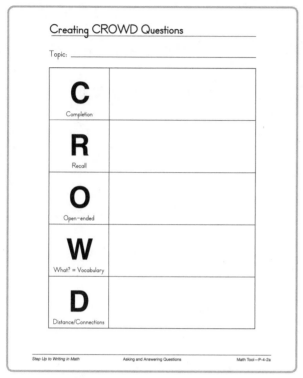

Math Tool P-4-2a

Math Tool P-4-2b

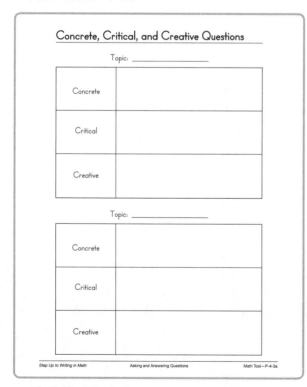

Math Tool P-4-3a

Math Tool P-4-3b

Math Tools: Primary–Intermediate

Great Short Answer

Name: _____ Date: _____

- Give a complete answer.
- Write a complete sentence(s).
- Use words from the question, but not question words.
    (Question words: How, Who, What, Where, When, Why)
- Include details and facts.

Question: _____

Math Tool P-4-4a

Great Short Answer

Name: _____ Date: _____

- Give a complete answer.
- Write a complete sentence(s).
- Use words from the question, but not question words.
    (Question words: How, Who, What, Where, When, Why)
- Include details and facts.

Question: __What is an even number?__

😞	2 or 4
😐	Numbers like 2, 4, 6, and 8
🙂	An even number is a number that can be divided by 2 without a remainder. The numbers 8, 14, and 22 are even numbers.

Math Tool P-4-4b

Great Short Answer

Name: _____ Date: _____

- Give a complete answer.
- Write a complete sentence(s).
- Use words from the question, but not question words.
    (Question words: How, Who, What, Where, When, Why)
- Include details and facts.

Question: __What is a triangle?__

😞	a shape
😐	A shape with just 3 sides
🙂	A triangle is a shape that has three sides. The sides can be the same or different lengths. Triangles come in all sizes.

Math Tool P-4-4c

Creating CROWD Questions

Topic: _____

C Completion	
R Recall	
O Open-ended	
W What? = Vocabulary	
D Distancing/Making Connections	

Math Tool I-4-2a

Math Tools: Intermediate (continued)

Creating CROWD Questions

Topic: _metric system_

C Completion	The metric system is based on the _____ system.
R Recall	What food or household products come labeled in the metric system?
O Open-ended	In what ways do you (or others) use the metric system?
W What? = Vocabulary	The metric system is a system of measurements. What does the word "system" mean?
D Distancing/Making Connections	Why is it hard for some Americans to use the metric system?

Math Tool I-4-2b

Concrete, Critical, and Creative Questions

Topic: _____

Concrete	
Critical	
Creative	

Topic: _____

Concrete	
Critical	
Creative	

Math Tool I-4-3a

Concrete, Critical, and Creative Questions

Topic: _pictograph_

Concrete	What is a pictograph and how is it created?
Critical	What kinds of pictographs are most useful?
Creative	What could you learn if you created a pictograph for the kinds of television shows that you watch each day, week, and month?

Topic: _scale factor_

Concrete	What is a scale factor?
Critical	When can a scale factor not be used?
Creative	How would you use a scale factor to make a model of your bedroom?

Math Tool I-4-3b

Great Short Answer

Name: _____   Date: _____

1. Give a complete answer.
2. Write in complete sentences.
3. Give details and specific information.
4. Use words from the question in the answer.
5. Do not use the "question" word.
6. Do not leave the reader guessing.

Question Words
- What?
- Why?
- How?
- Who?
- When?
- Where?

Question: _____

Math Tool I-4-4a

Math Tools: Intermediate–Secondary

Great Short Answer

Name: _____ Date: _____

1. Give a complete answer.
2. Write in complete sentences.
3. Give details and specific information.
4. Use words from the question in the answer.
5. Do not use the "question" word.
6. Do not leave the reader guessing.

Question Words
• What?
• Why?
• How?
• Who?
• When?
• Where?

Question: _What two geometric shapes make up a pyramid?_

☹	ones with 3 sides and ones with more sides
😐	It has triangles and a polygon.
☺	A pyramid is made of two shapes. It has a polygon as the base and triangles as the sides. The triangles come together at a point at the top of the pyramid.

Step Up to Writing in Math   Asking and Answering Questions   Math Tool—I-4-4b

Math Tool I-4-4b

Great Short Answer

Name: _____ Date: _____

1. Give a complete answer.
2. Write in complete sentences.
3. Give details and specific information.
4. Use words from the question in the answer.
5. Do not use the "question" word.
6. Do not leave the reader guessing.

Question Words
• What?
• Why?
• How?
• Who?
• When?
• Where?

Question: _What does it mean to average a set of numbers?_

☹	finding what the average number for all the numbers is
😐	Averaging is adding all the numbers and then dividing them.
☺	When we average a set of numbers, we add all of the numbers together. Then we divide the sum by the total number of numbers we added in the set. If we had a sum of 100 and we used 4 numbers to get the sum, our average would be 25.

Step Up to Writing in Math   Asking and Answering Questions   Math Tool—I-4-4c

Math Tool I-4-4c

Creating CROWD Questions

Topic: _____

C Completion	
R Recall	
O Open-ended	
W What? = Vocabulary	
D Distancing/Making Connections	

Step Up to Writing in Math   Asking and Answering Questions   Math Tool—S-4-2a

Math Tool S-4-2a

Creating CROWD Questions

Topic: _intercept_

C Completion	An intercept is the point where a line or curve crosses one of the _____.
R Recall	The y-intercept in a slope-intercept equation is represented by which letter?
O Open-ended	On a graph, what does/can the y-intercept tell you?
W What? = Vocabulary	The definition of an intercept includes the word _curve_. What is a curve?
D Distancing/Making Connections	What does changing the y-intercept of a graph do to its equation? How is this process similar or different in a quadratic equation?

Step Up to Writing in Math   Asking and Answering Questions   Math Tool—S-4-2b

Math Tool S-4-2b

Math Tools: Secondary *(continued)*

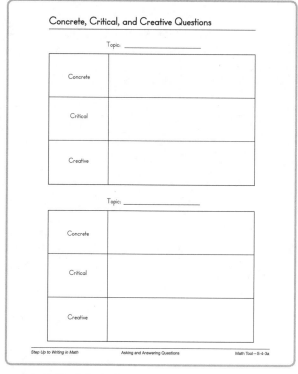

Concrete, Critical, and Creative Questions

Topic: _____

Concrete	
Critical	
Creative	

Topic: _____

Concrete	
Critical	
Creative	

Math Tool S-4-3a

Concrete, Critical, and Creative Questions

Topic: *Pythagorean theorem*

Concrete	What is the formula for the Pythagorean theorem?
Critical	How can you prove the Pythagorean theorem using area?
Creative	If you did not know the Pythagorean theorem, how could you find the missing lengths of a right triangle?

Topic: *polar coordinates*

Concrete	How do you define a point using polar coordinates?
Critical	When or why is it better to use polar coordinates instead of rectangular coordinates?
Creative	How could you use polar coordinates to define a point in three dimensions?

Math Tool S-4-3b

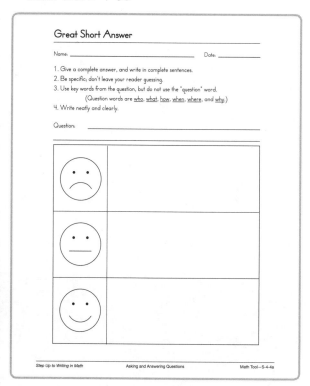

Great Short Answer

Name: _____ Date: _____

1. Give a complete answer, and write in complete sentences.
2. Be specific; don't leave your reader guessing.
3. Use key words from the question, but do not use the "question" word.
    (Question words are <u>who</u>, <u>what</u>, <u>how</u>, <u>when</u>, <u>where</u>, and <u>why</u>.)
4. Write neatly and clearly.

Question: _____

Math Tool S-4-4a

Great Short Answer

Name: _____ Date: _____

1. Give a complete answer, and write in complete sentences.
2. Be specific; don't leave your reader guessing.
3. Use key words from the question, but do not use the "question" word.
    (Question words are <u>who</u>, <u>what</u>, <u>how</u>, <u>when</u>, <u>where</u>, and <u>why</u>.)
4. Write neatly and clearly.

Question: *What is a variable?*

☹	*a symbol*
☺	*It's a symbol in a math problem that can change.*
☺	*A variable is a symbol whose value in an equation or in an expression can change. Often a letter is used as a symbol for a variable.*

Math Tool S-4-4b

Math Tools: Secondary *(continued)*

Great Short Answer

Name: _____ Date: _____

1. Give a complete answer, and write in complete sentences.
2. Be specific; don't leave your reader guessing.
3. Use key words from the question, but do not use the "question" word.
   (Question words are who, what, how, when, where, and why.)
4. Write neatly and clearly.

Question: *What is an irrational number?*

(frowning face)	*a number with a decimal*
(neutral face)	*It's a number with a decimal that never ends and never repeats.*
(smiling face)	*An irrational number is a number that cannot be written as a fraction. It has a decimal that never ends and has no repeating pattern.*

Step Up to Writing in Math   Asking and Answering Questions   Math Tool—S-4-4c

Math Tool S-4-4c

SECTION 5 WRITING FOR ASSESSMENTS

*M*ore and more classroom and high-stakes assessments in math include segments that require writing. Some written responses require only a few lines of text; others require students to explain processes or describe concepts in full-page, report format. Questions that require writing can include:

- **Explain**:

    – Explain how you would find the area of all the metal used to manufacture a can.

    – Explain what these graphs tell us about the number of families that own pets.

    – Explain how you figured out the answer to problem 12 in chapter 3.

- **Justify**:

    – In a short paragraph, give reasons why your answer is the correct answer.

    – Explain why your answer is a reasonable answer. Be specific; give examples.

    – Why does your answer make sense?

- **Illustrate:**

  - Solve problem 20. Make an illustration to show your math thinking. Explain your illustration in the space below.

  - Is the illustration for solving problem 14 accurate? Use the lines below to write your answer.

  - Describe the kind of illustration you would make for the problem about the train schedule. Explain how and why you would make those choices.

- **Define:**

  - Name and define two math terms that you would need to use if you were going to write about decimals.

  - Define *dividend* and *divisor*. Explain how each is used when you solve a division problem.

  - Write a paragraph defining and explaining ratios. Give examples.

- **Compare:**

  - Compare the bar graph with the line graph. Decide which one is easier to read and use. Use the space below to make the comparison.

  - What are some differences between prisms and pyramids? How are they alike? In two short paragraphs, describe the similarities and differences.

  - How are changes in perimeter different from changes in area when a figure is enlarged or reduced? Explain using the lines provided below.

- **Describe:**

  - In a paragraph, describe the steps needed to find the area of a rectangle.

  - Describe the chart about the cost of vegetables. Explain why the chart would be helpful to shoppers.

  - Describe two ways a teacher might use fractions.

- **Answer:**

  - Will a square with an area of 20 square inches fit inside a circle with a diameter of 6 inches? Explain your answer.

  - Complete the following sentence: It is easy to add fractions with the same denominators because . . .

  - Would a protractor be the best tool to use to solve this problem? Explain.

- **Reflect**:

    – How accurate was your estimate? Explain how you came up with your estimate.

    – Does the total amount of money needed for the school fair seem strange to you? Why or why not?

    – Do you think that three dozen apples will be enough for all of the baker's pies? Explain your answer.

Writing to explain math concepts and processes becomes more difficult when students have a limited amount of time and when the writing is part of an exam.

The strategies described in this section are designed to prepare students and save them time when they are writing in an assessment environment. More important, these strategies are structured to help make writing during an assessment automatic and predictable—so that students put little thought into the process of writing out their answers and instead pay most of their attention to the math computations and their explanations of them.

Step Up to Writing in Math strategies and activities are visual and tactile. The processes are easy for students to master and use independently. Because they do not add a great deal of time to assignments, they can be used often. The more students repeat these processes, the more their confidence and skills improve. That confidence can help them excel in an exam setting.

5-1 Explaining Steps Taken to Solve a Word Problem

Sometimes on tests, after students have solved a problem and entered their answer in their test booklets, they are asked to explain how they found the answer.

Unfortunately, as they solve a problem, most students do not stop to think about the many steps they complete in order to get that answer. In fact, students seldom stop to think about their problem-solving process, on tests or on daily assignments in math class.

Even advanced math students who "see" the answer to a problem before they do the actual math computation often do not realize how many small steps they took to solve the problem.

Fortunately, all students can learn a reliable method for quickly explaining how they found an answer. They can use this strategy on assessments, whether they are given only a few lines to write their explanation or they must write a detailed paragraph with explanations and examples.

The strategy involves folding a piece of paper into sections, then using those sections to organize the steps of problem solving. Here is how it works:

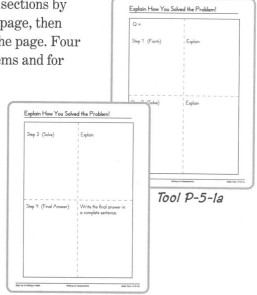

Tool P-5-1a

Tool P-5-1b

1. Divide a sheet of notebook paper into four or six sections by folding once on a line that runs the length of the page, then folding either once or twice across the width of the page. Four sections work well for most primary math problems and for a number of intermediate and secondary problems. But folding paper into six sections is the best option for upper intermediate and secondary students who must solve more sophisticated problems. Label each section on the front and back of the page to match **Math Tools 5-1a** and **5-1b**.

2. Restate the question from the word problem at the top of the page. Restating the question shows that you have read and understood the problem.

3. Step 1 in solving the problem is listing the facts. This is a good reading strategy, as well as a good way to start an explanation. As you list facts from a problem, you read closely for content and comprehension.

4. In the first *Explain* box, start the explanation with "First, I listed the facts about . . . " Just listing the facts in the left column is not enough; you should also describe and give information about the facts. When you do this, you show that you have comprehended the problem.

   Also, using the transitional phrase "First, I listed" will tell your reader that you are presenting the first step in your problem-solving process.

5. Solve the problem, using a separate box for each new operation. The number of boxes needed to solve problems will vary, but it is important to use a new one for each new operation. The goal is to work in "slow motion" and think about each separate step in the problem-solving process.

   After doing your work on the left, explain each step on the right-hand side. Use a transition with each explanation you write. Transitions (i.e., next, then, finally) are words that signal a new step in your problem-solving process.

6. State the final answer. It should be a complete sentence and should use key words from the math question, in order to put it into context. When the answer includes key words from the question, it is much easier to read and to check for reasonableness. Writing answers as complete sentences helps you prepare for formal math assessments. These tests ask you to write one- or two-sentence responses.

Students will seldom have the time or space during a test to complete all of these steps. The goal is not to have students show each step on an assessment; the goal, instead, is to encourage them to make a habit of and develop competence in explaining how they solve problems. When they do, they will be able to offer explanations of various lengths, in various forms, in test settings.

This strategy works because it:

- is easy to learn and easy to use;

- helps students organize information;

- includes practical and predictable steps that make sense;

- demands that students use accurate math vocabulary;

- requires students to think in slow motion;

- becomes a habit after only a few practice sessions;

- can be adjusted and adapted to fit a student's style and level of expertise;

- provides structure, yet is flexible so that it can be used for all types of problems;

- is visual and tactile; and

- promotes independence and builds confidence.

As students use and master this strategy, thinking about their process for solving a problem becomes a habit. They are then not surprised or frustrated in a testing situation when they are asked to explain how they solved a problem. Thinking through their problem-solving process and explaining the steps they took to reach an answer becomes second nature.

Reminders:

– Folding notebook paper into four or six parts is a tactile and kinesthetic activity that can help students begin breaking a process into small steps. The folding of the paper helps students visualize the process.

– Labeling the steps on notebook paper, rather than using a handout, is another good way for students to begin thinking about the steps they used as they solved a problem.

– Relying on a set of transitions (*First of all, Next, Then, Finally*) helps with organization and gives students confidence as they write. They write more quickly when they have a reliable strategy to follow. When students use transitions, scoring their responses and seeing their steps is also easier.

– Asking students to explain their steps is important. As students elaborate, they show how and why they solved a problem in a certain way.

– Writing the final answer in a complete sentence gives students one last chance to demonstrate their confidence in the way they solved a problem.

– Using and modeling the folded-paper activity frequently helps students master the skill of explaining their problem-solving processes.

Note: Like the note-taking strategies for problem solving presented in **Section 2: Reading and Taking Notes**, the "folded-paper activity" can, of course, be used during a lesson as students solve a problem and discuss their problem-solving processes.

However, using it often when students have already solved a problem will help them prepare for assessments that ask test-takers to solve a problem and then ask for a written explanation about how it was solved.

Before a Lesson

• Review **Math Tools 5-1a** through **5-1e**; make overhead transparencies and student copies as needed.

• Make several copies of **Math Tools 5-1a** and **5-1b** to use during demonstration and for practice.

• Select and practice with problems that you will use for demonstration, modeling, and guided lessons.

• Complete all of this strategy's steps for at least two problems, recording your work on overhead transparencies or chart paper.

- Anticipate questions or concerns that students might have as they use this strategy.

During a Lesson

- Remind students that tests often ask for more than just the answer to a math problem. Share examples of the types of directions that students might find on tests that you give or on formal tests given by the district or the state, such as:

  - **Explain how you solved problem 11.**
  - **In the space below, describe the steps you used to find the answer to problem B.**
  - **Explain your problem-solving process.**
  - **Tell how you found the answer to this problem.**

  Let students know that the explanations they give are an important part of the final score they receive on an exam. Remind them that just showing the right answer is not enough; explaining how they found the answer is just as important.

- Explain that your goal is to empower them to do well on these kinds of test questions by giving them a practical strategy that will remind them just what to do whenever they are asked to explain their steps for solving a problem on a test. Emphasize that visualizing steps and actively practicing this strategy will help them remember the process.

Note: Tell students that this strategy uses a few sheets of paper and takes up a lot of space that they will not have on an exam; but explain that mastering the strategy will give them the skills they need when they take an exam. When they have mastered the strategy, they will have memorized the steps—explaining their thinking will become automatic.

- Introduce the folded-paper format. Teach students how to fold and label notebook paper for explaining their problem solving. Display **Math Tools 5-1a** and **5-1b**. Explain that using the letter Q instead of the word *question* saves space, which leaves more space for rewriting the question that needs to be answered. Show students the "steps" and the "reasons for the steps" in each explanation.

- Display **Math Tool 5-1c**; read the problem to students.

- Display **Math Tools 5-1d** and **5-1e**. Read though all parts of the example: *question, facts, steps for solving the problem, explanations,* and *final answer*. Explain why each explanation on the right side of the page makes sense. Point out the organization and the thinking that is a part of the explanation.

Note: Also point out the fact that explanations include reasons—not just the steps.

- Reread each explanation. Point out the use of transitions and connector words (*first*, *next*, *then*, and *so on*) that help with the organization. Tell students that these words are important to use in a testing situation because they make an explanation clear and organized. When the reader looks at the response, he or she immediately sees the steps the student took and the matching explanations.

- Display **Math Tools 5-1a** and **5-1b** again. Read to students one of the math problems that you selected. With help from students, restate the question from the word problem in the space at the top of **Math Tool 5-1a**.

- Identify the facts from the word problem, and list them in the Step 1 box. Show students how to list the facts quickly.

- Then model for them how to explain why they selected those particular facts for inclusion.

- With student input, solve the problem, using a separate box for each new operation or step. Tell students that the goal is to identify all of the steps they take to get to the answer.

- Show students how to explain in writing how (and why) they solved the problem the way they did. Tell students that always starting their explanations the same way is a good idea. When students use the same phrase to start each explanation in class, they ensure that later, in a testing situation, they do not have to spend time wondering how to begin their response. Also tell students that "about" is one of several "magic words" that will remind them to be specific when they explain.

- Tell students that using transitions (connector and signal words) and math verbs will make writing explanations easier and faster.

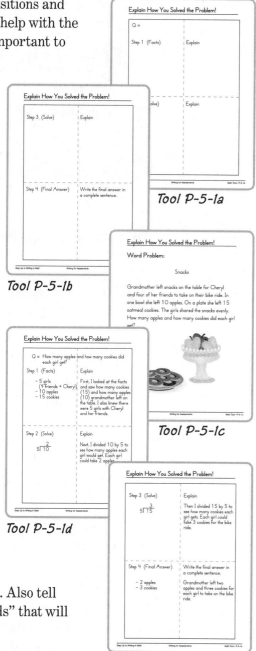

Tool P-5-1a

Tool P-5-1b

Tool P-5-1c

Tool P-5-1d

Tool P-5-1e

Post a list of transitions and verbs that work well for writing in math, such as the following:

Set 1	Set 2
<u>First</u>, I listed . . .	<u>First of all</u>, I listed . . .
<u>Next</u>, I subtracted . . .	<u>Then</u> I isolated . . .
<u>Then</u>, I added all of . . .	<u>Next</u>, I multiplied . . .
<u>Finally</u>, I subtracted the total . . .	<u>After that</u>, I added . . .
	<u>Finally</u>, I divided . . .

- Show students how to include the reason why they took the steps they did. For example:

  - Then I added 2 and 3 together <u>because</u> I needed to know the total number of pieces of candy that the children had.

  - Next, I divided the total cost by 12 months. I did this <u>in order to</u> figure out the monthly fee.

  - After that, I subtracted 6 from both sides <u>so that</u> I could isolate the variable.

- Keep a list of "magic" words and phrases that students can use in explanations to show why they took certain steps. Add to the list when you or your students discover new phrases. These words and phrases work well:

because	since	to find out	to show
to help me	to figure	in order to	so that
so I would know	I did this so	I wanted	I needed

- Explain that the final step in the process is to state the answer in a complete sentence. Demonstrate how to use key words from the math question in the answer. **It is fine for students to just write a complete sentence. But some students** might find it easier to start their final statements with phrases like *I figured out that . . .* or *I found that . . .*. For example:

<u>I figured out that</u> 14 cans of dog food would cost $27.02.

<u>I found that</u> apartment A would be the better deal, as it would cost $40 less per month.

- Remind students about the importance of labeling the numbers in their answers—with words like *inches*, *meters*, *square feet*, *yards*, *dollars*, and *o'clock*—so that they don't leave the reader wondering.

- With help from students, reread all of the explanation statements in the problem you just worked through. Discuss the strategy and its effectiveness.

- Model, as a guided lesson, the same process using a new problem. Include students' responses and suggestions.

- Let students practice a third problem in pairs. Help and encourage them as needed. Take time to share their results.

- Explain to students that although they would not complete all of the steps in this strategy in an actual exam, they would and should think about each of the steps as they write the explanation for an answer on an assessment. Essay-style test responses should include:

an introductory phrase such as:	First, I listed the facts . . .
explanations with transitions:	Next, I . . .. Then, I . . .
reasons why:	I did this so that I would know . . .
a final answer with labels and a lead:	I learned that . . .

Additional Ideas

- Plan for success by creating additional opportunities for practice. For example:
  - vary the type and difficulty level of problems;
  - do part of the work for students, and expect them to finish where you left off;
  - solve a problem, fill in the left half of the page, and have students work in pairs to write the explanations for your work;
  - complete all of the explanation steps orally; or
  - check students' work frequently, encouraging success by reviewing steps and demonstrating the process for students.

- Ask students to teach this strategy to each other as a way to review throughout the year.

- Use the scoring guide with examples (**Math Tools 5-3a** to **5-3e**) to show students the kind of writing that is expected on an assessment.

- Give students lists of math vocabulary (see **Math Tools 1-1a** and **1-1b**) to help them with spelling and to push them to use the right math terms.

- Have students practice writing math sentences. Students need practice and guidance to be able to write clear and accurate explanations.

  - Compare weak and strong sentences:

    > a. I put 5 with 72 and got 77.
    >
    >   I added 5 and 72, and the sum was 77.

    > b. I divided 182 and 7 to get the answer.
    >
    >   I divided 182 by 7 to find out how many apples each family would get.

    > c. I got rid of the 2 on both sides to get "x" alone.
    >
    >   I subtracted 2 from both sides of the equation to isolate the variable "x."

  - Watch for reversals:

    > I divided 4 by 440 to find the answer.

    when it should be:

    > I divided 440 by 4 to find the answer.

  - Encourage short, clear sentences:

    > I added all of my scores.
    > The total was 109.
    > I divided by 10 to find the average.

  - Give hints about how to use and place numbers:

    > I multiplied the number of students (30) by the number of cards (7) that each would need.
    >
    > I need 5 packs of note cards because when I divided 210 by 50 I had a remainder of 10.
    >
    > Four packs would not be enough.

- Have students practice speaking sentences orally. They benefit from hearing how words sound and what it sounds like to speak (or write) fluently.

- When students use everyday language to explain themselves, validate their thinking, then point out the mathematically precise way to express what they have said.

- Compare explanations. Share examples to point out that it is acceptable for students to approach problems and express themselves in different ways.

- Give students copies of problems that have been solved correctly and have good, clear explanations to keep in their math notebook for future reference.

5-2 Turning an Explanation Into a Formal Paragraph

To prepare students for test questions that require a partial or a full-paragraph response, share this strategy. Longer paragraphs, sometimes called extended responses, call for accurate and specific information. In an extended response, students must answer the question completely and correctly, and present information in a clear, organized way.

When students have learned and practiced the folded-paper strategy for explaining how they solved a problem (**5-1 Explaining Steps Taken to Solve a Word Problem**), they can fairly easily transfer their explanations into a full paragraph. In fact, once they have used the folded-paper method to explain the steps they took to solve a specific problem, students need only to add a topic sentence and copy their explanation sentences, editing as needed. The final statement, with the correct answer explained and labeled, becomes the paragraph's conclusion.

(With guidance this paragraph writing strategy can also be used with the note-taking strategies presented in Section 2. See examples on **Math Tools 2–9d, 2–9g, 2–11c,** and **2–12d.**)

The key skill, therefore, that students will still need to learn in order to successfully write an extended response on a math assessment is the ability to write a good topic sentence. To be able to think about and write topic sentences quickly during an exam, students must have a method that is reliable, makes sense, and is easy to remember.

Two strategies work well for writing topic sentences in paragraphs that explain problem solving:

1. Start the topic sentence with an infinitive. An infinitive is the word *to* plus a verb. For example:

> <u>To find</u> the answer to the problem about ticket sales for the school play, I used four steps.

> <u>To solve</u> problem 18 about buying paint, I followed these steps.

> <u>To figure</u> out how much money Brad would earn on his summer job, I completed these steps.

> <u>To get</u> the answer for this week's Challenge Problem, I completed five steps.

> <u>To complete</u> problem 6 in the unit exam, I used four simple steps.

2. Use an action verb that fits the task and creates organization for the rest of the paragraph.

> I <u>found</u> the answer to the geometry problem about triangles by doing three things.

> I <u>solved</u> problem 18 in four easy steps.

> I <u>completed</u> the circus word problem by using the following steps.

> I <u>answered</u> the Problem of the Week correctly by completing the following steps.

> I <u>determined</u> the answer to the volume problem with these steps.

Before a Lesson

- Make overhead transparencies and student copies (as needed) of **Math Tools 5-2a** through **5-2e**.

- Review the topic sentence and paragraph examples.

- Practice writing full paragraphs for problems that you used during the demonstration sessions for **5-1 Explaining Steps Taken to Solve a Word Problem**. Use the example on **Math Tool 5-2d** as a guide.

During a Lesson

- Use **Math Tools 5-2a** through **5-2d** to introduce students to the idea of turning their explanations into a formal paragraph. Display the question, read the steps taken and explanations on the folded paper, then talk about how the folded-paper exercise on **Math Tools 5-2b** and **5-2c** corresponds to the paragraph on **Math Tool 5-2d**. Point out that a topic sentence starts the paragraph.

- Display and read **Math Tool 5-2e** with students. Explain the purpose of a topic sentence.

- Point out the power of number words. Notice that many of the topic sentence examples use a number word. Explain to students that number words are important to use in an exam because they serve as a flag; the reader, the person scoring the paragraph, sees the number word and knows that a series of steps and explanations will follow. For example:

> I solved problem 18 in <u>four</u> easy steps.

> To get the answer for this week's Challenge Problem, I completed <u>five</u> steps.

- Have students copy examples of topic sentences that you create onto the back of their hard copies of **Math Tool 5-2e**.

- Have students work in pairs to write more topic sentences using both the infinitive (*to* plus a verb) strategy and the action verb strategy.

- Using one of your practice problems or a new problem, help students write out a formal paragraph with a topic sentence.

- Explain that they will usually not need to add other sentences to their paragraphs, but that they may want to smooth out their sentences and make small changes to the text on the folded paper as they write their paragraphs. At times students may feel that they need to add a bit more explanation in their final paragraph. Guide them and encourage independent choices, depending on the math and writing skills of your students.

- Give students a new problem. Have them complete all of the steps in the folded-paper activity. Then have them turn the explanations into a paragraph with a topic sentence.

- Use this strategy frequently to make sure that students are able to explain their problem-solving steps quickly and accurately. Keep in mind that this paragraph writing method works well with note-taking strategies (see **Math Tools 2-9, 2-11,** and **2-12**).

- Assess the final paragraph using the scoring guide on **Math Tool 5-3a**.

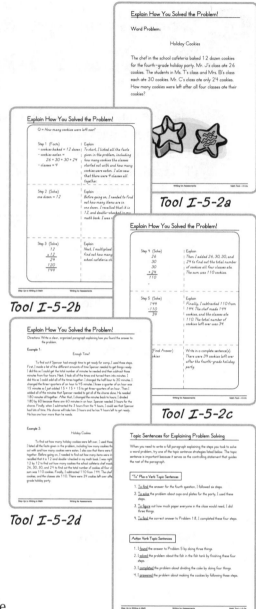

Tool I-5-2a

Tool I-5-2b

Tool I-5-2c

Tool I-5-2d

Tool I-5-2e

5-3 Scoring Paragraphs That Explain Steps in Problem Solving

Students must have direct, explicit instruction and access to numerous examples to build the skills and confidence they need to write paragraph responses quickly and accurately during a test.

The folded-paper activity for explaining problem solving (**5-1 Explaining Steps Taken to Solve a Word Problem**) gives students a structured method for learning this skill. In addition, they need student-friendly examples of the kind of writing that would score well on an exam. (This scoring guide can also be used with paragraphs written along with note-taking activities; see **Math Tools 2–9, 2-11, 2-12**.)

Math Tool 5-3a is a guide that you can use:

- to score student work;

- to set high expectations for all students;

- to give students helpful information about how you score papers;

- to give students goals for improving their work in order to reach a proficient or advanced level;

- to show students examples of below-basic, basic, proficient, and advanced work that help them judge their own work and learn more about writing paragraphs; and

- to support students as they prepare for assessments.

(See **6-5 Scoring Paragraph and Report Writing** for information about a scoring guide that can be used to evaluate more general assignments for writing about math.)

Before a Lesson

- Make overhead transparencies and student copies of **Math Tools 5-3a** through **5-3e**.

- Review the examples on **Math Tools 5-3b** and **5-3c**, and on **Math Tools 5-3d** and **5-3e**. Compare these examples with the scoring guide on **Math Tool 5-3a**; compare the examples with the kind of writing you expect from students. Decide whether the scoring guide needs any additions or changes in order to meet your goals and expectations.

- Consider writing a set of sample paragraphs (see **Math Tools 5-3b** to **5-3e**) for a math problem that you have used with the class. Students learn a great deal when teachers share their writing, and they appreciate knowing exactly what their teacher expects. When they have your examples, they are more likely to reach the goals that you set.

During a Lesson

- Display **Math Tool 5-3a**. Read each line on the scoring guide. Explain your expectations, define terms, and answer questions.

- Introduce students to the 16-point scale presented on the scoring guide. Explain that the number 16 is used because all parts of 16 are easy to add, subtract, multiply, and divide. More importantly, it sets goals for students; it provides guidance for improvement.

- Show them that they can earn up to 4 points in each of the four categories.

- Use the phrase "**over the line**" as you explain the numbers on the continuum. Let students know that the goal is for all of them to "get over the line," the center dark line, and write paragraphs that are **proficient** or **advanced**—in other words, clear, organized, and accurate.

- Explain that they should use the descriptions for earning 1, 2, 3, or 4 points to help them write; assure them that you will be helping them learn how to reach the proficient and advanced levels.

- Use **Math Tools 5-3b** through **5-3e** (and other examples that you have created) to demonstrate what you expect at each level on the continuum. Read and compare the examples with the scoring guide.

- Give students time to use the scoring guide to assess paragraphs that they have written.

- Using a problem that the class has solved, write a paragraph that has a clear topic sentence and an explanation for each step. Assess this paragraph using the scoring guide. Make changes, with student input, that would move the score to a higher number on the continuum.

- Have students keep copies of the scoring guide in their math notebook to refer to when they write. Have students assess their paragraphs before they turn in their work; have them compare their scores with grades you give.

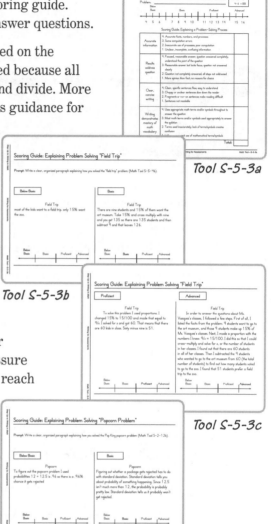

Tool S-5-3a

Tool S-5-3b

Tool S-5-3c

Tool S-5-3d

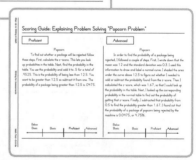

Tool S-5-3e

- Whenever possible, give students time to revise and improve paragraphs after they receive their first scores. This will push students to proficient and advanced levels—to do their best.

5-4 Using Framed Paragraphs to Practice for Writing in Math Assessments

You can create short and long framed paragraphs quickly and easily for any writing task, including paragraphs that explain how problems were solved.

Teachers create a frame by:

- Writing a clear topic sentence that shows the purpose of the paragraph and tells what the writer will either prove or explain.

- Using transition words and phrases as leads for each of the sentences in the body of the paragraph (*first, next, then, finally,* and *so on*).

- Writing the entire conclusion or a part of the conclusion.

For example:

Solving the Problem

To solve the problem about _____,
I followed these steps. First, I _____
_____
_____
because _____
_____. Next, I _____
_____. I did this _____
_____.
Then _____
_____
_____. After that _____
_____
_____ so I would _____

_____.

Finally, I found that _____

_____

_____.

Here is another example of a framed paragraph to explain a problem-solving process:

Finding the Answer

I found the answer to problem _____ in a few easy steps. First, I _____
_____. I did this to _____
_____.
Next, I _____
_____. This was an important step because
_____
_____. Finally, I _____
_____. I then figured out that the
answer was _____.

A framed paragraph works best when:

- the topic sentence is clear and specific. (See **5-2 Turning an Explanation Into a Formal Paragraph** for examples.)

- it uses only a few words. (Long, detailed sentences make it more difficult for students to follow the teacher's train of thought and complete the framed paragraph.)

- transitions are scattered throughout the frame in the way they would be in a completed paragraph. (If transitions are listed along the left side of the page, students may assume that they have a series of sentences to complete; they may not see the frame as a paragraph.)

- it is flexible and encourages students to make changes to fit the purpose of the assignment.

Ideas for Using Framed Paragraphs to Prepare for Assessments

- Make short framed paragraphs for specific purposes. Make copies to keep on hand and use for practice when time is limited.

- Hand out copies of a framed paragraph, and challenge pairs of students to complete the frame as quickly, creatively, and accurately as possible.

- Include framed paragraphs on quizzes and tests.

Note that framed paragraphs are not designed to be used exclusively. They should not replace the folded-paper strategy and accompanying paragraphs from sections **5-1 Explaining Steps Taken to Solve a Word Problem** and **5-2 Turning an Explanation Into a Formal Paragraph.** To be successful on class assignments and formal assessments, students need to think and write quickly on their own. They need reliable strategies that they understand and can use independently. Assessments that ask for extended responses are not going to include frames!

Practice Guides With Framed Paragraphs

A practice guide is a visual organizer that gives students a place to show math computations. You can use framed paragraphs and practice guides together.

The practice guides on **Math Tools 5-4a** to **5-4d** give students space to show their work and write about the steps they take to solve a problem.

Use these tools as they are, or create similar tools to meet your needs and the goals you have for a particular assignment.

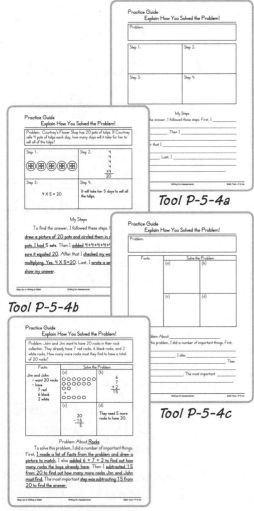

Tool P-5-4a

Tool P-5-4b

Tool P-5-4c

Tool P-5-4d

5-5 Preparing for Other Specific Types of Exam Questions

Students taking math assessments are often asked to complete writing tasks other than explaining how they solved word problems. The following strategies can help students anticipate other kinds of exam questions and give them strategies for responding.

Writing to Justify an Answer or a Process

Test questions that ask students to justify an answer require short but specific responses. These types of questions ask students to explain why an answer is reasonable. Sometimes the test-taker must solve a problem, then write to explain why the answer is correct and why it makes sense. At other times, students solve problems, select the correct answer in a multiple-choice format, then write to explain why the answer they selected is the best choice. For example:

In a short paragraph, give reasons why your answer is the correct answer.
Buying a spool of ribbon with 24 yards is definitely the right answer. The 12-, 15-, and 18-yard spools would not work. First, the girls need $2\frac{1}{2}$ yards for each holiday wreath. They need bows for 8 wreaths for the school play. Even doing mental math, I know that 8×2 is 16, and $8 \times \frac{1}{2}$ is 4. That means they need at least 20 yards of ribbon. None of the other spools would work.

Help students prepare for these types of questions by:

- Making sure that they understand, can explain, and can use the word *reasonable* when writing about answers to math problems.

  - Define *reasonable*. Tell students that something is reasonable if it: can be explained and/or understood, is not extreme, makes sense, falls within the bounds of reason, is rational, is justifiable, and shows correct thinking.

  - Discuss and give numerous examples of what it means for something to be called reasonable and/or unreasonable; use everyday experiences like playing in the street, eating 20 cookies in one sitting, doing 150 math problems for homework, or expecting to win every baseball game your team plays.

  - Demonstrate writing (or speaking) short explanations of why a given answer is reasonable. Use a very simple math problem that students can answer easily, so that they can see clearly that your answer is reasonable. Use more challenging problems once students have learned the strategy.

Do not assume that students know what *reasonable* means. Tell them that this word is often used on tests to find out what they know and do not know about the answers they give.

- List (and continue to add to the list) synonyms and phrases that have the same meaning as *reasonable* and elicit the same kind of response.

makes sense	*justify your answer*
give reasons	*explain why this is the best answer*
seems right	*rational answer*
reasonable response	*sounds right*
sensible	*logical*
fair	*just*

- Ask students to explain why an answer to a problem that the class has solved together is reasonable. Ask them to write their responses on index cards. Use index cards to save time in class, to mimic the amount of writing space students are likely to have on a test, and to make grading easier.

- End your demonstrations or lessons about word problems by having students explain why answers to problems were reasonable or unreasonable. Help one student start the response; call on others to add sentences to the response. Help as needed, and rephrase the response for the class when the students have finished. Speaking and listening will help students with their writing.

- Give students a quick, easy strategy to memorize and use in an exam:
  - Start with a short, strong statement that shows the purpose of the response.
  - Use transitions (connector words) for organization.
  - Use math vocabulary.

  For example:

  > My answer of 400 cookies makes sense. First, almost 35 kids are coming to the picnic on each of the 10 buses, and there are at least 2 teachers on each bus. This makes 370 people going to the picnic. When I round 370 up to the next hundred, I get 400. It makes sense to order 400. Finally, having 30 extra cookies left over is not too many. A few more kids and more teachers might show up at the picnic.

- Have students practice writing responses on the same number of lines, with the same spacing, that they will have on an exam. When students see a similar number of lines and the same amount of space on an exam, they will feel prepared.

Writing to Describe Illustrations or Representations

The strategy **2-10 Hints for Illustrating Word Problems** provides suggestions and examples for helping students illustrate and/or create visual representations—including symbols, pictures, graphs, tables, charts, equations, and sketches—that they can use in solving math word problems.

Occasionally, students are asked to explain or describe their own illustrations or to judge the effectiveness of math-related illustrations/representations made by someone else. For example:

> **Solve problem 20. Make an illustration to show your math thinking. Explain your illustration in the space below.**
>
> **Is the illustration for solving problem 14 accurate? Use the lines below to write your answer.**

Help students prepare for this type of written response by sharing examples and by providing time for practicing turning questions into topic sentences. A clear topic sentence gives students confidence to complete their response, and it gives those scoring the test a reason to keep reading. (See **5-2 Turning an Explanation Into a Formal Paragraph** for details on teaching strategies for writing topic sentences.) Using transitions makes it easy to complete the response. For example:

> My illustration for problem 20 shows how I plan to find the answer. First, ... The illustration also . . . . Finally, it . . ..
>
> Yes, it is accurate and helped me solve the problem. First of all, ... It also . . .. Most important, it . . ..

Defining Math Terms and Concepts

Section 1: Vocabulary provides strategies for helping students learn, remember, and use math terms. Four tools in particular can help students learn to give extended definitions that include examples and make connections to real-life situations:

- concept maps with detailed paragraphs,
- meaningful sentences,
- word maps with personal connections, and
- word banks.

Help students prepare for questions about definitions by:

- explaining that the answer needs more than a simple definition.
- modeling and giving examples.
- teaching students to make the best use of the allotted space without going outside the lines.
- rehearsing orally when new terms are introduced.

For example:

> ### Edge
>
> An edge is a line segment where two faces of a polyhedron meet. On blocks that babies play with, there are edges where the sides come together. On our kitchen countertop, there are edges where the large, flat top of the counter meets the small, two-inch trim that runs around the counter. Blocks and kitchen countertops are both polyhedrons.

Comparing or Contrasting

Many students can explain orally how two objects, examples, processes, or problems are alike, yet they struggle when trying to put that comparison into writing. Two strategies will help students learn to write compare and/or contrast responses:

- First are topic sentence strategies that make comparisons or draw contrasts. Give students a list of compare/contrast words to use in their topic sentences.

the same	*different*	*alike*	*similar*
differ	*similarities*	*differences*	*in common*
not alike	*unlike*	*vary*	*resemble*

Tell students to include key words from the question or prompt, along with compare/contrast terms, in their topic sentence. For example:

> **Compare the <u>bar graph</u> with the <u>line graph</u>, and decide which one is <u>easier to read</u> and use. Use the space below to make the comparison.**

> The <u>bar graph</u> and the <u>line graph resemble</u> each other, but the <u>bar graph</u> is <u>easier to read</u> because it gives two <u>different</u> types of information.

> **Explain how <u>decimals</u> and <u>fractions</u> are alike.**

> <u>Decimals</u> and <u>fractions</u> are <u>alike</u> in two important ways.

> **Describe how <u>squares</u> and <u>rectangles</u> are alike.**

> <u>Squares</u> and <u>rectangles</u> have three <u>similarities</u>.

- The second strategy that can help students craft compare/contrast responses is the informal outline. Ask students to use informal outlines with all compare/contrast writing assignments. When they use informal outlines, they can quickly organize the key/star ideas that will support their topic sentence. In a compare/contrast assignment, this means listing the ways that things are alike or different. For example:

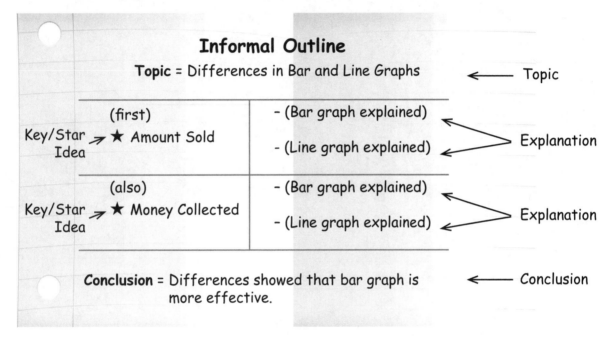

Informal Outline

Topic = Differences in Bar and Line Graphs   ← Topic

| Key/Star Idea → | ★ (first) Amount Sold | – (Bar graph explained) – (Line graph explained) | Explanation |
| Key/Star Idea → | ★ (also) Money Collected | – (Bar graph explained) – (Line graph explained) | Explanation |

Conclusion = Differences showed that bar graph is more effective.   ← Conclusion

(See **6-1 Accordion Paragraphs** for more details about informal outlines and the use of transitions for organization.)

Describing, Explaining, and/or Analyzing Processes, Content, or Concepts

The strategy presented in **6-1 Accordion Paragraphs** can help students write paragraphs on generic topics related to math.

The Accordion Paragraph strategy gives students specific information about creating topic sentences, making a plan for writing, using transitions, elaborating, and writing conclusions. Students can use the strategy to write short and long compositions. Once learned, the Accordion Paragraph strategy is the perfect tool to use during an assessment when general questions about math content are asked. Also, the term "Accordion" implies that paragraphs can be stretched or condensed in an "Accordion" style—students can write long or short paragraphs.

Math Tools: Primary

Explain How You Solved the Problem!

Q =	
Step 1 (Facts)	Explain
Step 2 (Solve)	Explain

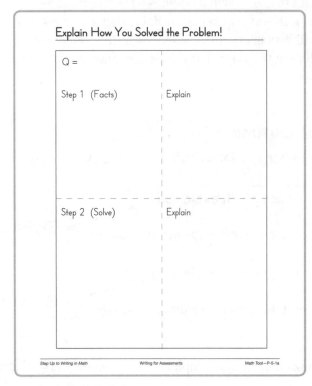

Step Up to Writing in Math — Writing for Assessments — Math Tool—P-5-1a

Math Tool P-5-1a

Explain How You Solved the Problem!

Step 3 (Solve)	Explain
Step 4 (Final Answer)	Write the final answer in a complete sentence.

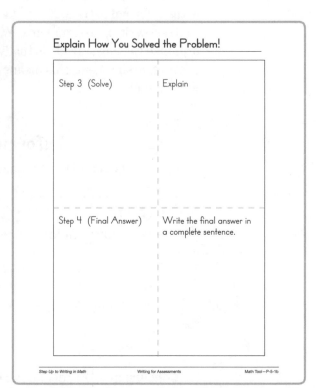

Step Up to Writing in Math — Writing for Assessments — Math Tool—P-5-1b

Math Tool P-5-1b

Explain How You Solved the Problem!

Word Problem:

Snacks

Grandmother left snacks on the table for Cheryl and four of her friends to take on their bike ride. In one bowl she left 10 apples. On a plate she left 15 oatmeal cookies. The girls shared the snacks evenly. How many apples and how many cookies did each girl get?

Step Up to Writing in Math — Writing for Assessments — Math Tool—P-5-1c

Math Tool P-5-1c

Explain How You Solved the Problem!

Q = How many apples and how many cookies did each girl get?	
Step 1 (Facts) – 5 girls (4 friends + Cheryl) – 10 apples – 15 cookies	Explain First, I looked at the facts and saw how many cookies (15) and how many apples (10) grandmother left on the table. I also knew there were 5 girls with Cheryl and her friends.
Step 2 (Solve) $5\overline{)10}$ with quotient 2	Explain Next, I divided 10 by 5 to see how many apples each girl would get. Each girl could take 2 apples.

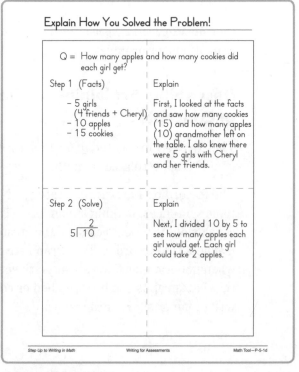

Step Up to Writing in Math — Writing for Assessments — Math Tool—P-5-1d

Math Tool P-5-1d

Math Tools: Primary *(continued)*

Explain How You Solved the Problem!

Step 3 (Solve)	Explain
$5\overline{)15}$ $\frac{3}{}$	Then I divided 15 by 5 to see how many cookies each girl gets. Each girl could take 3 cookies for the bike ride.
Step 4 (Final Answer) – 2 apples – 3 cookies	Write the final answer in a complete sentence. Grandmother left two apples and three cookies for each girl to take on the bike ride.

Step Up to Writing in Math · Writing for Assessments · Math Tool—P-5-1e

Math Tool P-5-1e

Explain How You Solved the Problem!

Word Problem:

Coins

Mallory had two nickels and two pennies. Her mom gave her two dimes for taking out the trash. How much money does Mallory have altogether?

Step Up to Writing in Math · Writing for Assessments · Math Tool—P-5-2a

Math Tool P-5-2a

Explain How You Solved the Problem!

Q = How much money does Mallory have?

Step 1 (Facts)	Explain
– 2 pennies – 2 nickels – 2 dimes	First, I listed how many pennies (2), nickels (2), and dimes (2) Mallory has.
Step 2 (Solve) – 2 pennies $1 + 1 = 2¢$ – 2 nickels $5 + 5 = 10¢$ – 2 dimes $10 + 10 = 20¢$	Next, I added each set of Mallory's coins together.

Step Up to Writing in Math · Writing for Assessments · Math Tool—P-5-2b

Math Tool P-5-2b

Explain How You Solved the Problem!

Step 3 (Solve)	Explain
$2¢ + 10¢ + 20¢ = 32¢$	Then I added all of the money together. I did this to see how much Mallory has altogether.
Step 4 (Final Answer) 32¢	Write the final answer in a complete sentence. Altogether Mallory has 32¢.

Step Up to Writing in Math · Writing for Assessments · Math Tool—P-5-2c

Math Tool P-5-2c

Step Up to Writing in Math · WRITING FOR ASSESSMENTS   **169**

Math Tools: Primary *(continued)*

Explain How You Solved the Problem!

Directions: Write a clear, organized paragraph explaining how you found the answer to the problem.

Example 1:

Snacks

To find out how many snacks each girl would get I used these steps. First, I looked at the facts. There were 10 apples to share and 15 cookies to share. There were 5 girls with Cheryl and her 4 friends. Next, I divided 10 by 5 to see how many apples each girl would get. Each girl would get 2 apples. Then I divided 15 by 5 to see how many cookies each girl gets. Each can have 3 cookies. Grandmother left two apples and three cookies for each girl to take on the bike ride.

Example 2:

Coins

To find out how much money Mallory has, I followed these steps. First, I listed the facts. Mallory has two pennies, two nickels, and two dimes. Next, I added each set of Mallory's coins together. Then, I added all of the money together. Altogether Mallory has 32 cents.

Step Up to Writing in Math   Writing for Assessments   Math Tool—P-5-2d

Math Tool P-5-2d

Topic Sentences for Explaining Math Steps

When you need to write a full paragraph explaining your steps in a word problem, try one of these topic sentence strategies. The topic sentence is important because it guides the rest of the paragraph.

"To" Plus a Verb Topic Sentences

1. <u>To find</u> the answer for the question, I followed these steps.
2. <u>To solve</u> the problem about the cookies, I used these steps.
3. <u>To figure</u> out how much sand the sandbox could hold, I did three things.
4. <u>To get</u> the answer for Problem 6, I used these four steps.
5. <u>To find</u> the total number of books read by each class during A+ Reading Week, our team used three easy steps.

Action Verb Topic Sentences

1. I <u>found</u> the answer to Problem 7 by doing three things.
2. I <u>solved</u> the problem about the fish by finishing these four steps.
3. I <u>answered</u> the problem about the wood with these steps.
4. I <u>completed</u> the second problem about art supplies in a few easy steps.
5. My partner and I <u>solved</u> Problem 29, the baseball problem, in five steps.

Step Up to Writing in Math   Writing for Assessments   Math Tool—P-5-2e

Math Tool P-5-2e

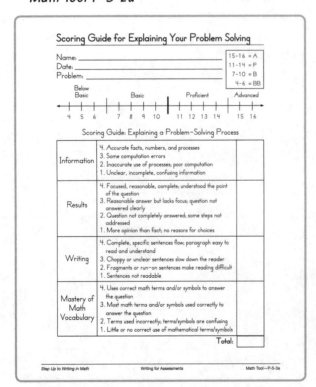

Math Tool P-5-3a

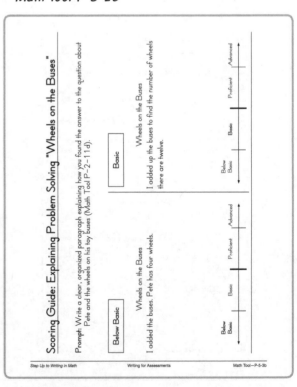

Math Tool P-5-3b

Math Tools: Primary *(continued)*

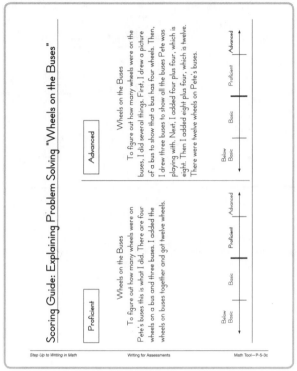

Math Tool P-5-3c

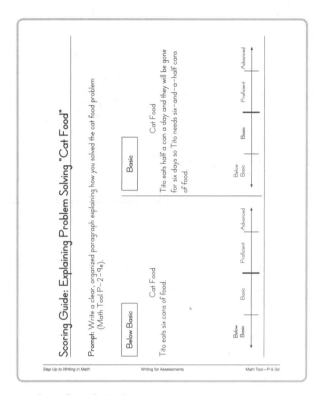

Math Tool P-5-3d

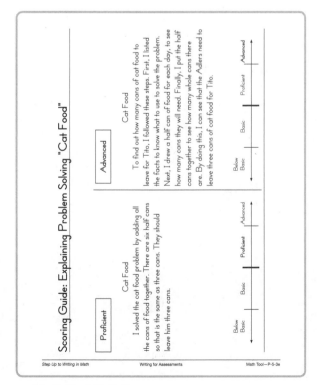

Math Tool P-5-3e

Practice Guide
Explain How You Solved the Problem!

Problem:	
Step 1:	Step 2:
Step 3:	Step 4:

My Steps

To find the answer, I followed these steps. First, I _____

_____. Then I _____

_____. After that I _____

_____. Last, I _____

_____

_____.

Math Tool P-5-4a

Math Tools: Primary–Intermediate

Practice Guide
Explain How You Solved the Problem!

Problem: Courtney's Flower Shop has 20 pots of tulips. If Courtney sells 4 pots of tulips each day, how many days will it take for her to sell all of the tulips?

Step 1:	Step 2:
⊞ ⊞ ⊞ ⊞ ⊞	$\begin{array}{r} 4 \\ 4 \\ 4 \\ 4 \\ +4 \\ \hline 20 \end{array}$

Step 3:	Step 4:
4 X 5 = 20	It will take her 5 days to sell all the tulips.

My Steps

To find the answer, I followed these steps. First, I _____ drew a picture of 20 pots and circled them in sets of 4 pots. I had 5 sets. Then I added 4+4+4+4+4 to make sure it equaled 20. After that I checked my work again by multiplying. Yes, 4 X 5=20. Last, I wrote a sentence to show my answer.

Math Tool P-5-4b

Practice Guide
Explain How You Solved the Problem!

Problem:

Facts:	Solve the Problem	
	(a)	(b)
	(c)	(d)

Problem About _____

To solve this problem, I did a number of important things. First, _____. I also _____. Then _____. The most important _____.

Math Tool P-5-4c

Practice Guide
Explain How You Solved the Problem!

Problem: John and Jim want to have 20 rocks in their rock collection. They already have 7 red rocks, 6 black rocks, and 2 white rocks. How many more rocks must they find to have a total of 20 rocks?

Facts:	Solve the Problem	

Jim and John
– want 20 rocks
– have
  7 red
  6 black
  2 white
	(a)
	○○○○○○○
	○○○○○○○
	○○
	+
	○○○○○
		(b)
		$\begin{array}{r} 6 \\ 7 \\ +2 \\ \hline 15 \end{array}$

	(c) $\begin{array}{r} 20 \\ -15 \\ \hline 5 \end{array}$	(d) They need 5 more rocks to have 20.

Problem About Rocks

To solve this problem, I did a number of important things. First, I made a list of facts from the problem and drew a picture to match. I also added 6 + 7 + 2 to find out how many rocks the boys already have. Then I subtracted 15 from 20 to find out how many more rocks Jim and John must find. The most important step was subtracting 15 from 20 to find the answer.

Math Tool P-5-4d

Explain How You Solved the Problem!

Q = _____

Step 1 (Facts)	Explain
Step 2 (Solve)	Explain
Step 3 (Solve)	Explain

Math Tool I-5-1a

Math Tools: Intermediate *(continued)*

Explain How You Solved the Problem!

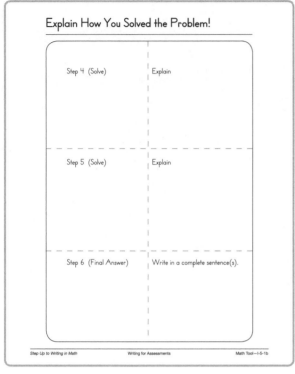

Step 4 (Solve)	Explain
Step 5 (Solve)	Explain
Step 6 (Final Answer)	Write in a complete sentence(s).

Step Up to Writing in Math · Writing for Assessments · Math Tool—I-5-1b

Math Tool I-5-1b

Explain How You Solved the Problem!

Word Problem:

Enough Time?

Each year the fifth-graders at High Point Elementary spend two days at Outdoor Camp. This year Spencer waited until the last moment to get ready. If he has only 4 hours to get ready and he needs 55 minutes for shopping, 25 minutes for a haircut, a half hour for lunch, three-quarters of an hour to pack, and 25 minutes for his family to drive him to the school, can he be ready on time?

Step Up to Writing in Math · Writing for Assessments · Math Tool—I-5-1c

Math Tool I-5-1c

Explain How You Solved the Problem!

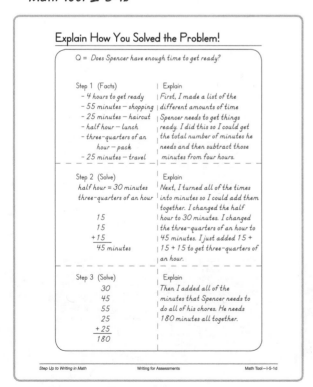

Q = *Does Spencer have enough time to get ready?*

Step 1 (Facts)	Explain
– 4 hours to get ready – 55 minutes – shopping – 25 minutes – haircut – half hour – lunch – three-quarters of an hour – pack – 25 minutes – travel	*First, I made a list of the different amounts of time Spencer needs to get things ready. I did this so I could get the total number of minutes he needs and then subtract those minutes from four hours.*
Step 2 (Solve) half hour = 30 minutes three-quarters of an hour 15 15 +15 45 minutes	Explain *Next, I turned all of the times into minutes so I could add them together. I changed the half hour to 30 minutes. I changed the three-quarters of an hour to 45 minutes. I just added 15 + 15 + 15 to get three-quarters of an hour.*
Step 3 (Solve) 30 45 55 25 + 25 180	Explain *Then I added all of the minutes that Spencer needs to do all of his chores. He needs 180 minutes all together.*

Step Up to Writing in Math · Writing for Assessments · Math Tool—I-5-1d

Math Tool I-5-1d

Explain How You Solved the Problem!

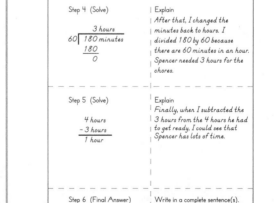

Step 4 (Solve) $\begin{array}{r} 3\ hours \\ 60\overline{)180\ minutes} \\ \underline{180} \\ 0 \end{array}$	Explain *After that, I changed the minutes back to hours. I divided 180 by 60 because there are 60 minutes in an hour. Spencer needed 3 hours for the chores.*
Step 5 (Solve) 4 hours – 3 hours 1 hour	Explain *Finally, when I subtracted the 3 hours from the 4 hours he had to get ready, I could see that Spencer has lots of time.*
Step 6 (Final Answer) *Yes.*	Write in a complete sentence(s). *Yes, Spencer has time. His chores will take him 3 hours, and he has 4 hours left to get ready. He has 1 hour more than he needs.*

Step Up to Writing in Math · Writing for Assessments · Math Tool—I-5-1e

Math Tool I-5-1e

Math Tools: Intermediate *(continued)*

Explain How You Solved the Problem!

Word Problem:

Holiday Cookies

The chef in the school cafeteria baked 12 dozen cookies for the fourth-grade holiday party. Mr. J's class ate 26 cookies. The students in Ms. T's class and Mrs. B's class each ate 30 cookies. Mr. C's class ate only 24 cookies. How many cookies were left after all four classes ate their cookies?

Math Tool I-5-2a

Explain How You Solved the Problem!

Q = How many cookies were left over?

Step 1 (Facts)	Explain
– cookies baked = 12 dozen	To start, I listed all the facts
– cookies eaten =	given in the problem, including
26 + 30 + 30 + 24	how many cookies the classes
– classes = 4	started out with and how many
	cookies were eaten. I also saw
	that there were 4 classes all
	together.

Step 2 (Solve)	Explain
one dozen = 12	Before going on, I needed to find
	out how many items are in
	one dozen. I recalled that it is
	12, and double-checked in my
	math book. I was right!

Step 3 (Solve)	Explain
12	Next, I multiplied 12 by 12 to
× 12	find out how many cookies the
24	school cafeteria chef made.
120	
144	

Math Tool I-5-2b

Explain How You Solved the Problem!

Step 4 (Solve)	Explain
26	Then I added 26, 30, 30, and
30	24 to find out the total number
30	of cookies all four classes ate.
+ 24	The sum was 110 cookies.
110	

Step 5 (Solve)	Explain
144	Finally, I subtracted 110 from
−110	144. The chef made 144
34	cookies, and the classes ate
	110. The total number of
	cookies left over was 34.

Step 6 (Final Answer)	Write in a complete sentence(s).
34 cookies	There were 34 cookies left over
	after the fourth-grade holiday
	party.

Math Tool I-5-2c

Explain How You Solved the Problem!

Directions: Write a clear, organized paragraph explaining how you found the answer to the problem.

Example 1:

Enough Time?

To find out if Spencer had enough time to get ready for camp, I used these steps. First, I made a list of the different amounts of time Spencer needed to get things ready. I did this so I could get the total number of minutes he needed and then subtract those minutes from four hours. Next, I took all of the times and turned them into minutes. I did this so I could add all of the times together. I changed the half hour to 30 minutes. I changed the three-quarters of an hour to 45 minutes. I knew a quarter of an hour was 15 minutes so I just added 15 + 15 + 15 to get three-quarters of an hour. Then I added all of the minutes that Spencer needed to get all of the chores done. He needed 180 minutes all together. After that, I changed the minutes back to hours. I divided 180 by 60 because there are 60 minutes in an hour. Spencer needed 3 hours for the chores. Finally, when I subtracted the 3 hours from the 4 hours, I could see that Spencer had lots of time. His chores will take him 3 hours and he has 4 hours left to get ready. He has one hour more than he needs.

Example 2:

Holiday Cookies

To find out how many holiday cookies were left over, I used these steps. To start, I listed all the facts given in the problem, including how many cookies the classes started out with and how many cookies were eaten. I also saw that there were four classes all together. Before going on, I needed to find out how many items were in one dozen. I recalled that it is 12 and double-checked in my math book. I was right! Next, I multiplied 12 by 12 to find out how many cookies the school cafeteria chef made. Then I added 26, 30, 30, and 24 to find out the total number of cookies all four classes ate. The sum was 110 cookies. Finally, I subtracted 110 from 144. The chef made 144 cookies, and the classes ate 110. There were 34 cookies left over after the fourth-grade holiday party.

Math Tool I-5-2d

Math Tools: Intermediate (continued)

Topic Sentences for Explaining Problem Solving

When you need to write a full paragraph explaining the steps you took to solve a word problem, try one of the topic sentence strategies listed below. The topic sentence is important because it serves as the controlling statement that guides the rest of the paragraph.

"To" Plus a Verb Topic Sentences

1. To find the answer for the fourth question, I followed six steps.
2. To solve the problem about cups and plates for the party, I used these steps.
3. To figure out how much paper everyone in the class would need, I did three things.
4. To find the correct answer to Problem 18, I completed these four steps.

Action Verb Topic Sentences

1. I found the answer to Problem 5 by doing three things.
2. I solved the problem about the fish in the fish tank by finishing these four steps.
3. I completed the problem about dividing the cake by doing four things.
4. I answered the problem about making the cookies by following these steps.

Step Up to Writing in Math · Writing for Assessments · Math Tool—I-5-2e

Math Tool I-5-2e

Scoring Guide: Explaining Problem Solving

Name: _____
Date: _____
Class: _____
Problem: _____

| 15–16 = A |
| 11–14 = P |
| 7–10 = B |
| 4–6 = BB |

Below Basic | Basic | Proficient | Advanced

4 5 6   7 8 9 10 11 12 13 14   15 16

Scoring Guide: Explaining a Problem-Solving Process

Accurate information	4. Accurate facts, numbers, and processes 3. Some computation errors 2. Inaccurate use of processes; poor computation 1. Unclear, incomplete, confusing information	
Results address question	4. Focused, reasonable answer; question answered completely; understood the point of the question 3. Reasonable answer but lacks focus; question not answered clearly 2. Question not completely answered; all steps not addressed 1. More opinion than fact; no reasons for choice	
Clear, concise writing	4. Complete, specific sentences flow; paragraph easy to read and understand 3. Choppy or unclear sentences slow down the reader 2. Fragments or run-on sentences make reading difficult 1. Sentences not readable	
Writing demonstrates mastery of math vocabulary	4. Uses appropriate math terms and/or symbols throughout to answer the question 3. Most math terms and/or symbols used appropriately to answer the question 2. Terms used inaccurately; lack of terms/symbols creates confusion 1. Little or no correct use of mathematical terms/symbols	
	Total:	

Step Up to Writing in Math · Writing for Assessments · Math Tool—I-5-3a

Math Tool I-5-3a

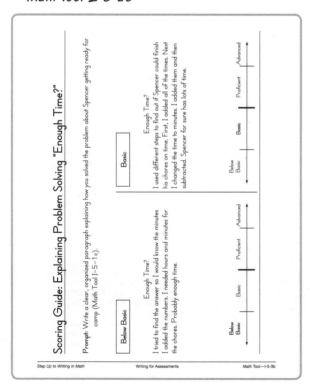

Math Tool I-5-3b

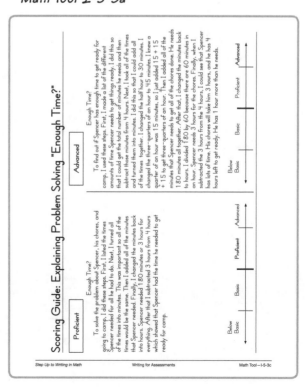

Math Tool I-5-3c

Math Tools: Intermediate (continued)

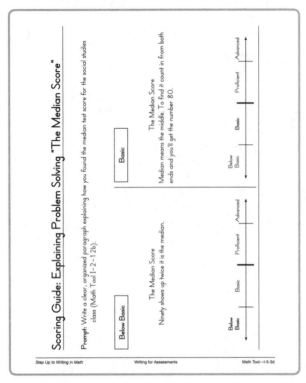

Scoring Guide: Explaining Problem Solving "The Median Score"

Prompt: Write a clear, organized paragraph explaining how you found the median test score for the social studies class (Math Tool I-2-12b).

Below Basic

The Median Score
Ninety shows up twice it is the median.

Basic

The Median Score
Median means the middle. To find it count in from both ends and you'll get the number 80.

Below Basic — Basic — Proficient — Advanced

Step Up to Writing in Math | Writing for Assessments | Math Tool—I-5-3d

Math Tool I-5-3d

Scoring Guide: Explaining Problem Solving "The Median Score"

Proficient

The Median Score
To find the median for the social studies test, first list the facts. Then put the numbers in order. Next, count in from each end and you get to the middle. When you do this you'll get 85 and 88 so the median is 86.5.

Advanced

The Median Score
To find the median score on Mrs. Jones' social studies test, follow these steps. First, list the facts so that you know what information you're working with. Then, arrange the scores in order so that you can "count in" to find the middle score. Starting from each end, count inwards to find the middle. Since there are two numbers in the middle of the data, you need to average them to find the median. The median score on Mrs. Jones' social studies test is an 86.5.

Below Basic — Basic — Proficient — Advanced

Step Up to Writing in Math | Writing for Assessments | Math Tool—I-5-3e

Math Tool I-5-3e

Practice Guide for Problem Solving

Problem:

Facts:

Use the following transitions to explain the steps you used to solve the problem:
—First of all   —Then
—Next   —Finally

Solve:

Solve:

Solve:

Final Answer:

Step Up to Writing in Math | Writing for Assessments | Math Tool—I-5-4a

Math Tool I-5-4a

Practice Guide for Problem Solving

Problem: Jane has $4.00. She wants to buy flowers for her aunt. Jane can buy four flowers for $0.55. She wants to buy two dozen. Will $4.00 be enough?

Facts:
J has $4.00
Flowers = 4 for $0.55
J wants 2 dozen

Use the following transitions to explain the steps you used to solve the problem:
—First of all   —Then
—Next   —Finally

Solve:
4 x 3 = 12

Solve:
3 x $0.55 = $1.65

Solve:
$1.65 x 2 = $3.30

Final Answer:
$4.00 - $3.30 = $0.70

I solved Problem 23 in a few easy steps. First of all, I listed all of the facts about Jane's money, how much the flowers cost, and how many flowers Jane wants. Next, I multiplied 4 x 3 in my head to remind myself that I need 3 groups of 4 flowers in order to have a dozen. Then I multiplied 3 times $0.55 so I would know how much each dozen would cost. Finally, I multiplied $1.65 (the cost for each dozen) times 2, since Jane wants 2 dozen. When I subtracted the $3.30 that it would cost for the two dozen from the $4.00 that Jane has, I saw that she definitely has enough money for all the flowers she wants with $0.70 left over.

Step Up to Writing in Math | Writing for Assessments | Math Tool—I-5-4b

Math Tool I-5-4b

Math Tools: Intermediate–Secondary

Practice Guide and Framed Response
Explain How You Solved the Problem!

Problem:

Facts:	Solve the Problem	
	(a)	(b)
	(c)	(d)

Problem # _____ About _____

To solve this problem, I did a number of important things. First, _____
_____. I also _____
_____. Another _____
_____. The most
important _____
_____.

Math Tool I-5-4c

Practice Guide and Framed Response
Explain How You Solved the Problem!

Problem: *Steve scored 12 points in the first basketball game and 9, 10, and 7 points in the last three games, respectively. What was his average number of points for the four basketball games?*

Facts:	Solve the Problem	
Steve —*played 4 games* —*scored points* *12* *9* *10* *7*	(a) 12 9 10 + 7 38	(b) 9.5 4⟌38.0 36 20 20 0
	(c) *average = 9.5*	(d) *Steve's average number of points is 9.5.*

Problem # <u>4</u> About <u>*Steve's Basketball Scores*</u>

To solve this problem, I did a number of important things. First, <u>*I listed the facts about Steve and the points he made.*</u> I also <u>*added all of the points that Steve made in the four games.*</u> Another <u>*step was dividing the total points by the number of games to find the average.*</u> The most important <u>*step was dividing because that's how to get the average.*</u>

Math Tool I-5-4d

Explain How You Solved the Problem!

Q = _____

Step 1 (Facts)	Explain
Step 2 (Solve)	Explain
Step 3 (Solve)	Explain

Math Tool S-5-1a

Explain How You Solved the Problem!

Step 4 (Solve)	Explain
Step 5 (Solve)	Explain
Step 6 (Final Answer)	Write in a complete sentence(s).

Math Tool S-5-1b

Math Tools: Secondary *(continued)*

Explain How You Solved the Problem!

Word Problem:

Buying Paper for the Office

Allison is ordering copy machine paper for the office. She can purchase a 10-pack box with 200 sheets in a pack for $18, or she can get a 5-pack box with 500 sheets in a pack for $20. The third option is to buy a box containing 10 packs of 600 sheets each for $55. Which is the best buy?

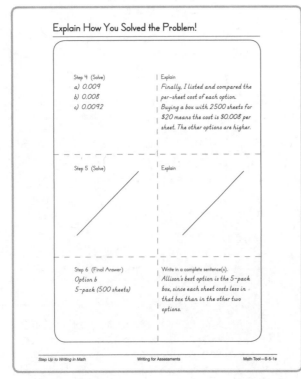

Math Tool S-5-1c

Explain How You Solved the Problem!

Q = Which option for paper is Allison's best buy?

Step 1 (Facts)	Explain
a) 10-pack (200) sheets $18.00 b) 5-pack (500 sheets) $20.00 c) 10-pack (600 sheets) $55.00	First, I listed all of the facts I knew about how many packs are in each box, how many sheets are in each pack, and how much each box costs. My goal was to compare all three options.

Step 2 (Solve)

$$\begin{array}{ll} a)\ \ 200 & c)\ \ 600 \\ \underline{\times\ 10} & \underline{\times\ 10} \\ 2000 & 6000 \end{array}$$

$$\begin{array}{l} b)\ \ 500 \\ \underline{\times\ 5} \\ 2500 \end{array}$$

Explain

Next, for each option I multiplied the number of packs per box times the number of sheets per pack to find out the total number of sheets for each option.

Step 3 (Solve)

$$a)\ \ 2000\overline{)18.00}\quad .009 \text{ per sheet}$$
$$b)\ \ 2500\overline{)20.00}\quad .008 \text{ per sheet}$$
$$c)\ \ 6000\overline{)55.0000}\quad .0092 \text{ per sheet}$$

Explain

Then I divided the price of the box by the number of sheets in the box to find out the price per sheet. The option with the lowest price per sheet will be the best buy.

Math Tool S-5-1d

Explain How You Solved the Problem!

Step 4 (Solve)
a) 0.009
b) 0.008
c) 0.0092

Explain

Finally, I listed and compared the per-sheet cost of each option. Buying a box with 2500 sheets for $20 means the cost is $0.008 per sheet. The other options are higher.

Step 5 (Solve)

Explain

Step 6 (Final Answer)
Option b
5-pack (500 sheets)

Write in a complete sentence(s).

Allison's best option is the 5-pack box, since each sheet costs less in that box than in the other two options.

Math Tool S-5-1e

Explain How You Solved the Problem!

Math Problem:

Directions: Solve the following algebraic equation. Solve for x.

Problem: $3(x + 4) = 10 + 2(x - 3)$

Math Tool S-5-2a

Math Tools: Secondary *(continued)*

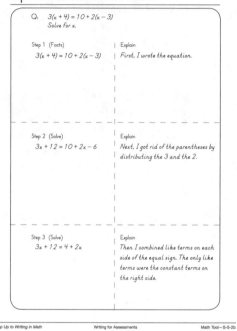

Explain How You Solved the Problem!

Q: $3(x + 4) = 10 + 2(x - 3)$
Solve for x.

Step 1 (Facts)	Explain
$3(x + 4) = 10 + 2(x - 3)$	First, I wrote the equation.

Step 2 (Solve)	Explain
$3x + 12 = 10 + 2x - 6$	Next, I got rid of the parentheses by distributing the 3 and the 2.

Step 3 (Solve)	Explain
$3x + 12 = 4 + 2x$	Then I combined like terms on each side of the equal sign. The only like terms were the constant terms on the right side.

Step Up to Writing in Math   Writing for Assessments   Math Tool—S-5-2b

Math Tool S-5-2b

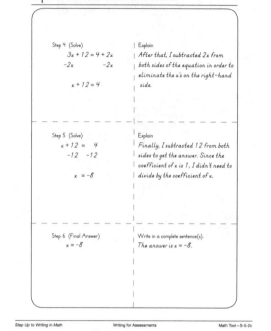

Explain How You Solved the Problem!

Step 4 (Solve)	Explain
$3x + 12 = 4 + 2x$ $\quad -2x \qquad -2x$ $x + 12 = 4$	After that, I subtracted 2x from both sides of the equation in order to eliminate the x's on the right-hand side.

Step 5 (Solve)	Explain
$x + 12 = \quad 4$ $\quad -12 \quad -12$ $x = -8$	Finally, I subtracted 12 from both sides to get the answer. Since the coefficient of x is 1, I didn't need to divide by the coefficient of x.

Step 6 (Final Answer)	Write in a complete sentence(s).
$x = -8$	The answer is $x = -8$.

Step Up to Writing in Math   Writing for Assessments   Math Tool—S-5-2c

Math Tool S-5-2c

Explain How You Solved the Problem!

Directions: Write a clear, organized paragraph explaining how you found the answer to the problem.

Example 1:

Buying Paper for the Office

To figure out which paper buying option offered the best deal, I completed the following steps. First, I listed facts about how many packs were in each box, how many sheets were in a pack, and how much each box costs. My goal was to compare all three options. Next, for each option I multiplied the number of packs per box times the number of sheets per pack to find out the total number of sheets per box for each option. Then I divided the price of the box by the number of sheets in the box to find the price per sheet. The option with the lowest price per sheet will be the best buy. Finally, I listed and compared the per-sheet cost of each option. Buying a box with 2500 sheets for $20.00 means the cost is $.008 per sheet. The other options are higher. Allison's best option, therefore, is the 5-pack box option since the sheets individually cost less than the other two options.

Example 2:

Solve for x

To solve the algebraic equation for x, I followed these steps. First, I wrote the equation. Next, I got rid of the parentheses by distributing the three and the two. Then I combined like terms on each side of the equal sign. The only like terms were the constant terms on the right-hand side of the equation. After that, I subtracted 2x from both sides of the equation in order to eliminate the "x"s on the right-hand side. Finally, I subtracted 12 from both sides to get x alone on the left-hand side. Since the coefficient of x is 1, I didn't need to divide by the coefficient of x. The answer is x equals −8.

Step Up to Writing in Math   Writing for Assessments   Math Tool—S-5-2d

Math Tool S-5-2d

Topic Sentences for Explaining Problem Solving

When you need to write a full paragraph explaining the steps you took to solve a word problem, try one of the topic sentence strategies listed below. The topic sentence is important because it serves as the controlling statement that guides the rest of the paragraph.

> Use an infinitive ("to" + a verb).

1. <u>To find</u> the answer to the pizza problem, I did four things.
2. <u>To solve</u> the problem, I followed these steps.
3. <u>To get</u> the answer to Problem 14, I completed six steps.
4. <u>To figure</u> out how much money everyone would need to contribute, I used this approach.
5. <u>To complete</u> Problem A on page 16, I used the following method.

> Use an action verb (make a statement).

1. I <u>found</u> the correct answer to the problem about the number of hours it would take to drive to Chicago by doing three things.
2. I <u>solved</u> Problem 2, which asked how many square yards of carpet Jeff and Jan would need, by completing these simple steps.
3. I <u>figured</u> out how much money Jared would need to contribute by executing four steps.
4. I <u>completed</u> the problem about the school schedule by using the following steps.
5. I <u>solved</u> the Problem of the Week in three easy steps.

Step Up to Writing in Math   Writing for Assessments   Math Tool—S-5-2e

Math Tool S-5-2e

Math Tools: Secondary *(continued)*

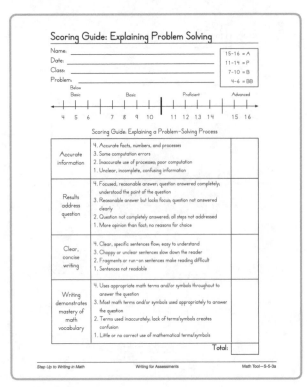

Scoring Guide: Explaining Problem Solving

Name: _____
Date: _____
Class: _____
Problem: _____

| 15–16 = A |
| 11–14 = P |
| 7–10 = B |
| 4–6 = BB |

Below Basic | Basic | Proficient | Advanced

4 5 6   7 8 9 10   11 12 13 14   15 16

Scoring Guide: Explaining a Problem-Solving Process

Accurate information	4. Accurate facts, numbers, and processes 3. Some computation errors 2. Inaccurate use of processes; poor computation 1. Unclear, incomplete, confusing information	
Results address question	4. Focused, reasonable answer; question answered completely; understood the point of the question 3. Reasonable answer but lacks focus; question not answered clearly 2. Question not completely answered, all steps not addressed 1. More opinion than fact; no reasons for choice	
Clear, concise writing	4. Clear, specific sentences flow; easy to understand 3. Choppy or unclear sentences slow down the reader 2. Fragments or run-on sentences make reading difficult 1. Sentences not readable	
Writing demonstrates mastery of math vocabulary	4. Uses appropriate math terms and/or symbols throughout to answer the question 3. Most math terms and/or symbols used appropriately to answer the question 2. Terms used inaccurately, lack of terms/symbols creates confusion 1. Little or no correct use of mathematical terms/symbols	
	Total:	

Step Up to Writing in Math — Writing for Assessments — Math Tool—S-5-3a

Math Tool S-5-3a

Math Tool S-5-3c

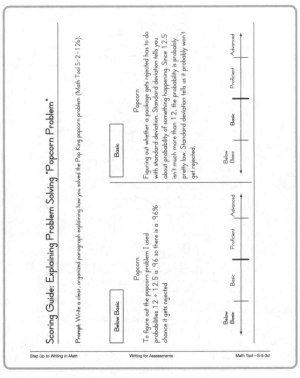

Math Tool S-5-3b

Math Tool S-5-3d

Math Tools: Secondary *(continued)*

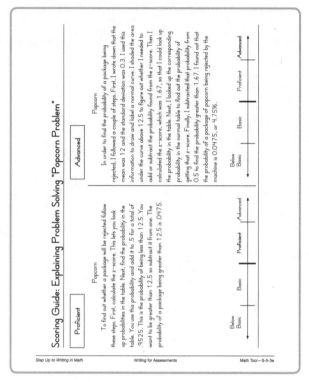

Scoring Guide: Explaining Problem Solving "Popcorn Problem"

Proficient

Popcorn

To find out whether a package will be rejected follow these steps. First, calculate the z-score. This lets you look up probabilities in the table. Next, find the probability in the table. You use this probability and add it to .5 for a total of .9525. This is the probability of being less than 12.5. You want to be greater than 12.5 so subtract it from one. The probability of a package being greater than 12.5 is .0475.

Below Basic — Basic — Proficient — Advanced

Advanced

Popcorn

In order to find the probability of a package being rejected, I followed a couple of steps. First, I wrote down that the mean was 12 and the standard deviation was 0.3. I used this information to draw and label a normal curve. I shaded the area under the curve above 12.5 to figure out whether I needed to add or subtract the probability found from the z-score. Then I calculated the z-score, which was 1.67, so that I could look up the probability in the table. Next, I looked up the corresponding probability in the normal table to find out the probability of getting that z-score. Finally, I subtracted that probability from 0.5 to find the probability greater than 1.67. I found out that the probability of a package of popcorn being rejected by the machine is 0.0475, or 4.75%.

Below Basic — Basic — Proficient — Advanced

Step Up to Writing in Math — Writing for Assessments — Math Tool—S-5-3e

Math Tool S-5-3e

Practice Guide for Problem Solving

Problem:

Facts:	Use the following transitions to explain the steps you used to solve the problem: —First of all —Then —Next —Finally
Solve:	
Solve:	
Solve:	
Final Answer:	

Step Up to Writing in Math — Writing for Assessments — Math Tool—S-5-4a

Math Tool S-5-4a

Practice Guide for Problem Solving

Problem: *Ms. Vasquez's seventh-grade classes voted to find out how many students wanted to go to the zoo and how many wanted to visit the art museum. If 15% of the classes, or 9 students, selected the art museum, how many students are in Ms. Vasquez's classes? How many students prefer a field trip to the zoo?*

Facts:
- 7th grade class
- 9 students want to go to art museum
- 9 = 15% of class

Solve:

$$\frac{9}{x} = \frac{15}{100}$$

$$900 = 15x$$

Solve:

$$15\overline{)900}$$
$$\underline{90}$$
$$0$$

$$60 = x$$

Solve:

$$60 - 9 = 51$$

Final Answer:
60 students in her classes
51 wanted to go to the zoo

Use the following transitions to explain the steps you used to solve the problem:
—First of all   —Then
—Next   —Finally

In order to answer the questions about Ms. Vasquez's classes, I followed a couple of steps. First of all, I listed the facts from the problem: 9 students wanted to go to the art museum, and those 9 students make up 15% of Ms. Vasquez's classes. Next, I made a proportion with the numbers I knew: 9/x = 15/100. I did this so I could cross-multiply and solve for x, or the number of students in her classes. I found out that there are 60 students in all of her classes. Then I subtracted the 9 students who wanted to go to the art museum from 60 (the total number of students) to find out how many students voted to go to the zoo. I found that 51 students prefer a field trip to the zoo.

Step Up to Writing in Math — Writing for Assessments — Math Tool—S-5-4b

Math Tool S-5-4b

Practice Guide With Framed Response

1. What is the problem asking? (Restate the problem.)	The problem about _____ _____ _____ is asking _____ _____ _____ .
2. What strategy will you use to solve the problem?	I will use the _____ strategy because _____ _____ _____ .
3. Solve the problem. Show all of your work using words, numbers, and/or pictures. Label or include units in your work.	
4. Explain how you solved the problem.	I solved the problem in _____ steps. First, I _____ _____ . Next, I _____ _____ . After that _____ _____ . Then _____ . Finally, _____ _____ .
5. Why is your answer reasonable?	My answer is reasonable _____ _____ _____ _____ .

Step Up to Writing in Math — Writing for Assessments — Math Tool—S-5-4c

Math Tool S-5-4c

Math Tools: Secondary (continued)

Practice Guide With Framed Response
_____

(My First Draft)

How Did You Solve the Problem?

I solved Problem #_____ in several steps. First, I _____

_____.

Next, I _____

_____. After that, _____

_____. Then _____

_____

_____. Finally, _____

_____.

(My Final Draft With Details and Elaboration)

_____

_____

_____

_____

_____

_____

_____

_____

_____

_____

_____

_____

_____

_____

_____

_____

_____

_____

Step Up to Writing in Math   Writing for Assessments   Math Tool—S-5-4d

Math Tool S-5-4d

SECTION 6 WRITING FOR GENERAL ASSIGNMENTS

Previous sections of *Step Up to Writing in Math* have covered strategies for writing in circumstances where students have a singular, specific purpose. Section 3 includes methods for organizing ideas, writing topic sentences, and structuring the text of summary paragraphs. Section 3 also includes instructions for using the summary strategy to write about graphs (interpreting, analyzing, and critiquing).

Section 5 covers strategies for writing to show problem-solving steps in an assessment setting (formal or informal) and preparing for exam essay questions.

In addition, Sections 1, 2, and 4 present approaches to learning and retaining vocabulary, reading thoughtfully, taking effective notes, and questioning—all of which are important skills that improve student performance on writing exercises.

Section 6 pulls together and extends many of the ideas from these previous sections and presents them in a way that makes them applicable to informational/expository writing. This section's strategies help students:

- organize information and ideas using informal outlines;

- write strong topic sentences (the controlling statements that establish a purpose for writing);

- support topic sentences with key ideas;

- use transitions effectively;

- elaborate, explain, and give examples;

- write appropriate and effective conclusions; and

- reach proficient and advanced levels in writing about math topics and concepts.

The structure for paragraph and report writing that this section presents is very visual and hands-on, and the tools that accompany the section's strategies minimize the amount of time that teachers must spend on them. Although the strategies can follow logically from the book's preceding, task-specific writing lessons, this section can be taught as a separate and self-contained unit.

Students learn these strategies in order to write about general math content or concepts. Examples include: reporting on the history of numbers, describing the work of a specific mathematician, explaining the types of math computation a seamstress might use, explaining the process used to multiply fractions, and defining math terms and explaining their importance.

Section 6 also provides a scoring guide* for informational/expository paragraphs and reports. The guide is designed to save teachers time and to give students the specific feedback they need in order to revise and improve their writing. The scoring guide assesses four traits: organization, content, style, grammar/mechanics/presentation.

When math teachers read what students have written, they gain insight into students' comprehension and thinking, identify students' strengths and weaknesses, and obtain valuable information to guide instruction. The goal for this section is to make writing doable in math classrooms where teachers are already pressed for time trying to cover all of the required content and meet curriculum goals.

*A separate scoring guide for assessing a student's ability to explain a problem-solving process is included in Section 5.

Objectives

- Provide teachers with practical tools for teaching the basic elements of paragraph and report writing

- Teach students how to write information/expository paragraphs and reports independently and successfully

- Give teachers a time-efficient way to teach students to write information/ expository paragraphs and reports

- Share an effective, four-part, easy-to-use scoring guide that is helpful to teachers and students

SECTION **6** CONTENTS

6-1 Accordion Paragraphs

The term "accordion paragraph" is used to emphasize to students that informational and expository paragraphs can be any length.

Like an accordion, or a piece of paper folded with accordion folds, paragraphs on most topics can be stretched or tightened. Some paragraphs are short, while others are quite long. Students learn to apply the "accordion effect" to their writing by learning to make decisions about how many key ideas and how much elaboration they need to include in a given writing assignment.

Students write accordion paragraphs whenever they are asked to explain, compare, contrast, sequence, critique, evaluate, justify, identify, describe, or inform. They learn to write accordion paragraphs by learning to organize information and ideas. They must learn two major skills before they can create quality accordion paragraphs and reports: organizing ideas and writing topic sentences.

Organizing Ideas

Several *Step Up to Writing in Math* strategies help students with organization:

1. **Informal outlines.** Informal outlines are key to success in informational/expository writing. The informal outline is a quick and easy-to-remember strategy writers can use before they begin writing. Jotting down a plan saves writers time and helps guarantee that their writing is clear and organized. Students can create an informal outline in six steps:

    *   Step 1: Fold paper into two columns. Then mark the fold lines to create a capital T. (The same type of form can organize ideas for writing a single, stand-alone paragraph or a longer report.)

    *   Step 2: At the top of the page, jot down a working title as a way to focus your thinking. Revise and improve this title later.

    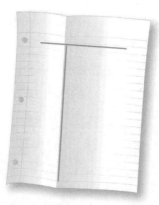

    *   Step 3: Write **Topic =** on the top line of the page. Jot down the topic you are writing about, or write out a draft of your topic sentence.

    *   Step 4: Add key ideas in the left column. These are the main ideas that will support, prove, and/or explain your topic sentence. Use a star to indicate each new idea. Leave ample space between the key ideas.

- Step 5: Add dashes and dots, as needed, in the right column to show the examples, evidence, or explanations to support the key ideas. Use only words and phrases. You will change these into complete sentences when you actually write your paragraph (or report).

- Step 6: After you have noted all of your key/star ideas and added the elaboration (the dashes and dots), add **Conclusion** = at the bottom of the page. Jot down a word or phrase that will help you remember that the final statement of a paragraph (or report) is important. That final statement reminds the reader of your topic.

The following example illustrates the parts of an informal outline: title, topic, key ideas, elaboration, and conclusion. This example also shows how an informal outline translates into a well-organized paragraph.

Title = Creating a Rectangular Coordinate System

Topic = rectangular (two-dimensional) coordinate system

★ draw vertical and horizontal axes	- establish origin - positive and negative directions - four quadrants
★ place uniform scale	- cover range of data - consistent grid
★ label	- horizontal - vertical

Conclusion = follow steps

	Creating a Rectangular Coordinate System
title ——————→	
topic sentence ——→	There are several steps involved in properly creating a rectangular (two-dimensional) coordinate system.
key/star idea ——→	First, you have to draw vertical and horizontal axes perpendicular to each other. This step establishes the origin,
elaboration ——→	the positive and negative directions, and the four quadrants of the x-y plane. Next, you place a uniform scale on both
key/star idea ——→	axes. The scale should be sufficient to cover the range of the
elaboration ——→	data, with increments that form a consistent grid. Finally, you
key/star idea ——→	need to label the axes. As a rule, the horizontal axis is the independent variable (x) and the vertical is the dependent
elaboration ——→	variable (y). To build an accurate rectangular coordinate
conclusion ——→	system, just follow the steps outlined above.

2. **Color-coding.** The informal outline goes hand in hand with another strategy, in which students mark a paragraph to show its organization using the colors of a traffic signal. The color-coding technique reinforces the informal outline and emphasizes organization of ideas in the paragraph by using the colors in this way:

– **Green**: Use green to indicate the topic sentence. Think of the green light as indicating what you are "<u>going</u> to prove or explain."

– **Yellow**: Use yellow to point to the key/star ideas and the transitions that connect one key/star idea with the next. Yellow means "<u>slow down</u>, and support the topic sentence with key or star ideas." Add transitions to help the reader with organization.

A transition tells the reader that you are introducing a new key/star idea. Here are some examples of useful groups of transitions:

one — another — next	*first — second — third*
first of all — another	*one — also*
to begin — then — next — finally	*first — next — then — finally*

Note: Students may not always choose or need transitions like those listed above; they may also make transitions by using repetition or synonyms.

– **Red**: Use red to indicate the examples, explanation, and elaboration for your key/star ideas. Red means "<u>stop</u>, and support each key or star idea with an example, an explanation, some evidence, or specific and helpful elaboration."

– **Green**: Finally, use green again to point to the conclusion. Here you can think of the green light as meaning "go back to the topic sentence and restate it in different words." It means go back and remind the reader of the topic.

This example shows how students can use an informal outline and traffic signal colors together to help organize their thoughts in informational/expository writing. The accompanying paragraph shows how the traffic signal colors are applied.

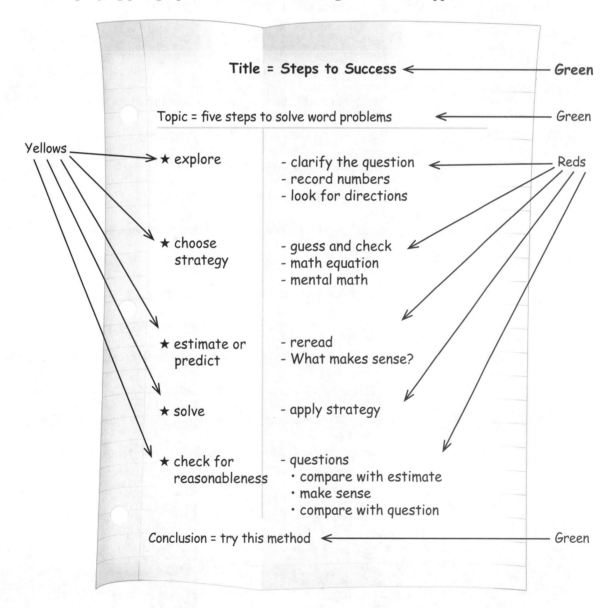

title
(green)

topic sentence
(green)

key/star idea
(yellow)

elaboration
(red)

key/star idea
(yellow)

elaboration
(red)

key/star idea
(yellow)

elaboration
(red)

key/star idea
(yellow)

key/star idea
(yellow)

elaboration
(red)

conclusion
(green)

Steps to Success

By using the following five-step plan, students can be more successful at solving word problems. To begin, explore the problem. Clarify what the problem is asking. When reading the problem, determine and record the pertinent information. Record numbers, units, and any directions. Example directions include "draw a picture," "label a diagram," or "develop a graph."

After exploring the problem, decide on an appropriate strategy for solving it. Different problem-solving strategies include guess-and-check, rewriting the words into a mathematical equation, and mental math. Next, predict or estimate what the answer to the problem will be. Reread the question and determine if the estimate makes sense. Now apply the decided upon strategy and solve the problem. Finally, be sure to check the answer for reasonableness. Using questions is a good way to check the solution: Was my final answer close to my estimate? Does the solution make sense? Did I answer the correct question? If students are struggling with word problems, the above steps can help lead them to the path of success.

3. **Folded or cut paper.** Another strategy students can use to organize their ideas involves physically either folding or cutting paper. The paragraph in the next example shows how organizing strips of paper or writing sentences on paper folded (accordion-style) can help students visualize the basic pattern of an informational/expository paragraph or report. Even when students are planning to write using strips of paper, they should start by creating an informal outline as a plan.

Title = Geometric Shapes

Topic = examples of geometric shapes

★ doors and windows
- squares in windows and panes
- rectangles for doors
- circles for knobs

★ clothes
- necklace with circle and rectangle
- shoes with black and white squares
- sweater and skirt with parallel lines

★ games
- dominoes
- chess

Conclusion = shapes everywhere

The paragraph (written on strips) found on the following page shows how students can write on strips to help with organization and to help with writing clear, complete sentences. Notice how the informal outline is used to write the paragraph.

Geometric Shapes

TS | In our search, my teammates and I found a number of geometric shapes.

★ | First, we noticed the shapes that make up the doors and windows in this room.

EX | The two windows facing west are squares, and the small panes inside those windows are also squares.

EX | The front and back doors to our classroom are both rectangles, but the signs on them with our room number are squares.

EX | The knobs on the doors are circles, and the brass plates holding the knobs are also circles.

★ | Next, we noticed the shapes on the clothes that some of our friends were wearing.

EX | The stones on Meg's necklace are all rectangles, but the latch is a circle.

EX | Jeremy and Nathan have similar shoes, which have alternating black and white squares.

EX | The diamond shapes on Simmy's sweater are rhombuses, just like the diamonds on Shanda's skirt.

★ | Finally, we saw shapes in the games that Ms. Miller has on the shelf.

EX | The dominoes are all rectangles covered with a number of small circles.

EX | The chess board has squares similar to the Scrabble game board.

EX | On both boards, we saw that we could take a number of the squares and count them off in different directions to make rectangles.

C | We could have found more examples, but we had to stop to head to art class, where we guessed we could find even more. Geometric shapes are everywhere.

4. **Practice (planning) guides.** The final method of organization for informational/expository writing is using a practice guide. A practice guide incorporates the same ideas as the previous three methods, but it provides a more structured visual tool for organizing the topic sentence, key/star ideas, and explanations of those ideas. Math Tools 6-1d and 6-1e provide the format for practice guides.

Writing the Topic Sentence

The other crucial element of an accordion information/expository paragraph or report is its topic sentence. After they have seen some examples of how informal outlines can turn into paragraphs, students are ready to learn practical approaches to writing topic sentences. A topic sentence can, of course, be written in any of a number of sentence structures. But to save time and to help students focus their writing, the accordion strategy for writing in math promotes four sentence structures that are easy to imitate:

1. **Action Verb topic sentences.** Sentences containing an action verb work well because the strong verb shows the purpose for the paragraph. For example:

> Today we <u>learned</u> to tell time.
>
> I <u>estimate</u> for several different reasons.

2. **Occasion/Position topic sentences are complex sentences.** The words on the following list help writers create topic sentences. Students might want to call these words "Starter Words and Phrases:"

If	When	As	While	Whenever
Even though	After	Until	Since	Unless
Before	Because	Although	Just as	Wherever

Examples:

> <u>When</u> we learned to tell time, we used two kinds of clocks.
>
> <u>Before</u> I try to solve word problems, I take time to estimate the answers.

3. **Power (number) topic sentences.** These sentences use a number or number word to focus the topic and let readers know that some kind of list will follow. The number word reflects the number of key/star ideas that will support the topic sentence.

two	three	four	several
some	many	a few	a number of

Examples:

> I know <u>two</u> different ways to tell time.

> Estimating answers before solving word problems helps me in <u>two</u> ways.

4. **Where or When, Plus What's Happening topic sentences.** These topic sentences are written by focusing on the "when" or "where" of the topic. The process is quite simple. Students fold a piece of paper into two columns. On the left, they write "where" or "when," and on the right they put "what's happening?" The phrase "what's happening?" stands for three questions: What is happening? What did happen? And what will happen? For example:

> (Where) <u>In math class</u> we practiced telling time when we went for a walk to different places in our school.

> (When) <u>Every day when I tackle the Problem of the Day</u>, I use estimation to help me find the right answer.

An Accordion Paragraph Student Sample

Together, the informal outline and these topic sentence writing strategies are powerful tools for improving student writing. The following informal outline and corresponding paragraph were written by a seventh-grader. This paragraph includes a clear topic sentence, key ideas with transitions, great examples, and exceptional elaboration. Students, like this student, are empowered to write when they have a structure to follow and methods for writing and organizing topic sentences and supporting sentences.

Title = Ratios

Topic = ratios in everyday activities

| ★ recipe | - flour to sugar
- doubling the batch |

| ★ recreation | - football
  • wins to losses
  • Broncos
  • ratio different from baking
    - characterization |

| ★ business | - systems of measurement
- inches to feet
  • like baking
  • will not change |

Conclusion = common

Ratios

Even though ratios are mostly used in math, they are commonly found in everyday activities. Such activities could be homemaking, recreation, and business. One example of a ratio for homemaking could be a recipe. This could mean that for every three cups of flour that a person adds, he would add one cup of sugar. This ratio would be "flour to sugar," and it would be written as 3:1. If you were baking cookies and the recipe called for 3 c. of flour and 1 c. of sugar, and you wanted to double the batch, then you would double both measurements. It would be 6 c. of flour and 2 c. of sugar. However, this is still a 3:1 ratio. Another example of a ratio could be in recreation, or more specifically in a sport such as football. The ratio could be in the number of wins to losses. Let's take the Broncos, who have won 10 and lost 3 so far. This ratio would be called "wins to losses" and would be written 10:3. However, this ratio is different from the first one involving baking. It is not necessarily the same as saying that for every 10 wins in the future the Broncos will lose 3. Instead, it is only a characterization of their current record. This ratio will change as they play more games, whether they win or lose. A third example of a ratio may be in business, used for systems of measurement. This ratio may be the amount of inches equal to one foot. The ratio would be described as "inches to feet" and written 12:1. This ratio is more like the first example in that it will not change. Even when it looks different (24:2, 36:3, etc.), it is still a ratio of 12:1. These three samples show some of the ways ratios are used on a daily basis.

Before a Lesson

- Review and make overhead transparencies or student copies, as needed, of Math Tools 6-1a through 6-1e. (See also **3-2 Practicing I-V-F Summary Topic Sentences** and **5-2 Turning an Explanation Into a Formal Paragraph** for more ideas on writing topic sentences.)

- Select a prompt or topic to use for demonstration and modeling. Reread directions and examples at the beginning of strategy **6-1 Accordion Paragraphs** to help ensure that your model matches the accordion style and examples.

- Practice creating an informal outline, topic sentence, and paragraph using the topic or prompt you have selected.

- Review the lesson that follows. Make changes as needed to fit your style, goals, and your students' needs. Keep in mind that you do not need to introduce all of the strategies and activities connected with accordion paragraphs in one lesson. However, it is almost always best to introduce informal outlines first. (The informal outline, at a glance, shows what will be included in the piece. Instead of worrying about how to fill blank lines on a page, students use the outline to write with confidence and a strong sense of purpose.)

During a Lesson

- Show students examples of informal outlines and their corresponding paragraphs. Use **Math Tools 6-1a** and **6-1b** or examples that you have created.

- Read through each example; help students match the sentences in the paragraph with the related parts of the informal outline.

- Explain that informal outlines can be made on notebook paper, or they can be jotted on index cards or small pieces of paper, such as self-stick notes. Tell students that the purpose of an informal outline is to visualize the contents of a paragraph (or report) before writing.

- Model the writing of an informal outline using an overhead transparency or chart paper. Have students mimic the steps as you write and explain.

- Show students how easily the outline can become an actual paragraph by talking through each line as you turn key/star ideas and supporting information (examples/elaborations) into complete sentences.

- Take time to write out the paragraph on chart paper or on the board. Ask for volunteers to read through the informal outline and the paragraph itself.

- Using the same informal outline and/or the examples on **Math Tools 6-1a** and **6-1b**, introduce students to the traffic signal color-coding system for marking and showing organization.

- Display **Math Tool 6-1c** to introduce topic sentences. Explain the strategies for writing topic sentences and the examples on **Math Tool 6-1c**; have students take notes. Encourage them to use empty space on the front of the page and all of the empty space on the back for topic sentence practice and for any examples you add in class.

- Have students practice informal outlines using **Math Tools 6-1d** and **6-1e**. These practice guides work for either paired or small-group activities. Give students copies of **Math Tools 6-1d** and **6-1e** to keep for reference when they write.

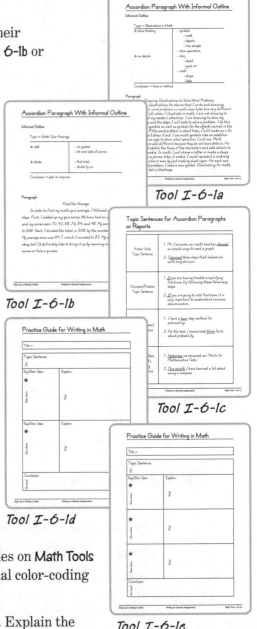

Tool I-6-1a

Tool I-6-1b

Tool I-6-1c

Tool I-6-1d

Tool I-6-1e

- Have students create their own guides on notebook paper if more than two or three key/star ideas are needed.

- Have students practice using an informal outline to write the first draft of a paragraph.

Additional Ideas

- Use the Paragraphs and Reports Scoring Guide—**Math Tools 6-5a** and **6-5b**—to assess students' work. Give students copies of the scoring guide. (See **6-5 Scoring Paragraph and Report Writing** for details and examples.)

- Keep in mind that it is not necessary to develop every informal outline into a full-blown paragraph (or report). Students learn, and demonstrate, a lot of information just by making informal outlines. Make outlines, then ask students to share the "paragraph" orally.

- Hand out informal outlines that you have partially filled in, and ask students to complete them. For example, you can fill in the topic sentence and the key/star ideas, leaving students to fill in the support for the key/star ideas and the conclusion. Ask students to use the completed outlines to write paragraphs or give informal speeches. Partially filled-in outlines provide students with the help they need to think and write quickly. Consider using partially filled-in informal outlines on assessments; for substitutes, paraprofessionals, or tutors; and for modification of assignments for students.

- Make large colored strips from poster board for use with the traffic signal color-coding activity. Laminate the strips, and put magnetic tape on the back. Use them as you model. Make several, and let students write on them using overhead markers. They can then display their work and share their writing with classmates.

- Make several overhead transparencies of **Math Tool 6-1d** or **6-1e**—enough for every two students to have one. Assign students to partners, and give each pair an overhead marker and a transparency. Give students a prompt or a topic sentence, and ask them to complete the outline within a given amount of time. Ask them to share their outlines using the overhead projector. This activity promotes writing practice, and you can give students points or a letter grade for their work without having to carry home a stack of papers for grading.

- Keep informational/expository transitions posted on the wall for easy access when students are writing or speaking.

- In secondary classrooms, have fun with formulas; try using them to help secondary students remember the design for a paragraph or report. Some students claim that they are good at math but not at writing. The math-like formulas on the following page may help some students see paragraph writing in a whole new light.

$$T + TS + 3(K + E) + C = \P$$

T	=	title
TS	=	topic sentence
3	=	three sets
(K + E)	=	key/star idea and explanation
C	=	conclusion
$\P$	=	paragraph

Along the same lines, you could use a formula that incorporates the traffic signal colors to show the organization of an informational/expository paragraph:

$$g_1 + g_2 + n(y + mr) + g_3 = \P$$

g_1	=	green (title)
g_2	=	green (topic sentence)
n	=	number of sets
y	=	yellow (key/star idea)
r	=	red (explanation, example, elaboration)
m	=	number of reds
g_3	=	green (conclusion)
$\P$	=	paragraph or report

Display these formulas, and explain to students that one way to look at accordion organization is as a formula for writing. Adhering to a formula for writing in math can sometimes save time and make it easier to concentrate on content. However, in most circumstances, paragraphs and reports are more flexible than these formulas suggest.

The Accordion Paragraph strategy encourages flexibility and creativity. Writers master paragraph writing by molding the basic accordion format to fit their style and the purpose for their writing. Still, it can be great fun—and sometimes useful—to apply a math concept like an equation to the process of writing about math concepts.

6-2 Accordion Reports and Essays

Writing reports using the accordion approach is very similar to writing individual accordion paragraphs that stand alone and address a single topic (**6-1 Accordion Paragraphs**).

Planning an accordion report is similar to planning an accordion paragraph. The two are different only in the added elaboration and examples.

- Both strategies call for students to plan before they write by making an informal outline.

- In an accordion report, students apply what they have learned about topic sentences (green), but their topic sentence becomes a part of the introductory paragraph (green).

- In a report, the key idea sentences (yellow) that support the topic sentence are the first sentences in the body paragraphs. They are called transition topic sentences (yellow). They are written in the same way as the key idea sentences in an accordion paragraph; only their position in the composition changes. They still include transitions (yellow) that help organize the information and ideas in the report.

- The transition topic sentences (yellow) are followed by several sentences that elaborate on the topic. These sentences (evidence, examples, and explanation—red) complete the body paragraphs; they add details and information that is the meat of the report.

- The major difference between the accordion paragraph and the accordion report is the quantity of red content that each includes. In a report, writers must present more evidence and more examples. The amount of elaboration (red) must also increase substantially.

- The conclusion (green) of a report may be only one, two, or three sentences long. It should restate and emphasize the purpose of the report. Students should use a new sentence structure for an accordion report's conclusion, rather than just copying the topic sentence, but they should not introduce a new topic. (Note: Not all reports need a formal conclusion. Sometimes writers "complete" the report with the final key idea and explanation.)

An accordion report and its informal outline look like this:

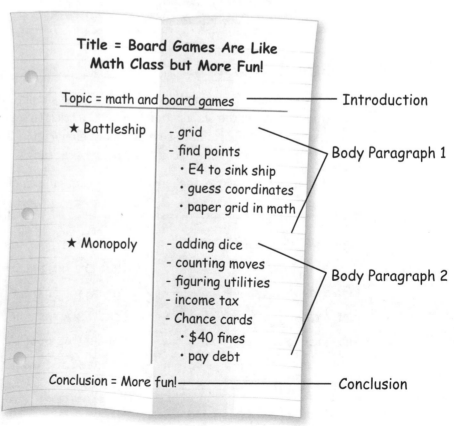

Title = Board Games Are Like Math Class but More Fun!

Topic = math and board games ——————— Introduction

★ Battleship
- grid
- find points
  • E4 to sink ship
  • guess coordinates
  • paper grid in math ⟩ Body Paragraph 1

★ Monopoly
- adding dice
- counting moves
- figuring utilities
- income tax
- Chance cards
  • $40 fines
  • pay debt ⟩ Body Paragraph 2

Conclusion = More fun!——————————— Conclusion

Board Games Are Like Math Class but More Fun!

My family likes to play board games. Friday night is family game night, but we play other times as well. I have noticed that when we play board games, we do a lot of math. Depending on the game, we add, subtract, multiply, learn about graphs, and even figure percentages.

Take the game of Battleship, for instance. This game is set up on a grid. Throughout the game, you have to find points on the grid to find the other player's ships. I love it when I call out "E4" and my sister says, "Hit!" Then I know that I have hit one of her ships. During my next turn, I guess the nearby coordinates. It is a lot like when we plot points on a graph.

Another game that teaches math skills is Monopoly. Of course, there is the adding of the two dice and counting out your move, but it gets much harder from there. When you land on a utility, you have to multiply to figure out how much you owe the person who owns the utility. For example, if someone owns one utility, you owe him/her four times your roll, and if he/she owns both Water Works and Electric, you owe that person 10 times your roll. That's nothing compared with figuring 10 percent of your wealth if you land on income tax! If you are really unlucky, like I was last time, you might draw the Chance card that says you have to pay $40 for each house you own! I ended up paying $440 and selling houses to the bank to pay the debt. That lost me the game.

Playing board games is a lot like math class, but it's much more fun. Especially when you win!

Stretch Your Ideas!

Moving from a paragraph to a report is quite simple. Use this example to show students that stretching the elaboration (red) is the trick to turning a paragraph into a report. Explain that reports have so much more elaboration that the information has to be broken into parts; these parts become the body paragraphs.

When it stands alone, the paragraph "Swimming in Math" is complete.

	Swimming in Math
title (green) ⟶	
topic sentence (green) ⟶	Perimeter, area, and volume are all measurements that are necessary to build a swimming pool.
key/star idea (yellow) ⟶	Perimeter is the distance around an object. It is
elaboration (red) ⟶	used to determine how many tiles you will need to
key/star idea (yellow) ⟶	border the pool. Area is the quantity of material you need to cover a space. It is used to figure out
elaboration (red) ⟶	how many tiles are needed to put on the bottom and

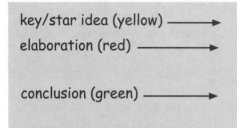

key/star idea (yellow) ⟶
elaboration (red) ⟶

conclusion (green) ⟶

the sides of the pool. Volume is the amount that a space can hold. The builders use volume to figure out how much water they will need to fill the pool. To successfully construct a pool, the workers must know how to calculate perimeter, area, and volume.

But comparing this paragraph with the following multiparagraph report on the same topic illustrates the accordion nature of informational/expository writing. Just add more details, and the paragraph expands dramatically.

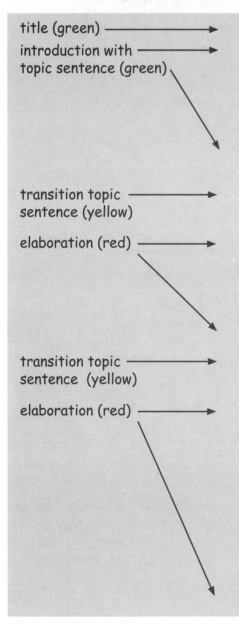

title (green) ⟶
introduction with ⟶
topic sentence (green)

transition topic ⟶
sentence (yellow)

elaboration (red) ⟶

transition topic ⟶
sentence (yellow)

elaboration (red) ⟶

Swimming in Math

Every summer, millions of people enjoy cooling off in swimming pools. Few of them consider the math knowledge that is necessary to provide this refreshing form of entertainment. Perimeter, area, and volume are all measurements that are used to construct a pool.

Perimeter is used to calculate the distance around the pool. This measurement is crucial for determining how many tiles are needed to create a border around the pool. If the pool is 50 ft. long by 20 ft. wide, then the perimeter is 50 + 50 + 20 + 20, which is equal to 140 ft. If the builders used 6 in. tiles, then they would need to buy at least 280 tiles.

When building a pool, workers use area to figure out how much material is needed to cover the bottom and sides of the pool. Area is equal to length x width. To determine the areas of the sides, you have to know the depth of the pool. In this case, it is 8 ft. The depth acts as the width when figuring out the area of the sides. Based on the dimensions above, the area of the bottom of the pool would be 50 x 20, which equals 1,000 ft^2. The area of the long side would be 50 x 8, which equals 400 ft^2. The area of the short side would be 20 x 8, which is equal to 160 ft^2. The builders would

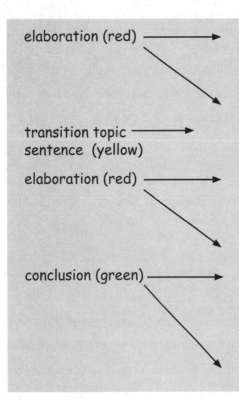

elaboration (red) ——→ count the area of the sides twice, as there are two short sides and two long sides. Altogether the builders would need 2,120 ft² of material to cover the bottom and sides of the pool.

transition topic sentence (yellow) ——→

elaboration (red) ——→ Volume is used to determine how much water is needed to fill the pool. To find out the volume, the workers would use the following formula: V = l x w x h. Plugging the above dimensions into the formula, 50 x 20 x 8, the builders would determine that they needed to order 8,000 ft³ of water to fill the pool.

conclusion (green) ——→ Is all this math making you want to take a break in the pool? Go ahead, but just remember to appreciate the mathematical knowledge that made it possible for overheated people everywhere to get relief from the heat.

After demonstrating for students the relationship between an accordion paragraph and an accordion report, display **Math Tools 6-2a** and **6-2b**. Ask students to make connections between the informal outline and the final report.

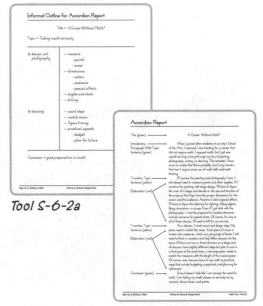

Tool S-6-2a

Tool S-6-2b

6-3 Accordion Races

Students enjoy working with classmates to complete an accordion race.

At the beginning of a race, students are divided into small groups. Each group of students receives an envelope with several strips of paper inside. On each strip of paper is a sentence. The envelope's sentences combine to make a good, organized paragraph. The groups race to read and organize the strips into a paragraph that makes sense. The word "race" is used primarily to motivate students, who enjoy the competition.

As students in each group read the strips of paper they've been given, they must find the topic sentence and the key/star supporting sentences. They must also decide which sentences explain or elaborate on each key/star idea. Finally, they must locate the sentence that makes sense as a conclusion to the paragraph.

When they sort the sentences, they see that the transition words help them organize the paragraph. They also see how pronouns and synonyms can connect ideas.

You can have students arrange the strips on their desks or tables, or copy the full paragraph onto chart paper. Another option is for students to tape the sentence strips in the correct order onto a large piece of construction paper to display for others to read. A fourth option is to have them stack the sentences in the correct order and staple the left side together so that the paragraph looks like a small booklet.

You can use accordion races to:

- promote careful reading,
- teach paragraph writing,
- show the purpose of a topic sentence,
- remind students how topic sentences and conclusions are connected,
- demonstrate the importance of transitions to readers and writers,
- initiate discussion about the importance of organization in writing, and
- have fun reviewing or learning new concepts or content.

Before a Lesson

- Review and make overhead transparencies and student copies, as needed, of **Math Tools 6-3a, 6-3b,** and/or **6-3c** or a paragraph of your own creation in a similar format. You will use this paragraph for a class demonstration.

- Create one or more additional paragraphs in accordion race format on a topic the class has studied. Copy and cut apart these paragraphs. Make enough sets for the number of groups that will participate in the activity.

- Consider storing cut-apart strips in legal-size envelopes to make it easier to pass out and retrieve strips.

During a Lesson

- Show students how most informational/expository paragraphs are controlled by a topic sentence.

- Remind them that informational text is usually organized with the aid of transitions (for example: *one, another, next; first, also, then, at last; one example, another example*).

- Display the demonstration paragraph with the sentences still intact on the same page.

- Point out the topic sentence, the key ideas that support the topic sentence, and the transitions that connect the sentences.

- Show students that explanations, examples, and elaboration constitute the meat of the text; they elaborate on the key ideas of a paragraph.

- Distribute a set of cut-apart sentences to use as practice with the entire class.

- Guide students as they try to organize the strips. Explain as you give them hints about how to find the correct order of the sentences.

- Read the entire paragraph in its correct order. Then discuss the activity and its purpose.

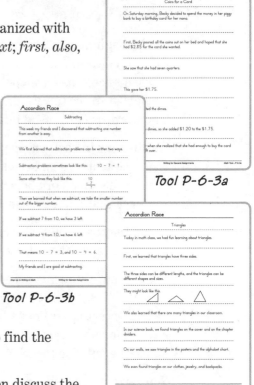

Tool P-6-3a

Tool P-6-3b

Tool P-6-3c

- Give students another set of strips, and begin an accordion race. Again, remind students to apply what they know about paragraphs and their organization.

- As students work, walk around the room and listen for comments and questions. Provide support as needed to ensure success for everyone.

- When all students have completed the task, engage them in a discussion, using some or all of the following questions:

    - What clues did you use to help you build the paragraph?

    - How much of the content were you comfortable with?

    - What content did this activity help you review or remember?

    - What questions did this activity make you ask?

    - What sentences did you find difficult? Why?

    - What content is still unclear to you?

    - How did piecing together a written explanation help you review this topic?

- Show an overhead transparency that has the paragraph in order (the sentences before you cut them into strips), and have students check their answers.

- Give students more opportunities to participate in accordion races.

- If students are struggling with a set of sentence strips, share this advice:
  – Use your knowledge of text structure. Look for the topic sentence, key ideas, support for the key ideas, and the conclusion. The topic sentence is not indented, as it normally would be, so you need to read closely.
  – Use your knowledge of math vocabulary, concepts, and processes that you have been studying in class.
  – Use constructive conversation to figure out the organization of the paragraph. Ask one another questions, and make good guesses.
  – After building the paragraph, read it to make sure it makes sense.

Additional Ideas

- See **2-6 Other Strategies for Improving Reading Comprehension** for ideas about using Accordion Races.

- Create an accordion race without capital letters or punctuation. Once students have pieced the paragraph together, ask them to write it in standard paragraph form, including capital letters and punctuation where appropriate.

- Create an accordion race out of a paragraph that explains the solution to a math word problem. Cut the page so that each step of the problem-solving process is on its own strip of paper. Include a strip for the problem. Include strips showing the computation; students can match these to strips with explanations and elaborations.

- Create an accordion race on an overhead transparency. Do this activity with shorter paragraphs, so that all of the strips will fit on the projector. Place the transparency sentence strips on the projector, and ask students to come up and put them in order. Require that students justify why they are putting strips in a certain place.

- Use an accordion race to introduce new vocabulary words.

- Use this strategy to review the content of a lesson. Design the activity as a cooperative learning opportunity in which students use their prior knowledge of informational/expository writing, plus their knowledge of the content of the lesson, to arrange the sentences.

- Label the backs of the strips to help with cleanup and to be able to reuse the same accordion race in other lessons or other classes. If you give students sets of sentences for several different paragraphs, code the backs of the sentence strips with a letter or number that indicates which set they belong to. This makes it easy to return them to the appropriate envelope. Put each set of sentence strips into a different envelope. Code the envelope with the same letter or number as its sentence strips.

6-4 Framed Paragraphs

With framed paragraphs, teachers provide the frame—the topic sentence and the first few words of the key idea sentences—of a paragraph in order to guide students as they write.

By using framed paragraphs, teachers can have students practice information/expository writing but spend minimal time teaching it. Framed paragraphs are also easy to complete and assess. (See **2-5 Framed Responses**, **3-5 Framed Paragraphs for Writing About Graphs**, and **5-4 Using Framed Paragraphs to Practice for Writing in Math Assessments** for examples of framed paragraphs used for other purposes.)

Framed paragraphs can be used to teach writing, support writing, and test for knowledge and understanding. You can create a framed paragraph in five easy steps:

Step 1: Give the paragraph a title.

Step 2: Write a topic sentence. Use topic sentence strategies presented on **Math Tool 6-1c** as models.

Step 3: Weave transitions throughout the paragraph frame to indicate where key/star ideas belong. Place the transitions as they might look in a full paragraph.

Step 4: Write the first few words for the elaboration sentences as needed, but keep in mind that framed paragraphs with a very limited number of words work best.

Step 5: Write out the conclusion or give a few words, followed by blank space, for a conclusion. (Sometimes formal conclusions are not needed at all.)

When teachers provide framed paragraphs for student writing, they are more likely to receive the correct and desired response from their students. Students benefit from framed paragraphs because they do not have to worry about the structure or organization of their writing and can, therefore, concentrate on the content. Framed paragraphs also help students produce paragraphs quickly and easily.

Example 1:

Counting by Tens

Counting by tens is easy if you just remember these two steps. First, ___
_____. Next, _____
_____.

Example 2:

A Dollar's Worth of Coins

In class we learned that there are many ways that a dollar bill can be
turned into coins. One way is to use dimes. Ten times $0.10 would make one
dollar. Another way to change a dollar into coins is to _____
_____. This works because _____
_____.
Finally, we could _____
_____. This would also work because _____
_____. Many different coins can be used to make a dollar.

Example 3:

New Strategies

In class today we learned two easy strategies for multiplying whole
numbers with fractions. First, we learned that _____
_____. After that, we practiced _____
_____. These
strategies make multiplying and working with fractions easier.

Example 4:

Choosing the Right Type of Graph

There are a number of ways to illustrate data in a graph format. Graphing methods include options like bar graphs, circle graphs, line graphs, histographs, and box-and-whisker plots. When it is time to create a graph, the designer must consider three factors. First, _____ _____ because _____ _____. It will also be important to _____ _____ since _____ _____. Finally, the designer will _____ _____. This will help _____ _____. Considering these factors will help the designer more successfully display data.

Before a Lesson

- Review **Math Tools 6-4a** through **6-4f**. Make overhead transparencies and student copies as needed to demonstrate the framed paragraph concept.

- Create two or three framed paragraphs to use for student practice. Use content that students know or are studying.

- Make copies of the framed paragraphs for students to use for practice.

During a Lesson

- Display a framed paragraph from **Math Tool 6-4**, leaving the blanks empty, to introduce students to the idea.

- Ask students to explain what they think is expected when they work with framed paragraphs. Clarify expectations, and answer questions.

- Explain to students that you have the same expectations for quality and content that you have in other paragraph-writing exercises. Show students that they should fill in the blanks with complete thoughts, details, and examples.

- With help from students, complete the frame.

- Ask for volunteers to read the full paragraph aloud. Discuss the content and the activity.

- Remind students that when they complete framed assignments, they will want to be accurate, use math language precisely, and write with clarity.

Additional Ideas

- If you want students to copy the framed paragraph into standard paragraph form, include blank lines below the frame (as exemplified by **Math Tool 6-4e**) or have students write their final drafts on notebook paper.

- Create a set of generic framed paragraphs for math. (**Math Tool 6-4a** is a good example of a generic frame.) Make enough copies for all students. Keep the frames handy for writing when you have a limited amount of time left in class.

- On pieces of chart paper, write a framed paragraph and then the completed paragraph. Post as an example for students to use for reference.

- Ask students to work in pairs or small groups to create framed paragraphs for units of study they have just completed. Then have them trade and complete the frames. This gives students a chance to show off their skills of paragraph writing, demonstrate mastery of math concepts and vocabulary, and prepare for assessments.

- Consider leaving a framed paragraph assignment with a substitute teacher. Students are more likely to be productive because they will have very clear directions, which means you are more likely to receive quality responses.

- When you feel confident about students' writing skills, tell them that they can make adjustments to your framed paragraphs as needed.

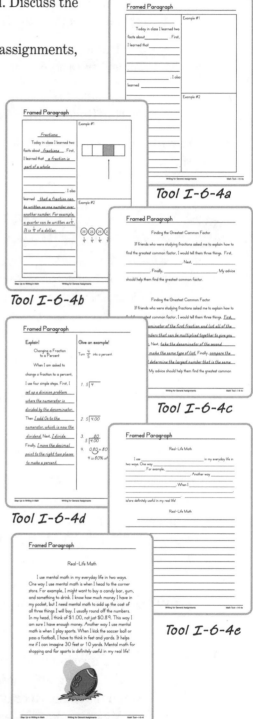

Tool I-6-4a

Tool I-6-4b

Tool I-6-4c

Tool I-6-4d

Tool I-6-4e

Tool I-6-4f

- Provide framed paragraphs to support English language learners. Expect quality responses, but use the frames to help students as they master a new language.

- Use framed paragraphs with students who have special needs and receive extra support from tutors, other teachers, or family members.

- Assess students' framed responses using the Math Paragraphs and Reports Scoring Guide on **Math Tools 6-5a** and **6-5b**.

Note: Framed paragraphs should always be considered as a supplement, not as a substitute for explicit instruction on paragraph writing.

6-5 Scoring Paragraph and Report Writing

The *Step Up to Writing in Math* scoring guide for paragraphs and reports is designed to make scoring papers less time-consuming and more effective. For students, this means that their papers are returned more quickly and that they receive information that helps them understand their scores. More important, it means they receive information they can use for revising and improving their writing.

This strategy gives paragraphs and reports scores in four categories: organization, content, style, and grammar/mechanics/presentation. Students can earn a maximum of four points in each category on a given assignment. The assignment receives an overall rating based on the total number of points it earns.

Below Basic (4–6)	Basic (7–10)	Proficient (11–14)	Advanced (15–16)

The scoring guide should serve as an incentive; students can watch their scores move to higher points on the continuum as they improve their informational/expository paragraph-writing technique. It can also serve as a guide for improving; students can look to their scores in each category to determine specific steps they can take to improve a piece of writing.

How to Use the Scoring Guide

- **Copying:**

  - The scoring guide consists of two pages: the prompt page (**Math Tool 6-5a**) and the scoring guide (**Math Tool 6-5b**). Make copies of both pages, back to back on the same paper before using them to score a student writing assignment. Make one copy for each student.

  - On the prompt page, fill the large, empty rectangle with the prompt for the assignment that you will use the scoring guide to grade; write it in before making copies, or else ask students to copy the prompt in this space before they begin the writing task.

- **Using the scoring guide**:

  - Notice the four traits being assessed on **Math Tool 6-5b**: organization, content, style, and grammar/mechanics/presentation.

  - Notice the four levels for scoring in each trait: advanced, proficient, basic, and below basic.

  - Notice the boxes on the right-hand side of the page. You will place a score for each trait in these boxes. There is a space for total points in the bottom right-hand corner.

  - Read the scoring guide by using another sheet of plain paper, a ruler, or some other straight edge. Lay the paper horizontally, and read the descriptors from left to right. At each row on the scoring guide, the descriptors address the same characteristic of student writing. For example, under "style," the first line at all four levels of competence addresses sentence quality and variety.

  - At the top of the *organization* section, there is an area that gives you the option to assess the plans (informal outline) that students have made for their writing. You may decide to consider the quality of a plan such as an informal outline when you assess a writing assignment's organization, or you may choose to let students know how well they did with their plans without scoring the plans.

- **Scoring with the 16-point grading scale**:

  - Students can earn a maximum of 16 points: four points for organization, four points for content, four points for style, and four points for grammar/mechanics/presentation. Score each trait separately.

  - As you score a student's writing assignment, consider the four options in each row. Place a check mark on the line in front of the applicable descriptor on each row of the grid.

  - For each category/trait, determine the number of points the student receives by figuring out which level (advanced, proficient, basic, or below basic) received the most check marks. For example, the *organization* category includes three areas for judging (excluding the plan). If a piece of writing gets two check marks in the proficient column and one in the basic column, it should receive three (of the four possible) points for the *organization* category.

  - Note that students do not receive a point for each check mark; they receive the score assigned to the column in which you gave them the most check marks. A writer who receives three check marks in *organization* in the advanced column gets four points for the *organization* trait.

Before a Lesson

- Make overhead transparencies and student copies of **Math Tools 6-5a** through **6-5f** as needed. Review each tool. Practice scoring paragraphs by rating the examples in **Math Tools 6-5c** to **6-5f** in each of the four categories on the scoring guide (**Math Tool 6-5b**). You can also practice using the scoring guide to assess math-related writing assignments that students have already completed.

- Choose a math concept/prompt based on content your class is currently learning. Create your own examples of below-basic, basic, proficient, and advanced responses. Your own examples will be helpful to students because they will accurately reflect what you are looking for in writing or math assignments.

Note: When you or your students create a set of "below basic, basic, proficient, and advanced" samples, take time to review and compare these samples to criteria on the scoring guide.

During a Lesson

- Display and describe the scoring guide (**Math Tools 6-5a** and **6-5b**). Introduce students to the continuum with four levels. Point out the placement of the sixteen points:

Below Basic (4–6)	Basic (7–10)	Proficient (11–14)	Advanced (15–16)

- Tell students that the scoring guide is based on a 16-point scale because all factors of 16 can easily be added and subtracted, which saves time for teacher and student.

- Explain that the scoring guide and the continuum were designed to help all students succeed and reach the proficient level on their writing.

- Explain that the purpose of the continuum and the scoring guide is to show students how to get "over the line"—the large, dark line in the middle of the continuum, which separates the below-basic and basic levels from the proficient and advanced levels in writing.

- Tell students that using the accordion strategies for writing paragraphs and reports will almost always improve their performance on the scoring guide. When a piece of writing is well-organized; has a strong topic sentence; is supported by well-thought-out key/star ideas; and contains accurate, detailed elaboration, it has the makings of a solid, proficient paragraph. Proficient and advanced scores come when students show mastery of math concepts and vocabulary. Both proficient and advanced scores are within reach.

- Display **Math Tools 6-5c** and **6-5d**. Ask students to compare the four levels of writing.

- Present your math prompt and examples of a response at each rating level. Discuss why you scored each response the way you did, and answer student questions.

- Tell students that it may take a bit of time in the beginning to learn to use the scoring guide, but that because it is so predictable, they will soon be able to refer to it easily.

- Ask students to score example prompts and responses using the scoring guide traits.

Additional Ideas

- Make extra copies of the scoring guide for students to store in their notebooks for reference throughout the year.

- Give students copies of the scoring guide to turn in with written assignments. Have them complete the form before turning in their work to show what score they think they have earned. Fill in the same form as you score their work, using a different color of ink. Use the scoring guide for discussion when you meet with students about their writing.

- After you have used the scoring guide and are familiar with the expectations at each level in each category, create labels or an ink stamp with the four categories on them. Then, when you grade papers, use the labels or the stamp instead of using the full-page copies of the scoring guide. This saves time and gets papers back to students even more quickly.

- Since the scoring guide is meant to give students explicit direction for improving their work, as often as possible have them revise and fix errors in an assignment, then return the piece for a higher score.

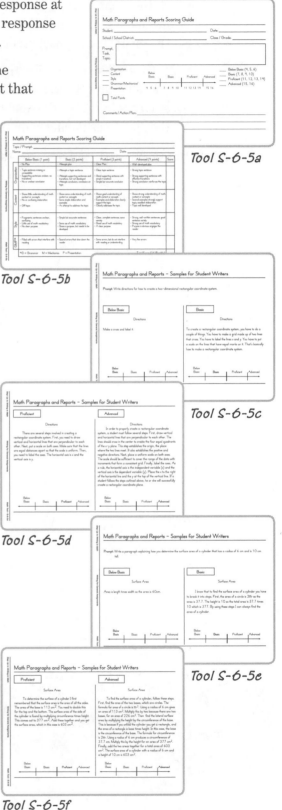

Tool S-6-5a

Tool S-6-5b

Tool S-6-5c

Tool S-6-5d

Tool S-6-5e

Tool S-6-5f

- Rather than making detailed notes on student work about mistakes in grammar or mechanics, just circle the mistakes; give students incentives to look for and correct the mistakes. Support students as needed.

- Have each student store graded papers in a large, legal-size envelope. Label each envelope with the student's name. Store the envelopes in crates. It is important for students to review the quality of their written work as it progresses over time. Use the envelopes during conferences with students or parents.

Note: Frequent assessments using every day assignments help students master writing skills.

Math Tools: Primary

Accordion Paragraph With Informal Outline

Informal Outline

Topic = Measurement

☆ rulers and tape measures	– inches and feet – small and big objects
☆ clocks and scales	– class clock – nurse's scale

Conclusion = tools help

Paragraph

Measurement

We have lots of tools that help us measure. Rulers and tape measures show inches and feet. I can use them to measure small and big objects. Clocks and scales have pointers to show the time or to show how much something weighs. Our class clock has hands that point to the minutes and the hours. The scale in the nurse's office points to show how many pounds I weigh. Lots of things need to be measured, and these tools help.

Math Tool P-6-1a

Accordion Paragraph With Informal Outline

Informal Outline

Topic = Making Bar Graphs

☆ labels	– title – numbers – girls and boys

☆ bars	– skyscrapers
	– show
	  • boys
	  • girls

Conclusion = show facts

Paragraph

Bar Graph

This morning we made a bar graph to compare boys and girls in this class. First, we drew a large rectangle on lined chart paper and labeled all sides. At the top, we put the title of the graph. On the left side, we put numbers to show how many were girls and how many were boys. Along the bottom, we wrote "girls" and "boys." Then we drew the bars. The bars were tall like skyscrapers. The bar for the girls shows 11 girls, and the bar for the boys shows 9 boys. The bar graph is like a picture that shows facts.

Math Tool P-6-1b

Topic Sentences for Accordion Paragraphs or Reports

Action Verb Topic Sentence	1. My friends and I <u>drew</u> different geometric shapes in math class. 2. I <u>know</u> how to tell time.
Number (Power) Topic Sentence	1. I use nickels, dimes, and quarters in <u>many</u> ways each week. 2. Our class discovered <u>two</u> different ways to measure the length of an object.
Where or When Plus What's Happening Topic Sentence	1. <u>In our math lesson today</u> we compared four different coins. 2. <u>In our school store</u> we practice buying and selling school supplies.

Math Tool P-6-1c

Practice Guide for Writing in Math

Name: _____ Date: _____

Title = _____

Topic Sentence Go	
Key/Star Idea ★ *Slow Down.*	Explain. *Stop!*
Key/Star Idea ★ *Slow Down.*	Explain. *Stop!*
Conclusion Go Back!	

Math Tool P-6-1d

Math Tools: Primary (continued)

Practice Guide for Writing in Math

Name: _____ Date: _____

Title = _____

Topic Sentence Go!	
Key/Star Idea ★ Slow Down.	Explain. Stop!
★ Slow Down.	Stop!
★ Slow Down.	Stop!
Conclusion Go Back!	

Math Tool P-6-1e

Informal Outline for Accordion Report

Title = Learning About Shapes

Topic = Shapes

☆ cube	– sugar cube – six sides
☆ cylinder	– juice can, glass, garbage can – circle top and bottom
☆ sphere	– apple, bowling ball, light bulb – my basketball
☆ cone	– funnel, tornado – ice-cream cone – snow cone

Conclusion = looking for pictures

Math Tool P-6-2a

Accordion Report

Title (green) ———→ Learning About Shapes

Topic Sentence ———→ This week in class we learned about four
(green) common shapes.

Transition Topic ———→ A cube looks like this. [ ] A
Sentence (yellow)
Explain (red) cardboard box and sugar cubes both
———→ come in the shape of a cube. Cubes have six
sides.

Transition Topic ———→ A cylinder looks like this. [ ] A fruit
Sentence (yellow)
juice can , a glass , and a garbage can
Explain (red) are examples of cylinders. Cylinders have
circles at the top and on the bottom.

Transition Topic ———→ A sphere looks like this. ◯ Many
Sentence (yellow)
items like apples , bowling balls , and
Explain (red) light bulbs look like spheres. My basketball is a
sphere.

Transition Topic ———→ A cone looks like this. ▽ Two cone-
Sentence (yellow)
shaped things are a funnel and a
Explain (red) tornado . I eat snow cones and ice-cream
cones.

Conclusion (green) —→ My friends and I are now looking for
pictures of different shapes. When we find
them, we cut them out and put them on our
"shapes" bulletin board.

Math Tool P-6-2b

Accordion Race

Coins for a Card

- -

On Saturday morning, Becky decided to spend the money in her piggy
bank to buy a birthday card for her nana.

- -

First, Becky poured all the coins out on her bed and hoped that she
had $2.85 for the card she wanted.

- -

She saw that she had seven quarters.

- -

This gave her $1.75.

- -

Then she counted the dimes.

- -

She had twelve dimes, so she added $1.20 to the $1.75.

- -

She was happy when she realized that she had enough to buy the card
with $0.10 left over.

Math Tool P-6-3a

Math Tools: Primary *(continued)*

Accordion Race

Subtracting

This week my friends and I discovered that subtracting one number from another is easy.

We first learned that subtraction problems can be written two ways.

Subtraction problems sometimes look like this: $10 - 7 = ?$

Some other times they look like this:
$$\begin{array}{r} 10 \\ -\ 7 \\ \hline ? \end{array}$$

Then we learned that when we subtract, we take the smaller number out of the bigger number.

If we subtract 7 from 10, we have 3 left.

If we subtract 4 from 10, we have 6 left.

That means $10 - 7 = 3$, and $10 - 4 = 6$.

My friends and I are good at subtracting.

Math Tool P-6-3b

Accordion Race

Triangles

Today in math class, we had fun learning about triangles.

First, we learned that triangles have three sides.

The three sides can be different lengths, and the triangles can be different shapes and sizes.

They might look like this.

We also learned that there are many triangles in our classroom.

In our science book, we found triangles on the cover and on the chapter dividers.

On our walls, we saw triangles in the posters and the alphabet chart.

We even found triangles on our clothes, jewelry, and backpacks.

Math Tool P-6-3c

Math Tool P-6-4a

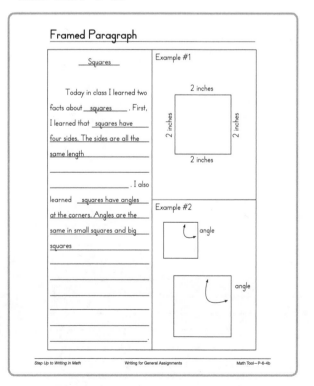

Math Tool P-6-4b

Math Tools: Primary *(continued)*

Framed Paragraph _____

New Skill

Today in math class, I learned to _____

_____. The steps are easy.

Start by _____

_____

_____. Then _____

_____. Next, _____

_____

_____.

See! Learning to _____

_____ is easy.

Math Tool P-6-4c

Framed Paragraph _____

New Skill

Today in math class, I learned to _read word problems___

_____. The steps are easy.

Start by _carefully reading the problem once to help you get the

big idea___

_____. Then _read the problem

again to find the facts and to pay attention to the question. If you can,

underline the facts and put a box around the question. Next, write

down the facts and start solving the problem one step at a time.

Sometimes it helps to draw a picture to show the problem .

See! Learning to _read a word problem_____

_____ is easy.

Math Tool P-6-4d

Framed Paragraph _____

Real-Life Math

I use _____ in my life in

two ways. One way _____

_____. Another way _____

_____

_____.

Real-Life Math

_____

_____

_____

_____

_____

_____

_____

_____

_____.

Math Tool P-6-4e

Framed Paragraph _____

Real-Life Math

I use subtraction in my life in two ways. One way
subtraction helps me is when I hang up my clothes. If
I have five things to hang but only have two hangers, I
can subtract. I subtract two from five and know that
I need three more. Another way I use subtraction is
when I read. If I want to read ten pages and I have
read seven pages, I see that I must read three more
pages.

Math Tool P-6-4f

Math Tools: Primary *(continued)*

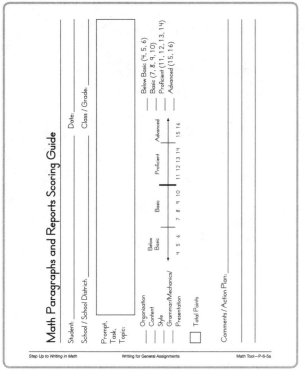

Math Tool P-6-5a

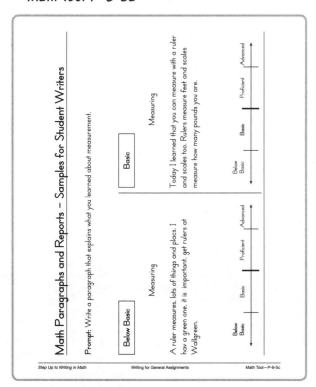

Math Tool P-6-5c

Math Tool P-6-5b

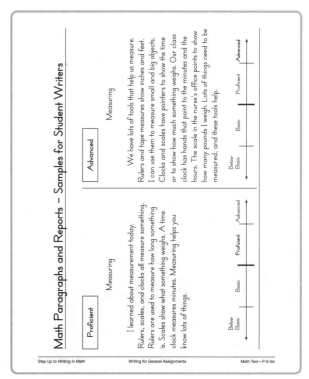

Math Tool P-6-5d

Math Tools: Primary–Intermediate

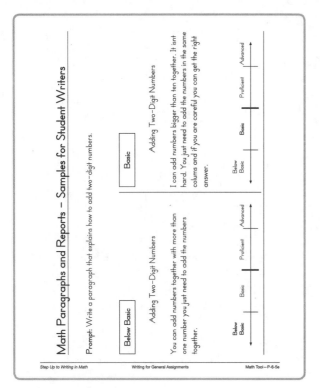

Math Tool P-6-5e

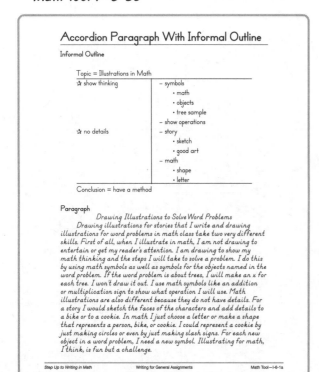

Math Tool P-6-5f

Accordion Paragraph With Informal Outline

Informal Outline

Topic = Illustrations in Math

☆ show thinking	– symbols
	• math
	• objects
	• tree sample
	– show operations
☆ no details	– story
	• sketch
	• good art
	– math
	• shape
	• letter

Conclusion = have a method

Paragraph

Drawing Illustrations to Solve Word Problems

Drawing illustrations for stories that I write and drawing illustrations for word problems in math class take two very different skills. First of all, when I illustrate in math, I am not drawing to entertain or get my reader's attention. I am drawing to show my math thinking and the steps I will take to solve a problem. I do this by using math symbols as well as symbols for the objects named in the word problem. If the word problem is about trees, I will make an x for each tree. I won't draw it out. I use math symbols like an addition or multiplication sign to show what operation I will use. Math illustrations are also different because they do not have details. For a story I would sketch the faces of the characters and add details to a bike or to a cookie. In math I just choose a letter or make a shape that represents a person, bike, or cookie. I could represent a cookie by just making circles or even by just making slash signs. For each new object in a word problem, I need a new symbol. Illustrating for math, I think, is fun but a challenge.

Math Tool I-6-1a

Accordion Paragraph With Informal Outline

Informal Outline

Topic = Math Quiz Average

☆ add	– six quizzes
	– list and add all scores
☆ divide	– find total
	– divide by six

Conclusion = plan to improve

Paragraph

Find the Average

In order to find my math quiz average, I followed a couple of steps. First, I added up my quiz scores. We have had six quizzes so far, and my scores were 70, 92, 88, 76, 84, and 98. My scores added up to 508. Next, I divided the total, or 508, by the number of quizzes. My average score was 84.7, which I rounded to 85. My average is okay, but I'd definitely like to bring it up by receiving some higher scores on future quizzes.

Math Tool I-6-1b

Math Tools: Intermediate *(continued)*

Topic Sentences for Accordion Paragraphs or Reports

Action Verb Topic Sentence	1. Mr. Camacho, our math teacher, <u>showed</u> us simple ways to read a graph. 2. I <u>learned</u> three steps that helped me with long division.
Occasion/Position Topic Sentence	1. <u>If</u> you are having trouble simplifying fractions, try following these three easy steps. 2. <u>If</u> you are going to add fractions, it is very important to understand common denominators.
Number (Power) Topic Sentence	1. I have a <u>two</u>-step method for estimating. 2. For the test, I memorized <u>three</u> facts about probability.
Where or When Plus What's Happening Topic Sentence	1. <u>Yesterday</u> we reviewed our "Hints for Mathematics Tests." 2. <u>This month</u> I have learned a lot about using a compass.

Math Tool I-6-1c

Practice Guide for Writing in Math

Title =		
Topic Sentence *Go!*		
Key/Star Idea ★ Slow down.	Explain. Step!	
Key/Star Idea ★ Slow down.	Explain. Step!	
Conclusion *Go back!*		

Math Tool I-6-1d

Practice Guide for Writing in Math

Title =	
Topic Sentence *Go!*	
Key/Star Idea ★ Slow down.	Explain. Step!
★ Slow down.	Step!
★ Slow down.	Step!
Conclusion *Go back!*	

Math Tool I-6-1e

Informal Outline for Accordion Report

Title = *Comparing Rectangles and Squares*

Topic = *Rectangles and squares are similar, but they have some important differences.*

☆ similarities	— four sides
	— angles
	   • corners
	   • 90 degrees
	   • right angles
	— pick up a square/put in a rectangle
	   • show how they're alike
	— parallel sides

☆ differences	— rectangles
	   • two sides longer
	   • same length as each other
	— show the difference
	   • line up 6 kids shoulder to shoulder
	     – on each of the four sides
	     – show a square
	   • add three kids on two of the sides
	     – expand it into a rectangle
	     – see the difference

Conclusion = *close but not the same*

Math Tool I-6-2a

Math Tools: Intermediate *(continued)*

Accordion Report

Title (green) ——→ Comparing Rectangles and Squares

Introductory ——→ From a distance, some rectangles and
Paragraph with Topic squares might seem the same. The window panes
Sentence (green) in our classroom, for example, look like squares.
But when I measured, they were really rectangles.
Rectangles and squares are similar, but they have
some important differences.

Transition Topic ——→ The similarities are pretty obvious. Rectangles
Sentence (yellow) and squares each have four sides. They each have
four angles called corners. These angles are all
Elaboration (red) ——→ 90-degree angles. They are called right angles.
You could actually pick up a square cut from paper
and put it in a rectangle to show how their angles
are alike. Another way they are alike is their
parallel sides. The lines on both sides of a square or
a rectangle are parallel because they do not meet.

Transition Topic ——→ The differences between a square and
Sentence (yellow) rectangle are not always so obvious. This is true
Elaboration (red) ——→ especially if a rectangle has sides that almost seem
the same. Rectangles have two sides that are
longer but still the same length as each other. It is
easy to show the difference between a square and
a rectangle. Start by lining up six kids shoulder to
shoulder on each of the four sides to show a square.
Then add three kids on each of the two sides that
are across from each other. This will expand it into
a rectangle. The rectangle will look different than
the square. Two of its sides will be longer—three
kids longer.

Conclusion (green) ——→ As you can see, rectangles and squares are
close but not the same.

Step Up to Writing in Math Writing for General Assignments Math Tool—I-6-2b

Math Tool I-6-2b

Accordion Race

Buying Clothes

It's important to understand and figure percentages when you're out shopping for clothes.

First of all, understanding percentages will help you know how much you can save.

For example, if a shirt that costs $29 is on sale for 10% off, you will save $2.90.

If shoes are on sale for 25% off, you can save $10 on a pair that costs $40.

Percentages can also help you figure out how much you will pay for each item at the checkout stand.

You will pay $29.70 for a $27 sweatshirt if tax is 10%.

If tax is 8%, a $50 pair of pants will cost a total of $54.

Learning to figure percentages quickly and accurately is definitely a valuable skill.

Step Up to Writing in Math Writing for General Assignments Math Tool—I-6-3a

Math Tool I-6-3a

Accordion Race

Subtracting Decimals

Subtracting numbers with a decimal is a snap.

Start by arranging the numbers in a vertical form so that the decimals line up.

If you are subtracting 0.05 from 1.371, it will look like this:

$$\begin{array}{r} 1.371 \\ -\ 0.05 \\ \hline \end{array}$$

Next, add zeros to make both numbers have the same number of digits behind the decimal point.

In our problem, we need a zero after the number 5.

$$\begin{array}{r} 1.371 \\ -\ 0.050 \\ \hline \end{array}$$

Once the problem is set up this way, subtract as you usually do.

$$\begin{array}{r} 1.371 \\ -\ 0.050 \\ \hline 1.321 \end{array}$$

The answer to our subtracting numbers with a decimal example is 1.321.

Step Up to Writing in Math Writing for General Assignments Math Tool—I-6-3b

Math Tool I-6-3b

Accordion Race

Measuring the Area of a Triangle

Follow these simple directions if you want to find the area of a triangle.

First, you measure the height of your triangle.

You figure the height by measuring the length from the top of the triangle straight down to the bottom line, which is called the base.

The line you measure will look like this:

You can check to make sure that your line is straight by making sure you have a 90° angle where the height line meets the base line.

Next, you measure the length of the base, or the bottom line, of the triangle.

Once you know the base and height of the triangle, multiply these two numbers, and then multiply the answer by 0.5, or $\frac{1}{2}$.

In other words, plug those numbers into the formula for the area of a triangle: Area $= \frac{1}{2}$ b x h.

For example, if a triangle has a base of 4 feet and a height of 2 feet, multiply 4 x 2 and get 8 square feet.

One half of 8 is 4, so the area in this triangle is 4 square feet.

The area is then labeled as 4 sq. ft.

Finding the area of a triangle is really quite easy.

Step Up to Writing in Math Writing for General Assignments Math Tool—I-6-3c

Math Tool I-6-3c

Math Tools: Intermediate *(continued)*

Framed Paragraph

Math Tool I-6-4a

_____

    Today in class I learned two

facts about _____ . First,

I learned that _____

_____

_____

_____ . I also

learned _____

_____

Example #1

Example #2

Math Tool I-6-4a

Framed Paragraph

    Fractions

    Today in class I learned two

facts about _*fractions*_ . First,

I learned that _*a fraction is*_

*part of a whole*

_____

_____ . I also

learned _*that a fraction can*_

*be written as one number over*

*another number. For example,*

a quarter can be written as $\frac{1}{4}$.

It is $\frac{1}{4}$ *of a dollar.*

_____

_____

_____

_____

Example #1

Example #2

25 25 25 25 = $\boxed{\$1.00}$
$\frac{1}{4}$ $\frac{1}{4}$ $\frac{1}{4}$ $\frac{1}{4}$

Math Tool I-6-4b

Framed Paragraph

    Finding the Greatest Common Factor

    If friends who were studying fractions asked me to explain how to

find the greatest common factor, I would tell them three things. First,

_____ . Next, _____

_____ . Finally, _____ . My advice

should help them find the greatest common factor.

    Finding the Greatest Common Factor

    If friends who were studying fractions asked me to explain how to

find the greatest common factor, I would tell them three things. _First,_

take the denominator of the first fraction and list all of the

different numbers that can be multiplied together to give you

that number. Next, _take the denominator of the second_

fraction and make the same type of list. Finally, _compare the_

two lists and determine the largest number that is the same

in both lists. My advice should help them find the greatest common

factor.

Math Tool I-6-4c

Framed Paragraph

Explain!

    Changing a Fraction
    to a Percent

    When I am asked to

change a fraction to a percent,

I use four simple steps. First, I

set up a division problem

where the numerator is

divided by the denominator.

Then _I add 0s to the_

numerator, which is now the

dividend. Next, _I divide._

Finally, _I move the decimal_

point to the right two places

to make a percent.

Give an example!

Turn $\frac{4}{5}$ into a percent.

1. $5\overline{\smash{)}4}$

2. $5\overline{\smash{)}4.00}$

3. $\dfrac{.80}{5\overline{\smash{)}4.00}}$

4. $0.80 = 80\%$
    4 is 80% of 5

Math Tool I-6-4d

Math Tools: Intermediate *(continued)*

Framed Paragraph

Real–Life Math

I use _____ in my everyday life in
two ways. One way _____
_____. For example, _____
_____. Another way _____
_____. When I ____
_____,
is/are definitely useful in my real life!

Real–Life Math

_____
_____
_____
_____
_____
_____
_____
_____
_____
_____
_____
_____
_____

Step Up to Writing in Math   Writing for General Assignments   Math Tool—I-6-4e

Math Tool I-6-4e

Framed Paragraph

Real–Life Math

I use mental math in my everyday life in two ways.
One way I use mental math is when I head to the corner
store. For example, I might want to buy a candy bar, gum,
and something to drink. I know how much money I have in
my pocket, but I need mental math to add up the cost of
all three things I will buy. I usually round off the numbers.
In my head, I think of $1.00, not just $0.89. This way I
am sure I have enough money. Another way I use mental
math is when I play sports. When I kick the soccer ball or
pass a football, I have to think in feet and yards. It helps
me if I can imagine 30 feet or 10 yards. Mental math for
shopping and for sports is definitely useful in my real life!

Step Up to Writing in Math   Writing for General Assignments   Math Tool—I-6-4f

Math Tool I-6-4f

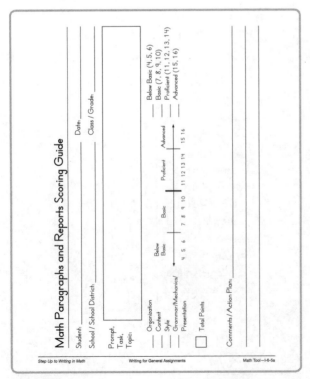

Math Tool I-6-5a

Math Tool I-6-5b

Math Tools: Intermediate *(continued)*

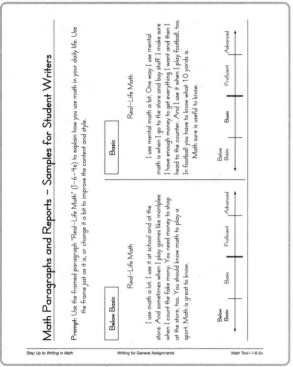

Math Paragraphs and Reports – Samples for Student Writers

Prompt: Use the framed paragraph "Real–Life Math" (I–6–4e) to explain how you use math in your daily life. Use the frame just as it is, or change it a bit to improve the content and style.

Below Basic

Real–Life Math

I use math a lot. I use it at school and at the store. And sometimes when I play games like monkplee when I count the fake money. You need money to shop at the store, too. You should know math to play a sport. Math is great to know.

Basic

Real–Life Math

I use mental math a lot. One way I use mental math is when I go to the store and buy stuff. I make sure I have enough money to get everything I want and then I head to the counter. And I use it when I play football, too. In football you have to know what 10 yards is. Math sure is useful to know.

Math Tool I-6-5c

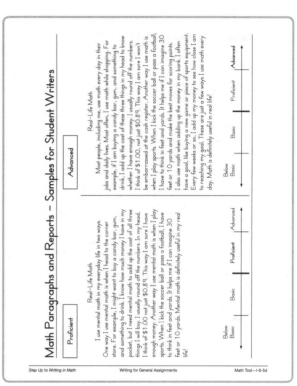

Math Paragraphs and Reports – Samples for Student Writers

Proficient

Real–Life Math

I use mental math in my everyday life in two ways. One way I use mental math is when I head to the corner store. For example, I might want to buy a candy bar, gum, and something to drink. I know how much money I have in my pocket, but I need mental math to add up the cost of all three things I will buy. I usually round off the numbers. In my head, I think of $1.00, not just $0.89. This way I am sure I have enough money. Another way I use mental math is when I play sports. When I kick the soccer ball or pass a football, I have to think in feet and yards. It helps me if I can imagine 30 feet or 10 yards. Mental math is definitely useful in my real life!

Advanced

Real–Life Math

Most people, including me, use math every day in their jobs and daily lives. Most often, I use math while shopping. For example, if I am buying a candy bar, gum, and something to drink, I add up the cost of these three things in my head to know whether I have enough money. I usually round off the numbers. I think of $1.00, not just $0.89. This way I am sure I won't be embarrassed at the cash register. Another way I use math is when I play sports. When I kick the soccer ball or pass a football, I have to think in feet and yards. It helps me if I can imagine 30 feet or 10 yards and make the best moves for scoring points. I also use math when adding up the money in my bank. I often have a goal, like buying a new game or piece of sports equipment. Every few weeks or so, I add up my money to see how close I am to reaching my goal. These are just a few ways I use math every day. Math is definitely useful in real life!

Math Tool I-6-5d

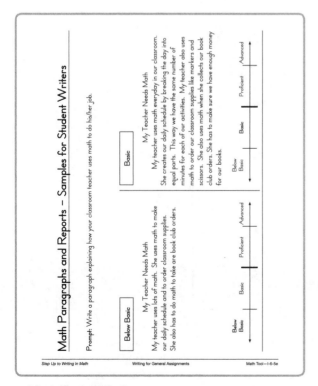

Math Paragraphs and Reports – Samples for Student Writers

Prompt: Write a paragraph explaining how your classroom teacher uses math to do his/her job.

Below Basic

My Teacher Needs Math

My teacher uses lots of math. She uses math to make our daily schedule and to order classroom supplies. She also has to do math to take are book club orders.

Basic

My Teacher Needs Math

My teacher uses math everyday in our classroom. She creates our daily schedule by breaking the day into equal parts. This way we have the same number of minutes for each of our activities. My teacher also uses math to order our classroom supplies like markers and scissors. She also uses math when she collects our book club orders. She has to make sure we have enough money for our books.

Math Tool I-6-5e

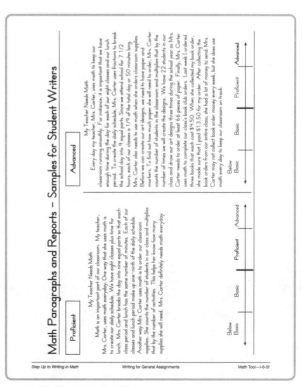

Math Paragraphs and Reports – Samples for Student Writers

Proficient

My Teacher Needs Math

Math is on important part of our classroom. My teacher, Mrs. Carter, uses math everyday. One way that she uses math is to create our daily schedule. We have eight classes plus time for lunch. Mrs. Carter breaks the day into nine equal parts so that each class period and lunch period make up one-ninth of the daily schedule. Another way Mrs. Carter uses math is to order our classroom supplies. She counts the number of students in our class and multiples that by the number of activities. This helps her know how many supplies she will need. Mrs. Carter definitely needs math everyday.

Advanced

My Teacher Needs Math

Every day my teacher, Mrs. Carter, uses math to keep our classroom running smoothly. For instance, it is important that we have enough time during the day for each of our eight classes and our lunch period. To create the daily schedule, Mrs. Carter uses fractions to break the school day into 9 equal parts. Since we attend school for 7 1/2 hours, each of our classes is 1/9 of the total day or 50 minutes long. Mrs. Carter also needs to use math when she orders classroom supplies. Before we can create our art designs, we need to have paper and markers. To find out how much paper she will need to order, Mrs. Carter counts the number of students in the classroom and multiplies that by the number of times we will create the designs. We have 22 students in our class and draw our art designs three times during the school year so Mrs. Carter needs to order 66 pieces of paper. Finally, Mrs. Carter uses math to complete our class's book club orders. Last week I ordered three books that would cost $1.50. When she collected my book order, she made sure that I paid $13.50 for my order. After collecting the book orders from our entire class, she had a lot of money to send. Mrs. Carter may not collect book order money every week, but she does use math every day to keep our classroom on track.

Math Tool I-6-5f

Math Tools: Secondary

Accordion Paragraph With Informal Outline

Informal Outline

Topic = Angles Test

☆ obtuse	– half an O
☆ acute	– capital A
☆ straight	– lay flat – half circle – 180°

Conclusion = visualizing helps

Paragraph

Angles Test

To help myself study for the geometry test on angles, I decided to try to see the angles in my head. I had no problem with the right angles (⌐), but I needed a trick to remember the obtuse angle. When I drew it (⟍), it looked like half of an O or the sun sneaking up in the morning. To remember the acute angle, I drew an example (∠) and realized that if I stood it up, it would like a capital A; capital A for acute and capital O for obtuse. I drew straight angles that were flat (◠) or stood up tall (⌐). Drawing the half circles reminded me that these angles measure 180 degrees. It doesn't always work perfectly, but if I make drawings and try to see ideas in my head, I feel more prepared for a quiz.

Step Up to Writing in Math   Writing for General Assignments   Math Tool—S-6-1a

Math Tool S-6-1a

Accordion Paragraph With Informal Outline

Informal Outline

Topic = Transformations

☆ translation	–moves object from one position to another • no change in size or orientation • also called a slide
☆ rotation	–rotates object around point • like placing object on hand of clock
☆ reflection	–flips object over line • line is like a mirror

Conclusion = important concepts in geometry

Paragraph

Transformations

A transformation is a change in the size, shape, location, or orientation of a figure. There are several types of transformations. One kind of transformation is called a translation. A translation moves an object from one position to another without changing its size or orientation. It is also called a slide because when a figure is translated it appears to have slid across a plane. Rotations are another type of transformation. Rotations turn an object around a point. Rotating an object is like placing it on one hand of a clock. A third type of transformation is a reflection. Reflections flip an object over a line. The line is like a mirror and the reflection is what a person would see if he looked into the mirror. Translations, rotations and reflections are important concepts in geometry.

Step Up to Writing in Math   Writing for General Assignments   Math Tool—S-6-1b

Math Tool S-6-1b

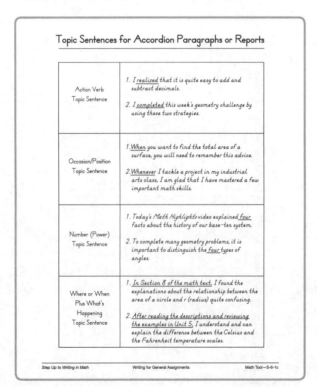

Topic Sentences for Accordion Paragraphs or Reports

Action Verb Topic Sentence	1. I *realized* that it is quite easy to add and subtract decimals. 2. I *completed* this week's geometry challenge by using these two strategies.
Occasion/Position Topic Sentence	1. *When* you want to find the total area of a surface, you will need to remember this advice. 2. *Whenever* I tackle a project in my industrial arts class, I am glad that I have mastered a few important math skills.
Number (Power) Topic Sentence	1. Today's *Math Highlights* video explained *four* facts about the history of our base-ten system. 2. To complete many geometry problems, it is important to distinguish the *four* types of angles.
Where or When Plus What's Happening Topic Sentence	1. *In Section 8 of the math text*, I found the explanations about the relationship between the area of a circle and r (radius) quite confusing. 2. *After reading the descriptions and reviewing the examples in Unit 5*, I understand and can explain the difference between the Celsius and the Fahrenheit temperature scales.

Step Up to Writing in Math   Writing for General Assignments   Math Tool—S-6-1c

Math Tool S-6-1c

Practice Guide for Writing in Math

Title =

Topic Sentence Go!		
Key Idea ★	Explain.	
Slow down.		Stop!
Key Idea ★	Explain.	
Slow down.		Stop!
Conclusion Go back!		

Step Up to Writing in Math   Writing for General Assignments   Math Tool—S-6-1d

Math Tool S-6-1d

Math Tools: Secondary *(continued)*

Practice Guide for Writing in Math

Title =

Topic Sentence

Go!

Key Idea	Explain.
★ Slow down.	Stop!
★ Slow down.	Stop!
★ Slow down.	Stop!
Conclusion Go back!	

Math Tool S-6-1e

Informal Outline for Accordion Report

Title = *A Career Without Math?*

Topic = *Taking math seriously*

☆ *design, art,* *photography*	— *measure* · *paints* · *areas* — *dimensions* · *actors* · *audience* · *special effects* — *angles and shots* — *billing*
☆ *dancing*	— *count steps* — *match music* — *figure timing* — *practical aspects* · *budget* · *plan for future*

Conclusion = *good preparation in math*

Math Tool S-6-2a

Accordion Report

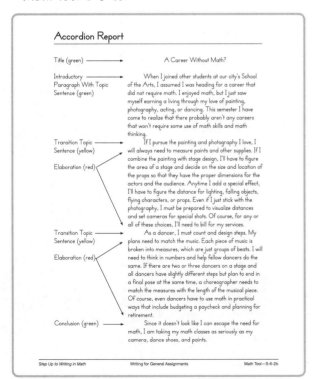

Title (green) ⟶ A Career Without Math?

Introductory Paragraph With Topic Sentence (green) ⟶ When I joined other students at our city's School of the Arts, I assumed I was heading for a career that did not require math. I enjoyed math, but I just saw myself earning a living through my love of painting, photography, acting, or dancing. This semester I have come to realize that there probably aren't any careers that won't require some use of math skills and math thinking.

Transition Topic Sentence (yellow) ⟶
Elaboration (red) ⟶ If I pursue the painting and photography I love, I will always need to measure paints and other supplies. If I combine the painting with stage design, I'll have to figure the area of a stage and decide on the size and location of the props so that they have the proper dimensions for the actors and the audience. Anytime I add a special effect, I'll have to figure the distance for lighting, falling objects, flying characters, or props. Even if I just stick with the photography, I must be prepared to visualize distances and set cameras for special shots. Of course, for any or all of these choices, I'll need to bill for my services.

Transition Topic Sentence (yellow) ⟶
Elaboration (red) ⟶ As a dancer, I must count and design steps. My plans need to match the music. Each piece of music is broken into measures, which are just groups of beats. I will need to think in numbers and help fellow dancers do the same. If there are two or three dancers on a stage and all dancers have slightly different steps but plan to end in a final pose at the same time, a choreographer needs to match the measures with the length of the musical piece. Of course, even dancers have to use math in practical ways that include budgeting a paycheck and planning for retirement.

Conclusion (green) ⟶ Since it doesn't look like I can escape the need for math, I am taking my math classes as seriously as my camera, dance shoes, and paints.

Math Tool S-6-2b

Accordion Race

The Money Exchange

After their plane landed in Mexico City, the members of the Pleasantville High School soccer team realized that the first thing they needed to do was exchange their U.S. currency for Mexican currency.

All of the boys were happy that they could get 10.4 pesos for every $1.00 they had.

Jim had $120.00 but decided to exchange only half of it.

He jumped in line first and walked away with $60.00 and 624 pesos.

After Jim was finished, Larry exchanged $85.00.

He then stuffed the 884 pesos into his pocket.

Marcus was not sure how much of his $125.00 he wanted to exchange.

But finally he decided to exchange all but $20.00.

He counted the 1092 pesos, grabbed his bags, and ran to join the others, who were hailing cabs and heading for the hotel.

Math Tool S-6-3a

Math Tools: Secondary *(continued)*

Accordion Race

Miles Per Gallon

- -

Some people might argue that EPA gas mileage estimates on cars are inflated.

- -

It is a good idea to do some calculating on your own if you really want to get an idea of your car's fuel performance.

- -

First, fill your tank to its capacity using a gas pump's automatic shutoff.

- -

After that, reset your travel odometer and drive until the tank is almost empty.

- -

But remember, it is always a good idea to have a spare gallon of gas in your car to get you to a gas station if you need it.

- -

Next, refill your tank to its capacity, making note of how many gallons you put in the tank. This is how many gallons you consumed since the last fill-up.

- -

Now you have all the information you need to calculate the miles per gallon.

- -

To determine the miles per gallon, take the number of miles that you have driven (trip odometer) and divide it by the number of gallons it took to fill the tank.

- -

The formula looks like this: MPG = distance traveled ÷ gallons consumed.

- -

The quotient is your average number of miles per gallon.

- -

While finding out exactly how many miles per gallon your car gets is a science, it is fairly simple to get a good estimate.

Step Up to Writing in Math   Writing for General Assignments   Math Tool—S-6-3b

Math Tool S-6-3b

Accordion Race

Triangular Prism

- -

To find the surface area of a triangular prism, you need to go through all of the following steps.

- -

The first step is determining the area of the base (bottom) of the prism, plus the top (roof) of the prism, which are two identical triangles.

- -

The formula for finding the area of a triangle is $\frac{1}{2}$ base x height, so for two identical triangles it would look like this: $2(\frac{1}{2} b_s \times h_b)$ or $(b_s \times h_b)$. (The "$_s$" on the variables shows that they are lengths for the base side of the prism.)

- -

Once you have figured out the area of the base and the top, determine the area of the rest of the prism, which consists of three rectangular walls (sides).

- -

Since the walls are rectangles, you have to use the formula for finding the area of a rectangle, which is base x height.

- -

All three rectangles will have the same height—the height of the prism—but they may have different base lengths.

- -

Once you have determined the area of all the rectangles, you can add them together. This is called the lateral surface area. (Lateral surface area = $b_1h_p + b_2h_p + b_3h_p$.)

- -

Finally, complete the formula: surface area of a triangular prism = $b_1h_p + b_2h_p + b_3h_p + 2(\frac{1}{2} b \times h)$, or $b_1h_p + b_2h_p + b_3h_p + (b_s \times h_b)$.

- -

To further simplify the equation, you could factor out the height of the prism (h_p) from the first three terms to get the following formula: surface area of a triangular prism = $h_p(b_1 + b_2 + b_3) + (b_s \times h_b)$.

- -

Once you understand what "area" is and how to find the area of different shapes, it is simple to find the surface area of a triangular prism.

Step Up to Writing in Math   Writing for General Assignments   Math Tool—S-6-3c

Math Tool S-6-3c

Framed Paragraph

_____	Example #1
Today in class I learned two facts about _____ . First, I learned that _____ _____ _____ _____ _____ . I also learned _____ _____ _____ _____ _____ _____ _____ _____ _____ _____	
	Example #2

Step Up to Writing in Math   Writing for General Assignments   Math Tool—S-6-4a

Math Tool S-6-4a

Framed Paragraph

Decimals	Example #1
Today in class I learned two facts about _decimals_ . First, I learned that _a fraction may be changed to a decimal by dividing the numerator by the denominator_ _____ . I also learned _that I can change the decimal to a percent by moving the decimal point two places to the right_	$\frac{1}{8} = 8\overline{)1.00}$ $8\overline{)1.000}$ $\begin{array}{r} 0.125 \\ \underline{8} \\ 20 \\ \underline{16} \\ 40 \\ \underline{40} \\ 0 \end{array}$ 0.125
	Example #2
	0.125 = 12.5%

Step Up to Writing in Math   Writing for General Assignments   Math Tool—S-6-4b

Math Tool S-6-4b

Math Tools: Secondary (continued)

Framed Paragraph

Converting a Quadratic Equation From Standard Form to Vertex Form

Converting a quadratic equation into vertex form can seem difficult, but following the steps involved in completing the square greatly simplifies the process. First, _____ _____. Next, _____ _____ _____ _____. Finally, _____ _____ _____.

Converting a Quadratic Equation From Standard Form to Vertex Form

Converting a quadratic equation into vertex form can seem difficult, but following the steps involved in completing the square greatly simplifies the process. First, _divide the coefficient of the linear term in half, and use this new number to make a squared binomial expression._ _____ Next, _expand that expression to compare its value with the original quadratic expression. Determine what number needs to be added to or subtracted from the new expression so that it matches the original._ Finally, _add or subtract that number to or from the squared binomial expression to create a vertex form expression that is equivalent to the original._ _____

Math Tool S-6-4c

Framed Paragraphs

The Perimeter of a Rectangle

I realized that it would be easy to find the perimeter of a rectangle if I just followed these steps. To begin, _____ _____. I do this because _____. Next, _____ _____. This is an important step because _____ _____. Finally, _____.

The Area of a Rectangle

I realized that it would be easy to find the area of a rectangle if I just followed these steps. To begin, _____. Next, _____ _____. After that, _____ _____. Finally, _____ _____.

The Perimeter of a Rectangle

I realized that it would be easy to find the perimeter of a rectangle if I just followed these steps. To begin, _I measure the length and width of the rectangle._ I do this because _to find the perimeter I need to know both the length and the width._ Next, _I multiply the length by 2 and the width by 2._ This is an important step because _to find a perimeter I need to find the total length of all 4 sides, which is the same as 2 lengths and 2 widths._ Finally, _I add the results together to find the total length of all 4 sides, which is the perimeter._

The Area of a Rectangle

I realized that it would be easy to find the area of a rectangle if I just followed these steps. To begin, _I measure the length of the rectangle._ Next, _I measure the width of the rectangle._ After that, _I multiply the length by the width._ Finally, _I label my answer with the correct unit of measurement._

Note: The paragraph on the left is longer because it includes explanations: "I do this because ... " and "This is important ... ." In general, math students should include more, not less, explanation.

Math Tool S-6-4d

Framed Paragraph

Real-Life Math

In math class, we have just finished studying _____. _____ are used in the real world. One way _____ _____. _____ _____. Another way _____ _____ _____. In addition, _____ _____. _____. is/are definitely useful outside of the math classroom.

Real-Life Math

_____ _____ _____ _____ _____ _____ _____ _____ _____ _____ _____ _____

Math Tool S-6-4e

Framed Paragraph

Real-Life Math

In math class, we have just finished studying percentages. Percentages are used in the real world. One way that I use them is to tell how well I did on a test. If I score 60 points on a 100-point test, that means that I only got 60% correct. Another way that I use percentages is to find out which sports team is doing the best. I divide the number of games each team has won by the number of games they have played and multiply by 100 to find each team's winning percentage. In addition, I use percentages to figure out how much money I'll make when I invest it. If I invest $1,000 at 5% interest, then $50.00 will be added to my account after one year. Percentages are definitely useful to me outside of the math classroom.

Math Tool S-6-4f

Math Tools: Secondary *(continued)*

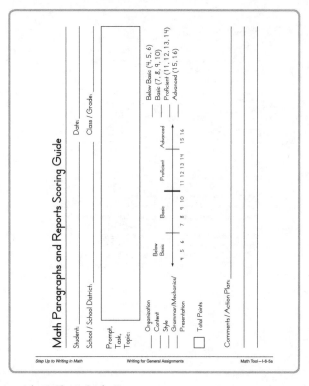

Math Tool S-6-5a

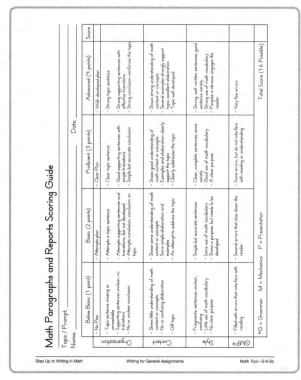

Math Tool S-6-5b

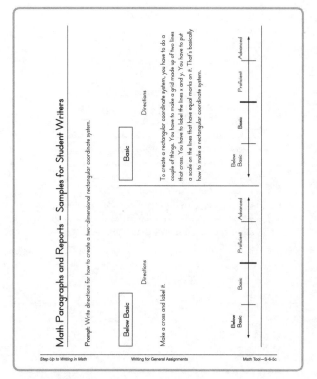

Math Tool S-6-5c

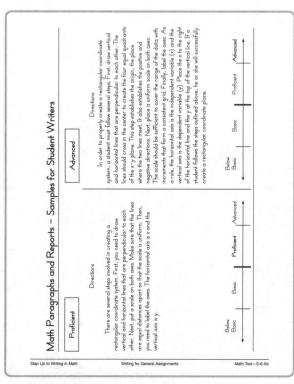

Math Tool S-6-5d

Math Tools: Secondary *(continued)*

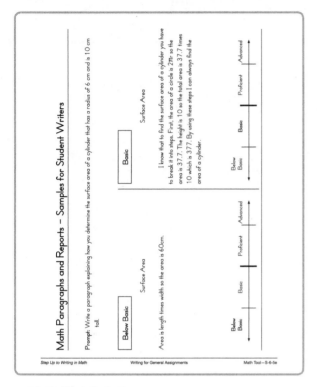

Math Paragraphs and Reports – Samples for Student Writers

Prompt: Write a paragraph explaining how you determine the surface area of a cylinder that has a radius of 6 cm and is 10 cm tall.

Below Basic

Surface Area

Area is length times width so the area is 60cm.

Basic

Surface Area

I know that to find the surface area of a cylinder you have to break it into steps. First, the area of a circle is $2\pi r$ so the area is 37.7. The height is 10 so the total area is 37.7 times 10 which is 377. By using these steps I can always find the area of a cylinder.

Below Basic · Basic · Proficient · Advanced

Math Tool S-6-5e

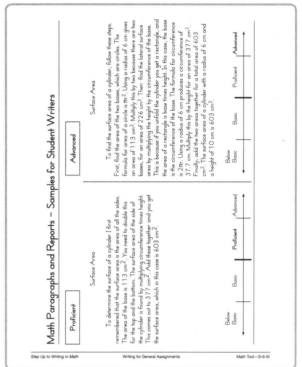

Math Paragraphs and Reports – Samples for Student Writers

Proficient

Surface Area

To determine the surface area of a cylinder I first remembered that the surface area is the area of all the sides. The area of the base is 113 cm². You need to double this for the top and the bottom. The surface area of the side of the cylinder is found by multiplying circumference times height. This comes out to 377 cm². Add these together and you get the surface area, which in this case is 603 cm².

Advanced

Surface Area

To find the surface area of a cylinder, follow these steps. First, find the area of the two bases, which are circles. The formula for area of a circle is πr^2. Using a radius of 6 cm gives an area of 113 cm². Multiply this by two because there are two bases, for an area of 226 cm². Then find the lateral surface area by multiplying the height by the circumference of the base. This is because if you unfold the cylinder you get a rectangle, and the area of a rectangle is base times height. In this case, the base is the circumference of the base. The formula for circumference is $2\pi r$. Using a radius of 6 cm produces a circumference of 37.7 cm. Multiply this by the height for an area of 377 cm². Finally, add the two areas together for a total area of 603 cm². The surface area of a cylinder with a radius of 6 cm and a height of 10 cm is 603 cm².

Below Basic · Basic · Proficient · Advanced

Math Tool S-6-5f

*C*reative writing is not an activity many students—or teachers—associate with math class. But math-related writing assignments can be very creative. Often, the more creativity students are able to express through their writing, the more interesting they find math writing assignments.

One way to show creativity is to present information from an unexpected point of view. The RAFTS strategy for creative writing, which this section explains, gives math students a structure for writing from a completely new point of view. RAFTS assignments ask students to write about math topics from the perspective of someone or something outside themselves, and to write for an audience other than their math teacher. Students have to put thought into the tone and structure of the composition and figure out how best to fulfill the specific purpose of the assignment. When they write in RAFTS mode, students demonstrate higher-level thinking skills and show off what they know about math concepts and content.

Composing word problems is another way in which creative writing is a natural fit with math class. When students write word problems, they demonstrate knowledge of math concepts and show that they can apply their understanding of math content. Creating word problems also improves students' reading skills. As they piece together their own ideas for a problem, they learn more about how word problems are structured. Then they are able to read word problems more carefully and with more comprehension. Finally, students are sometimes asked to create word problems on assessments. They can prepare by practicing in class using details and numbers that the teacher provides. Strategies in this section help students recognize the elements of a word problem and follow simple steps for writing their own.

Learning logs and journal entries are two forms of personal writing that can also benefit math instruction. In learning logs, students reflect upon their math understanding in short paragraphs. Teachers can use these logs to inform future lessons.

The Teaching Principle from *Principles and Standards for School Mathematics* states, "Effective mathematics teaching requires understanding what students know and need to learn, and then challenging and supporting them to learn it well" (NCTM, 2000–2004, p. 370). Paragraphs that students create using the Learning Logs strategy show how well they have comprehended new information, important concepts, or math processes.

Journals require less formal writing. They can include lists, brainstorming, stream-of-consciousness writing, short paragraphs, or imaginative writing. Teachers can ask students to journal for a variety of purposes: to share their level of understanding, their feelings toward math, or their frustrations and areas of confusion.

As students think and write, they grow as mathematicians. When teachers read their students' writings, they grow too, gaining insights that they can use to improve and individualize their math instruction. In addition, journals can act as an alternative form of dialogue between teachers and students.

As with all academic tools, students need to learn how to effectively use learning logs and journals. Section 7 of *Step Up to Writing in Math* offers concrete suggestions for setting up and using these communication tools.

Objectives

- Encourage students to think creatively and apply what they have learned

- Teach students to write about math from various points of view

- Give students the opportunity to reflect on their learning and show what they know

- Empower students to write with confidence and clarity

- Improve students' skills for communicating about math and about what they understand or do not understand

SECTION 7 CONTENTS

7-1 Writing From a Different Point of View

The RAFTS strategy gives students an opportunity to use their imagination and demonstrate their creativity. At the same time, it encourages them to demonstrate their knowledge of math terms, concepts, and processes.

RAFTS is an acronym for:

R **Role.** Before they can write a RAFTS composition, students must answer the question "Who, or what, are you as you write?" They then write from the point of view of the selected role. This activity requires students to step into the shoes of someone or something else and use their imaginations.

A **Audience.** Students using the RAFTS approach also must answer the question "To whom, or for whom, are you writing?"

F **Format.** In math class, the format for writing assignments is usually fairly standard, but consider these different forms of writing:

acceptance letter	diary entry	rap
advertisement	dispatch	riddle
brochure	editorial	sign
bumper sticker	flyer	speech
cartoon	invitation	sympathy note
children's story	memoir	telegram
complaint letter	petition	wanted poster
dialogue	poem	will

RAFTS requires students to answer the question "What type of writing are you doing?" before they begin.

T **Topic.** A RAFTS writer must answer one of two topic-related questions: either "What are you writing about?" or "What are you planning to prove or explain in your writing?" It is best to write the topic in a complete sentence because this puts the writer into the chosen role and clarifies the message and/or intent of the RAFTS composition. Without a clear message, writing is not strong or effective.

S **Strong Verb.** The final question that a writer must answer before writing in the RAFTS method is "What is the purpose of your writing?" Choosing a strong verb helps students set the tone, focus their writing, and get their point across to readers. Examples of strong verbs and strong purposes for a creative RAFTS text include:

to show excitement	to beg	to complain
to convince	to plead	to persuade
to inform	to warn	to entertain

Note: The verb does not need to be used in the final written piece; it merely serves as a tool to set the tone and/or mood of the piece.

Being specific reminds students of the purpose of their writing. A complete sentence helps. Consider the difference in clarity of purpose between:

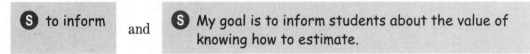

S to inform   and   **S** My goal is to inform students about the value of knowing how to estimate.

When students follow the RAFTS approach, creative ideas usually flow. For example:

Role	(Who or what are you?)	A castle
Audience	(To whom, or for whom, are you writing?)	A king
Format	(What type of writing are you doing?)	Letter response to a want ad
Topic	(What are you writing about? What are you proving or explaining?)	My response letter will explain how to find the area of a unique shape using the metric system.
Strong Verb	(What is the purpose of your writing?)	My goal is <u>to encourage</u> the king to live in my castle.

Dear King:

This letter is in regard to a recent want ad for a castle to fit a king. I can clearly demonstrate that I am the castle for you. I am the size of a castle that is truly fit for a king.

My unique shape is what you would call a "U shape" with right angles. It is as if I have two arms to wrap around you and keep you protected. My two sides stick farther out than my backside. My total width on each side is 100m, and my total length is 150m. So as you can see, you would have plenty of room for your court.

If you are concerned with total area, the enormity of me is quite easily determined. As I mentioned, my sides are 100m on the outside. The dimensions of the inside of my "U" are 40m wide and 40m long. To find my area, you can split me up into three separate rectangles.

First, imagine removing my "arms." Since we know that these rectangles are 40m by 40m, we can easily find the area by multiplying 40 times 40 to get 1600m². Since there are two of these rectangles, multiply 1600 times 2 to get an area of 3200m².

Now we need to find the area of the final rectangle. Since my sides are 100m long and we already counted the 40m from my "arms," that leaves 60m to multiply with the length of 150m. That means this section has an area of 9000m². To find the total area, add 3200m² to 9000m² for an area of 12,200m².

Surely, you can see that I provide enough room for a king and his court! Please consider me for the castle of your dreams. It is obvious that no other castle has the area or the charm of me. I look forward to you acquiring me and making me your home.

Regards,
The Castle

Before a Lesson

- Determine the purpose (message and/or intent) of the RAFTS assignment. The purpose might be:

  - to explain how to subtract,

  - to explain the meaning of probability, or

  - to describe the relationship among classes of two- and three-dimensional geometric objects.

- Decide how many elements of the RAFTS assignment you want to specify and how many you want to leave up to students' creativity. This decision depends on the ability levels of the students and the amount of time they have for writing. You can present a RAFTS assignment in one of three ways:

  1. Provide words and phrases explaining the purpose of the assignment. For example:

role:	bottom number in a subtraction problem
audience:	top number in a subtraction problem
format:	letter
topic:	explain what it means to borrow
strong verb:	apologize

2. Explain the purpose of the RAFTS assignment in complete sentences. For example:

role:	I will be the bottom number in a subtraction problem.
audience:	I will write to the top number in a subtraction problem.
format:	I will use a letter format for an apology.
topic:	In my letter, I will explain how to borrow in a subtraction problem.
strong verb:	My goal is to apologize for making the number above me borrow from its neighbor.

3. Specify only some of the RAFTS elements. Let students answer some of the RAFTS questions and establish their own purpose for their RAFTS writing.

role:	bottom number in a subtraction problem
audience:	top number in a subtraction problem
format:	letter
topic:	_____
strong verb:	_____

- Review and make overhead transparencies of **Math Tools 7-1a** to **7-1d** and student copies, as needed.

- Choose examples from the tools provided (or create your own) to use during your demonstration and explanation of the RAFTS strategy.

During a Lesson

- Display **Math Tools 7-1a** and **7-1b**, or examples you have created, to introduce the RAFTS concept.

- Explain the meanings of the letters in the RAFTS acronym.

- Share and discuss the examples.

- Using **Math Tools 7-1c** and **7-1d**, create some possible RAFTS assignments with student input. **Math Tool 7-1c** can serve as a template or overhead transparency for demonstrations and guided lessons. **Math Tool 7-1d** provides examples you can share with students to show them the potential for expressing their creativity in applying the RAFTS strategy.

- Share RAFT ideas with students and ask students for ideas. Then write a RAFTS composition as a class. Use topics students have studied, and/or give students time to work in pairs or small groups to brainstorm ideas. Let students know that they can start by filling in any part of the RAFTS form. Starting with the topic, for example, is effective because students will focus on the purpose (message and/or content) of their RAFTS.

- Have students write their own RAFTS composition using one of the RAFTS examples you've discussed, with or without making changes, or ask them to create a RAFTS task of their own. Another option is to have all students write using the same RAFTS assignment. When they share their final products, students will see how their classmates applied the same set of criteria in slightly different ways.

- Remind students that the goal for the assignment is to show their math knowledge in a creative way. This means using math terms, language, and concepts as they write.

- Take time to share results and assess the value of the activity.

Tool P-7-1a

Tool P-7-1b

Tool P-7-1c

Tool P-7-1d

Additional Ideas

- Look for (on your own and with help from students) examples of RAFTS-type writing assignments in other classes. Social studies, history, and science materials frequently lend themselves to these types of assignments.

- Give students a RAFTS assignment in the form of a prompt. Use the RAFTS acronym to help you write the prompt. For example:

> **R** = algebraic equation
>
> **A** = students
>
> **F** = speech
>
> **T** = In my speech, I will include the steps of how to solve me, why I am important, and how they will use me in the real world.
>
> **S** = to inform students and convince them I am important

- Use **Math Tool 7-1c** at the end of a unit of study to brainstorm with students about possibilities for RAFTS compositions related to the content they just learned. Make several overhead transparencies of **Math Tool 7-1c**. Have students work in pairs to create RAFTS assignments using the terms, concepts, and topics presented in the unit. Provide time for students to share their ideas using the overhead projector. Use this as a fun way to review content from the unit.

- Encourage students to submit their best RAFTS writing to the school's literary magazine or newspaper.

- Combine RAFTS writing with school-wide goals; create an interdisciplinary, math-based project with a language arts, social studies, science, or art class.

- Make booklets of RAFTS compositions that students have created. Use the booklets to help other students generate RAFTS ideas, to share during family conferences, and to celebrate students' creativity.

- Ask students to explain (to their classmates) how they come up with ideas for a RAFTS project. Students learn from each other and often learn to take risks with encouragement from their classmates.

7-2 Creating Word Problems

Math textbooks, math teaching materials, and district or state assessments sometimes ask students to create word problems as a way to demonstrate mastery of a process or a concept.

In class, math students can create word problems to learn more about reading and solving these kinds of problems, and to show off their comprehension of math content in a way that is unusual and fun.

Writing word problems is challenging for students of all ages and ability levels. Word problems have a unique structure, they demand that the writer know and be able to use math vocabulary, and they serve a special purpose. The writer of a word problem must organize it around four important points:

1. The *who* or the *what* involved, which is determined by the purpose of the word problem.

2. The important numbers and/or terms that give hints or direct information.

3. The situation(s), issue(s), or circumstance(s) that creates the problem.

4. The question that the problem solver needs to answer—in other words, the problem that needs to be solved.

For example, before creating this word problem:

> ### Paying for the Fuel
>
> The Little Town School District owns 41 buses. Each bus uses an average of 34 gallons of gas a week. Last year fuel cost $1.20 a gallon. This year the cost jumped to $2.23 a gallon. How much more money will the school district need to budget for gas this year?

the writer must have thought through all of the following:

1. The *who* or the *what* involved in the problem:

    –   The school district, the buses, and the gas are the *what* in the problem. They are like the key players in a story.

    –   The *purpose* for this word problem is to test for mastery of multiplication skills. In addition, it checks for knowledge of the number of weeks in a year and the ability to subtract decimal numbers.

2. The *numbers* and *terms* that give hints or present the facts:

    –   The district has 41 buses that use an average of 34 gallons a week. Since no other information is given, it is safe to assume the buses are used 52 weeks a year.

    –   The cost of gas has increased from $1.20 a gallon to $2.23 a gallon.

3. The *situation*, *issue*, or *circumstance* that creates the problem:

    –   A school district must budget for the fuel to run its buses, and fuel costs are rising.

4. The *question* that needs to be answered:

    –   How much money must Little Town School District budget for gas this year?

A teacher assigning students the task of writing a word problem can give them a prompt that includes details on some combination of these four key elements. For example:

> –   Will and Bill are brothers.
>
> –   Will and Bill have 86 building blocks.
>
> –   Will wants half of the blocks to build a skyscraper.
>
> –   He wants 12 more blocks to build a road to the skyscraper.
>
> –   Use all of these facts to write a word problem that will need division and addition to solve the problem.

Or a prompt can be less structured and encourage more creativity:

> Suppose a new student joins your class when you have just finished several lessons on finding the area of a circle. This new student tells you that she has not learned to find the area of a circle. Write a word problem that you could use to teach her to find the area of a circle.

Either way, students will enjoy the challenge of writing word problems and will fare better on formal exams when they have practiced creating word problems based on prompts like these. Use this strategy to help students build the confidence they need to write word problems, even in stressful situations like taking tests. Change and add steps to the process to meet your students' needs and your class goals.

Before a Lesson

- Decide on your goals for having students write word problems.

- Select math skills and concepts that you want students to apply as they write their problems.

- Analyze several word problems, looking for their four key elements (the *who* or *what*; the important *numbers* or *terms*; the *situation, issue,* or *circumstance*; and the *question* that the problem solver needs to answer).

During a Lesson

- Have students fold a sheet of notebook paper into two columns. Ask them to divide the page into five rows. Then label the rows with these headers:

purpose
who/what
facts
situation
question(s)

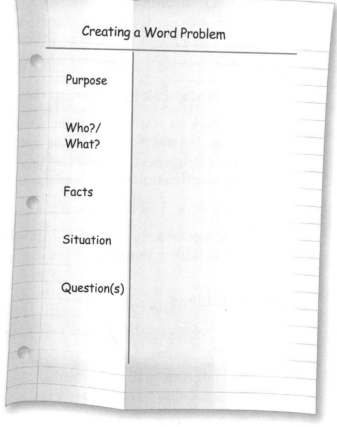

Creating a Word Problem

Purpose

Who?/ What?

Facts

Situation

Question(s)

- Using chart paper or an overhead transparency, guide the class through the creation of a word problem. Together come up with:
  - a purpose for the problem;
  - the *who* and the *what* for the problem;
  - *numbers*, *terms*, and *facts* that identify the problem;
  - a *situation*, *circumstance*, or *issue* that creates the problem; and
  - a *question(s)* that needs to be answered.

- Have students use the responses that this exercise generates and work with partners to write the actual word problem.

- Remind them to be neat, accurate, detailed, and organized.

- Encourage students to use action verbs to make their word problems clear and easy to understand. Action verbs convey the situation, issue, or circumstance of the problem. A good way to encourage students to use action verbs in their word problems is to point out the action verbs in other word problems. For example, in the "Paying for the Fuel" word problem, the action verbs are:

> ### Paying for the Fuel
>
> The Little Town School District <u>owns</u> 41 buses. Each bus <u>uses</u> an average of 34 gallons of gas a week. Last year fuel <u>cost</u> $1.20 a gallon. This year the cost <u>jumped</u> to $2.23 a gallon. How much more money will the school district <u>need</u> to budget for gas this year?

- Give time for students to solve and check these problems.

- Have students share their problems, explaining how their word problems fit their purpose and how they included the mathematical operation(s) that were intended. Discuss the process. Give students time to make suggestions for changing or improving the strategy and to ask questions.

- Ask students to create problems independently. Share the results.

- Encourage students to create word problems that the class can use as a way to practice skills or prepare for assessments.

Additional Ideas

- Have students practice writing word problems at home with family members or friends.

- Have them use (in their word problems) the names of classmates and neighborhood places that all students will recognize.

- Apply the RAFTS strategy (**7-1 Writing From a Different Point of View**). The format for the composition will always be *word problems*, but the role and audience will vary. The topic statement will give the purpose for the word problem.

- Ask students to rewrite problems incorporating different facts and a different purpose.

- Give students opportunities to teach others how to write a word problem.

- Have students analyze word problems, looking at the same features they consider in creating their own word problems.

- Give students a question and then have them develop a word problem to go along with the question.

Note: See Section 2, strategies **2-7 Marking Word Problems to Improve Understanding** and **2-8 Highlighting or Underlining Word Problems**, for more ideas for reading and/or writing problems.

7-3 Learning Logs

This strategy asks students to process information from lessons, and then record what they know in short written responses. The responses provide valuable information that the teacher can use to inform future instruction.

Learning logs give students a chance to write about what they have learned as a form of reflection; as a way to organize information for use later in reviewing and preparing for tests; and as a way to demonstrate comprehension. The steps to writing a learning log entry are:

Step 1: Read the prompt or question. For example:

> **In a short paragraph, explain the rules of the order of operations.**

Step 2: Turn the prompt into a topic sentence, such as:

> The order of operations involves four rules.

Step 3: Make a list of two, three, or four key ideas to support the topic sentence.

> ★ parentheses
> ★ multiplication and division
> ★ exponents
> ★ addition and subtraction

Step 4: Give the response a practical title that shows the topic.

Step 5: Use your topic sentence and key ideas to write the learning log response.

Order of Operations

The order of operations involves four rules. First, perform any calculations inside parentheses. Next, simplify all exponents, working from left to right. After that, multiply and divide in order from left to right. Finally, perform all additions and subtractions—once again moving from the left of the expression to the right.

Students master this skill by completing several learning log responses as a class, with the teacher's guidance, before working on their own. Once students have practiced this strategy, completing a learning log response should take only a few minutes. Encourage students to work and think quickly.

Before a Lesson

- Review the learning logs on **Math Tool 7-3**.

- Make an overhead transparency and student copies (as needed) of **Math Tool 7-3**.

- Make plans for how and when students will use the Learning Logs strategy. Options include:

  - student notebooks that can hold all learning log entries;

  - index cards, which are easy to collect, review, and return to students;

  - e-mail entries; and

  - handouts created specifically for learning log responses.

- Using content that the class has studied, create sample questions or prompts with corresponding topic sentences on an overhead transparency or chart paper to use during demonstration. For example:

Prompt:	In a short paragraph, explain the rules of the order of operations.
Topic sentence:	The order of operations involves four rules.
Question:	How do you prove a geometric concept?
Topic sentence:	Proving a geometric concept is easy if you follow the two-column proof format.
Question:	What are two facts about telling time that you remember?
Topic sentence:	I remember two facts about telling time.

Question:	How are triangles different from squares?
Topic sentence:	Triangles are different from squares in at least two ways.
Question:	How might you use what you have learned about percentages in your other classes?
Topic sentence:	I know I'll use the information I've learned about percentages in at least two other classes.

- Select topics that students can use for practice.

During the Lesson

- Emphasize that students will use learning logs exclusively to write short responses.

- Review the purpose of learning logs:
  - for reviewing the main ideas of a lesson;
  - to help in the processing of new information;
  - to increase retention of information learned;
  - as practice for writing short-constructed responses in a short time frame;
  - to maintain a record of important concepts students have learned; and
  - to demonstrate comprehension.

- Explain to students that at times you will give them a prompt or a question to guide the learning log entry; at other times they will write constructed responses on their own about the content that they have studied.

- Explain that sometimes you may give them a topic sentence to use, but that the ultimate goal is for them to create clear, focused, and accurate learning log responses on their own.

- Tell students that you will model and guide them through the process several times before you will expect them to complete learning logs on their own.

- Display **Math Tool 7-3**. Explain the format for organizing information for a learning log response.

- Take students slowly through each step of the process of creating a learning log response: writing the topic sentence, listing the key ideas, creating a title, and then composing the response.

Tool I-7-3

- Guide students as they respond to prompts or questions that you have created. Model the strategy on the overhead exactly as you expect students to record their responses in their logs. As students perfect this skill, they will develop their own style and steps for completing a learning log response, but when they first begin they will need and appreciate your guidance.

- Ask students to share their final short paragraphs. Celebrate appropriate use of math language, demonstrations of understanding, and fluency in writing.

- Collect students' logs; assess and make plans to review or reteach the concepts that students have not mastered.

Additional Ideas

- Suggest that students use their learning logs to study for assessments, as they often contain explanations of the major concepts from a unit of study.

- Use learning logs at family conferences as evidence of student learning.

- Place students in small groups, and ask them to share their responses to a learning log prompt. Doing this gives students time to process what they've learned and time to think about the learning log process, and exposes them to the ways other students express themselves on the topic of mathematics. It also gives some students the repetition they need to master a concept.

- Use the following topic sentences as models for writing your own learning log prompts and/or corresponding topic sentences; change as needed to fit your lesson:

1. When you work with fractions, there are a few important math terms you must know.

2. Spheres and circles have two characteristics in common.

3. If I want to find the total cost of electricity for our school in the months of June, July, and August, there are two operations that I must do.

4. There are two facts to remember about telling time.

5. Keeping score in volleyball includes these two steps.

6. The game we played today taught me how to find the probability.

7. I know I'll use the information I've learned about percentages in at least two other classes.

8. Today we learned two important symbols used in division.

9. I have learned a number of math terms that relate to multiplication.

10. Hexagons have two features.

11. Graphs have a number of practical uses.

12. Creating a table can help you understand a pattern.

13. There are times when estimating is the right choice.

14. Improving my "mental math" skills is important for two reasons.

15. The article about Russia explained how the abacus is used to estimate.

16. Three steps are necessary in solving an equation.

17. I use math every day in a number of ways.

18. Adding fractions is easy if you just follow these instructions.

19. Today I learned three important math terms.

20. You can use division to solve many real-world problems.

21. When I go shopping, I need math.

22. Today's newspaper illustrates two important math concepts.

23. My mom and dad use math every day in many different ways.

24. You can compare fractions using two different methods.

25. Determining whether the answer to a problem needs to be exact or estimated is easy when you use two simple clues.

26. In science, we use math for different purposes.

27. The career I would like to have would require me to use math in at least three ways.

28. Learning about different geometric shapes is important.

29. Interpreting data is easy when you consider all the information that is provided.

30. Mr. Visser's two examples helped me understand ratios.

Note: See strategy **5-2 Turning an Explanation Into a Formal Paragraph** for more examples and explanation about topic sentences.

7-4 Journal Entries

Use journals when you want to give students an opportunity to write informally about their understanding, feelings, or frustrations related to math.

Journal writing can take many forms and be used for a variety of purposes. Journals give students time to reflect; journal entries give teachers valuable information about students' learning and attitudes. For example:

Primary journal entries:

- I am good at adding, but it is hard for me to subtract. I am trying to remember most of them. Each night I practice a little while. It is easier when I can use counters.

- If I use counters, it takes me a long time to do each problem. I like it when I get problems that I know right away. I can't wait until I can remember all of the facts.

Intermediate journal entries:

- When I did my homework last night, I was very confused about how to order decimals. I know that the whole number is to the left of the decimal and that the numbers at the right are parts of a whole. It is really confusing when they are written as words and I have to remember whether I need a decimal for tens or tenths.

- I wish we could go into adding, subtracting, and multiplying decimals. I am really excited about learning to use decimals in a new way.

Secondary journal entries:

- Working in a group today was a lot of fun. We were able to find old statistics online, and then we searched for more current statistics. We then worked together to determine how the data had changed. Each of us determined which statistic we were interested in and completed the research.

- When we work in a group, I usually get frustrated. Sometimes I want to go at my own speed. It can be fun helping others and getting help from friends. Today I helped my group complete the statistics project, and there were a couple of other students who did the research. Unfortunately, there were also some students who did not help much.

Journaling does not need to be an everyday activity to be effective. Writing journal responses at the end of a unit or just after you have presented new information gives students a forum for asking questions and explaining any frustration or confusion they may be feeling. These types of responses would then help you with lesson planning.

That said, use journaling only if the time seems well-spent and the outcome of the activity is beneficial for you and for the students. Journaling can be helpful, but time spent on building skills for explaining processes and writing about math concepts may be more important.

Before a Lesson

- Determine how you will use journaling. Consider the following:

Defining the Purpose

- Why am I asking my students to journal?
- Will the journal-writing tasks vary, or will the purpose for journaling remain the same?
- Will journals be used for students to explain their math thinking or just for reflecting on the affective aspects of learning—joy, success, frustration, confusion, confidence, enlightenment, growth, struggle, fun, curiosity, etc.?
- Will journals be a place for students to ask for help?
- Will journals be used as a record of growth?

Defining the Task

- When will I ask students to journal?
- When will students write in their journals—at the beginning of class, at the end of class, or at home?
- How often will students write in their journals?
- Will students consistently journal, or will it be random?

Defining the Assessment

- How will I assess students' journals?
- How often will I collect and read students' journals?
- Will I respond to students' journal entries in writing?
- What parameters will I use to assess the journal entries?
- What are my expectations regarding spelling and punctuation?

- Create journal entries of your own, or use the examples in this section for demonstration. Copy the example(s) on the board or on chart paper.

- Determine the journal-writing task for the demonstration lesson.

During a Lesson

- Describe and define a journal entry; explain why you will be asking students to journal.

- Let students know that journal entries are informal. Explain that the goal for journaling in math is to spend just a few minutes sharing a success, a concern, or asking a question in order to get clarification and improve their math understanding.

- Share and discuss your expectations with your class.

- Display copies of example journal questions and responses.

- Ask students to evaluate the examples; ask them to explain why the entries might be helpful to both student and teacher.

- Model journaling by presenting a task and then completing the task using chart paper or an overhead transparency. As you write, explain to students why and how you have decided what to write. Give students time to comment and/or ask questions.

- Explain how you will use and assess the journal entries. Students will value journaling if they know that their entries will be read, respected, and addressed.

Additional Ideas

- Keep journaling time short. Consider providing small slips of paper that will give students space to share but will enable you to read and return the responses quickly.

- Provide a list of response starters like these to help students get started and to promote better journal responses.

As we were	If
When	Whenever
While the class	I'm still struggling
I have a question	Before
I wonder	The word _____ confuses me
I am confused	If only
I think _____ but	I do not think I will ever
During	I appreciate

During the film	I wish
I finally realized	My teammates
Working in a group	Trying the problems on my own
Using the computer	The calculator sometimes
I am good at _____, but I wish	I want to
To improve, I know	Every day when I leave math
When I do my math homework	I am excited about

Post the list, or make copies of the list for students to use as a reference.

- Ask students to journal about the same important topic several times throughout the school year. Compare the responses—and ask them to do the same—to see how their knowledge, reactions, attitudes, or concerns have changed.

- Give students a minute or two to journal at the beginning of class. Have them write about the previous day's lesson or homework assignment as a way to refresh their thinking and encourage discussion.

- Use journaling at the end of a class as a "ticket out." Give students index cards or small sheets of paper. Ask them to journal about what they want you to review, what they understand, how they plan to use what they have learned, or other topics that will help you plan for the next day's lesson.

Math Tools: Primary

Writing From a Different Point of View
Playing "Pretend" With RAFTS

Role Who or what are you?	
Audience To whom or for whom are you writing?	
Format What type of writing are you doing?	
Topic What are you writing about? What are you proving or explaining?	
Strong Verb What is the purpose of your writing?	

Math Tool P-7-1a

Writing From a Different Point of View
Playing "Pretend" With RAFTS

Recipe for Solving a Problem

Role	R = a word problem
Audience	A = friends
Format	F = recipe
Topic	T = problem-solving steps
Strong Verb	S = learn

Problem Solving Recipe
1 C Careful Reading
2 C Information in Problem
3 Tbsp Act It Out — optional
2 tsp Draw A Picture — optional
1 C Use Real Objects — optional
1 C Check Your Work
2 C Write and Label Your Answer Correctly

Start by reading me carefully. Look for the facts. To solve me, take out all the unimportant ingredients. Then determine what it is you are supposed to mix together to solve me. Next, add all the extra information and mix. Choose the tool that works best. Finally, take your answer and put it in the oven. Don't forget to check over your work and answer when I am done. Serve me in a complete sentence when you give my answer.

Math Tool P-7-1b

Writing From a Different Point of View
Playing "Pretend" With RAFTS

Using a Map Scale

Role	R = Mrs. Silbert's 2nd grade class
Audience	A = map scale
Format	F = thank you letter
Topic	T = purpose and helpfulness of a scale
Strong Verbs	S = appreciate

Dear Map Scale,
    Thanks for helping me figure out the distance from the school to the swimming pool. You told me that one inch is equal to one mile. The distance on the map between the school and the pool is three inches, so I know it is only three miles away. You were very helpful.

           Sincerely,
           Mrs. Silbert's second graders

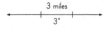

3 miles

3"

Math Tool P-7-1c

RAFTS Idea Cards

R = toy soldier A = toy box F = list T = sorting S = determine	R = dictionary A = dictionary reader F = dictionary definition T = polygons S = describe
R = cartoon character A = television set F = cartoon T = determine how big the TV is and have him or her ask for more room S = grumble	R = first grader A = mother nature F = e-mail T = report on daily temperatures – beg mother nature to warm up! S = plead
R = pyramid A = first grade students F = picture dictionary T = define the words: <u>face</u>, <u>edge</u>, <u>side</u> S = brag	R = graham cracker A = students F = memo T = add and subtract halves and fourths S = inform
R = number patterns A = another number F = want ad T = find the next number in a pattern S = announce, explain	R = fire chief A = tire salesman F = order form T = 3 fire trucks need new tires. Each truck has 10 tires. How many tires are needed? S = identify

Math Tool P-7-1d

Math Tools: Primary–Intermediate

Learning Log

Example 1:

Today in math we learned four facts about time.
– minutes in an hour
– hours in a day
– days in a week
– weeks in a year

Today in math we learned four facts about time. First, we learned there are sixty minutes in an hour and twenty-four hours in a day. Then we learned that there are seven days in a week. Last, we learned there are 52 weeks in a year.

Example 2:

I learned that the different coins we use are worth different amounts.
– penny
– nickel
– dime
– quarter

I learned that the different coins we use are worth different amounts. A penny is worth one cent. A nickel is worth five cents. A dime is worth ten cents. A quarter is worth twenty-five cents.

Math Tool P-7-3

Writing From a Different Point of View
Playing "Pretend" With RAFTS

Role Who or what are you?	
Audience To whom or for whom are you writing?	
Format What type of writing are you doing?	
Topic What are you writing about? What are you proving or explaining?	
Strong Verb What is the purpose of your writing?	

Math Tool I-7-1a

Writing From a Different Point of View

R	Papa Dollar
A	primary students
F	introduction
T	tell students about members of the Coin family
S	describe, inform

The Coin Family

Hello class! I am Papa Dollar. Let me introduce myself and the other members of my family. You may already know some of us and might even have a few of us in your pocket or backpack, right now.

To start, I am Papa Dollar. I am big and heavy. I am a beautiful gold color. I have a picture of that famous Native American girl on me—Sacagawea. I am the biggest coin around. You might not know it, but I am just as valuable as that green paper guy, Mr. One Dollar Bill. Also, I have the strength of 4 quarters, 10 dimes, or 20 nickels.

I have a great little lady as my wife. Everyone calls her Precious because she is a silver half-dollar. She may be just worth one-half of me, and it takes only two quarters to equal her, but she is always silver and worth a lot. She is a rare beauty! People don't find her in piggy banks or purses too often. That's something we have in common, wouldn't you say?

We have four super kids. Quarter is our teenage son. He likes to hang out at candy and soda machines. He enjoys getting some friends together and playing pinball, skee ball, and car racing games at the mall. He sure likes to get out and about! In fact, you can find him almost everywhere. Some say he is the favorite coin of all those in the Coin family. He and three of his strong friends equal the likes of me!

Dime is our lovely daughter. I could take 10 of her, she is so great. In fact, it would take 10 of her to equal me! I have heard that long ago you could make a phone call with her, but those days are gone. You can't buy much with Dime these days, maybe a pencil or a large piece of bubble gum. Even though she isn't worth much, I still love to hold her. She is as light as a feather.

Nickel is our playful preschooler. He is very jolly and round. If you hold him, you'll see how thick and wide he is. He never lets us forget how big he is. He likes to brag. After all, he equals five pennies. And, he comes in handy when people make change at a store.

Penny is our darling little baby girl. She has such pretty skin—all brown and copper. The world might not think she is worth much because it takes 100 of her to equal one dollar, but she means a lot to us. If you think about it, she can do a lot, like help kids get rides on the horse at the grocery store and buy penny gumballs.

Now that you know all about my family, go ahead and use us! Give us a ride in your pocket or put us in your piggy bank. We'll add value to your life!

Math Tool I-7-1b

Writing From a Different Point of View
Playing "Pretend" With RAFTS

Topic = Protractor

Role	R = protractor
Audience	A = fifth-grade students
Format	F = rap
Topic	T = show how a protractor is used
Strong Verb	S = inspire

Protractor Rap

A protractor is what I am.
I'm more useful than a can of Spam.
Bein' me is super cool.
Determinin' angles, I'm a measurin' fool.
Using me won't make you frown.
Put my center at the vertex; it's time to get down.
Up to 90 degrees is a big fat hoot.
I like measurin' angles that are acute.
If it's bigger than that, no need to get juiced.
I also work if the angle's obtuse.
Measurin' angles is easy, as easy as pie.
So get me out, and give me a try!

Math Tool I-7-1c

Math Tools: Intermediate–Secondary

RAFTS Idea Cards

R = number 8	R = two-dimensional shape
A = number 183,570	A = one-dimensional shapes
F = e-mail	F = letter
T = place value	T = different characteristics
S = brag	S = protest, convince
R = word problem	R = student
A = problem solver	A = other students
F = test question	F = poem
T = determine correct strategy for solving	T = add fractions with unlike denominators
S = justify	S = encourage
R = pints	R = octagon
A = cups	A = scientists
F = greeting card	F = lab report
T = how to convert	T = determine symmetry and congruence
S = inform	S = describe
R = bar graph	R = mom
A = students	A = her children
F = graffiti	F = commercial
T = use art and words to show when to use bar graphs and when to use pie graphs	T = use estimates when shopping to make sure you have enough money
S = convince	S = nag

Math Tool I-7-1d

Learning Log

Example 1:

Adding and subtracting fractions is simple when you follow some easy steps.
   – examine fractions
   – find common denominator
   – multiply numerator
   – add or subtract

Adding and subtracting fractions is simple when you follow some easy steps. You will first want to look and see if the fractions can be added or subtracted the way they are. If the fractions have different denominators, then you cannot add and subtract them. Next, you need to find a common denominator, and that means finding a multiple of both denominators. The numerator needs to be multiplied by the same number as the denominator. The last thing you do is add or subtract the fractions.

Example 2:

Today I learned four new things about lines.
   – line
   – line segment
   – ray
   – vertex

Today I learned four new things about lines. A line is a straight path that goes in two directions. I also learned that a line segment is part of a line and that it has two ending points. Next, we learned about rays. Rays are like line segments except that they only have one endpoint. Then we learned about a vertex. We learned that the vertex is where two rays meet at the same endpoint.

Math Tool I-7-3

Writing From a Different Point of View

Playing "Pretend" With RAFTS

Role	
Who or what are you?	
Audience	
To whom or for whom are you writing?	
Format	
What type of writing are you doing?	
Topic	
What are you writing about? What are you proving or explaining?	
Strong Verb	
What is the purpose of your writing?	

Math Tool S-7-1a

Writing From a Different Point of View

Playing "Pretend" With RAFTS

Topic = Estimation

Role	R = waiter
Audience	A = police officer
Format	F = monologue
Topic	T = estimation
Strong Verb	S = accuse, explain, advise

Sam, the waiter at the Silver Platter restaurant, talking to Officer Valdez:

Listen, I don't know what this young man was thinking. He is a thief. He comes in here with his girlfriend and orders a fancy meal barring no expense, and then when it comes time to pay, he realizes he hasn't enough money.

What am I to do? Make him do dishes?

Like I told him, all he really had to do was some estimation. They both ordered the New Maine Lobster Tail with creamy butter sauce, which was $32.50. He could have rounded that easily up to $33 or even $35 to be safe. Unfortunately I think he rounded everything down.

Then they ordered a bottle of sparkling juice for $17.95, and I think he rounded down to $15, instead of up to $18—or, more quickly, up to $20.

Finally, he and his girlfriend had the nerve to order the chocolate soufflé, one for each of them. The soufflé was $8.75 and quite easily could have been rounded to $9, or even $10 for simplicity.

So as you can see, if he would have rounded correctly, he would have seen that his mere $90 was not going to cover this exquisite meal. He not only forgot to round up instead of down, he didn't take his final total times 0.10 to get the amount of tax, and he didn't take it times another 0.20 to get the 20% he should have added to pay me the tip I deserved.

If he had rounded correctly, he would have known he needed approximately.
   meal – $35 + 35 + 20 + 10 + 10 = $110
   tax – $110 x 0.10 = $11
   tip – $110 x 0.20 = $22
   total – $110 + 11 + 22 = $143.

What am I to do about this big problem? The kid can't estimate! Does that make him a thief?

Math Tool S-7-1b

Math Tools: Secondary *(continued)*

Math Tool S-7-1c

Writing From a Different Point of View

Playing "Pretend" With RAFTS

Topic = Circumference and Diameter

Role	R = diameter of a circle
Audience	A = my circle
Format	F = empathy note
Topic	T = explain how the circumference of a circle depends on the diameter
Strong Verbs	S = explain, describe, apologize

Dear Circle,

I am sorry for your loss. I know that it is a difficult time for you. It is going to take some time to get through this. When I shrunk by two inches, I wasn't thinking about the fact that you would shrink, too. I forgot that you are approximately 3.14 times my actual length. I'm sure it's hard to get used to your new size. Maybe you didn't even shrink that much. To find out, you can take my length times pi and determine your new circumference. If you want, you can take your old circumference minus your new one to know how much you have shrunk. Maybe it isn't as bad as you think. Either way, you're still my favorite circle. Again, I am sorry. Let me know if I can help.

Your friend,
Diameter

Step Up to Writing in Math · Creative and Personal Writing · Math Tool—S-7-1c

Math Tool S-7-1d

RAFTS Idea Cards

R = solution/answer A = algebraic equation F = travel brochure T = order of operation S = assist	R = three-dimensional shape A = other shapes F = contest entry T = explain and analyze attributes S = entice
R = real-world issue A = society F = speech T = compute increases and decreases in percents S = incite	R = student A = teacher F = petition T = use and misuse of statistics in society S = enlighten
R = composite number A = prime, odd, even numbers F = yearbook entry T = describe characteristics S = divulge	R = Pythagorean theorem A = students F = satire T = develop and use S = entertain
R = number 1.81 A = number line F = campaign speech T = locate rational numbers S = challenge	R = fractions A = decimals F = marriage proposal T = equivalence S = convince

Step Up to Writing in Math · Creative and Personal Writing · Math Tool—S-7-1d

Math Tool S-7-3

Learning Log

Example 1:

I learned several rules about how to perform operations with exponents.
- multiplying and dividing like bases
- raising an exponent by an exponent
- fractional exponents

I learned several rules about how to perform operations with exponents. The first rule concerned what to do when multiplying or dividing like bases. If you want to multiply like bases, you add the exponents and keep the base the same. Dividing like bases is similar to multiplying them, except you subtract the exponents instead of adding them. Next, I learned what to do when an exponent is being raised by another exponent. In this case you keep the base the same and multiply the two exponents. Finally, I learned what it means when you have a fractional exponent. The numerator of the fraction is the power you raise the number to and the denominator is the root that you take of the number.

Example 2:

Today I learned the definitions for four math terms: mean, median, mode, and range.
- mean
- median
- mode
- range

Today I learned the definitions for four math terms: _mean_, _median_, _mode_, and _range_. The _mean_ is the average of a group of numbers. The _median_ is the number that is located in the middle of a set of numbers. The _mode_ is the number or value that most often occurs, and the _range_ is the difference between the highest and lowest numbers. Statisticians use the terms to share information about whatever it is that they are compiling data on. For example, I can use these definitions to find out how I am doing in class. My scores so far are 70, 75, 80, 80, 80, and 100, so my average, or mean, is about 81. The median of my scores is 80, the mode is 80, and the range is 30.

Step Up to Writing in Math · Creative and Personal Writing · Math Tool—S-7-3

BIBLIOGRAPHY

Association for Supervision and Curriculum Development. "'Radical' Math Becomes the Standard: Emphasis on Algebraic Thinking, Problem Solving, Communication." <u>Education Update</u> 48.4 (Apr. 2006): 1+.

Auman, Maureen. *Classroom Reproducibles*. 2nd ed. Longmont, CO: Sopris West Educational Services, 2003.

- - -. *Step Up to Writing*. 1st, 2nd, 3rd ed. Longmont, CO: Sopris West Educational Services, 2008.

Auman, Maureen, et al. *Primary Steps Reproducibles*. 2nd ed. Longmont, CO: Sopris West Educational Services, 2003.

Bell, Max, et al. *Everyday Mathematics*. 2 vols. The University of Chicago School Mathematics Project. Chicago: Everyday Learning Corporation, 1999.

Companion to Principles and Standards for School Mathematics. Ed. Jeremy Kilpatrick, W. Gary Martin, and Deborah Schifter. Reston, VA: The National Council of Teachers of Mathematics, Inc., 2003.

Cooper Foreman, Linda. *Starting Points for Implementing Visual Mathematics*. Salem, OR: The Math Learning Center, 1995.

Council for Exceptional Children. "Teaching Math to Students with Disabilities." *Today* 9.5 (Jan. 2003): 1+.

Council for Learning Disabilities. "Secondary Students with Learning Disabilities in Reading: Vocabulary Development." *CLD Infosheets* 21 Mar. 2007. 2 June 2008 <http://iris.peabody.vanderbilt.edu/info_briefs/cld/cld_vocabulary.html>.

Countryman, Joan. *Writing to Learn Mathematics: Strategies That Work*. Portsmouth, NH: Heinemann, 1992.

ED Thoughts: What We Know about Mathematics Teaching and Learning. Ed. John Sutton and Alice Krueger. Aurora, CO: Midcontinent Research for Education and Learning, 2002.

Ellsworth, Peter, and Vincent Sindt. *What Every Teacher Should Know about How Students Think: A Survival Guide for Adults.* Eau Claire, WI: Thinking Publications, 1992.

Forsten, Char. "The Problem with Word Problems." *Principal* (Nov.–Dec. 2004): 20–23.

Hiebert, James, et al. *Making Sense: Teaching and Learning Mathematics with Understanding.* Portsmouth, NH: Heineman, 1997.

Hogan, Bob. "Singapore Math: A Problem-Solving Approach." *Principal* (Nov.–Dec. 2004): 22.

Lappan, Glenda, et al. *Covering and Surrounding: Two-Dimensional Measurement.* Connected Mathematics. N.p.: Dale Seymour Publications, 1998.

O'Brien, Thomas C., and Ann Moss. "What's Basic in Mathematics?" *Principal* (Nov.–Dec. 2004): 25–27.

O'Connell, Sue. *Writing About Mathematics: An Essential Skill in Developing Math Proficiency (Grades 3-8).* Bellevue, WA: Bureau of Education and Research, 2001.

Principles and Standards for School Mathematics. Reston, VA: The National Council of Teachers of Mathematics, 2000–2004.

Richardson, Joan. "Japanese Method has Benefits for all Teachers." *Results* (Dec.–Jan. 2001): 1+.

Sanchez, Wendy, and Nicole Ice. "Open-Ended Items Better Reveal Students' Mathematical Thinking." *NCTM News Bulletin* July–Aug. 2004. 3 July 2008 <http://www.nctm.org/news/release.aspx?id=754>.

Schielack, Jane F., et al. *Curriculum Focal Points for Prekindergarten through Grade 8 Mathematics: A Quest for Coherence.* Reston, VA: The National Council of Teachers of Mathematics, Inc., 2006.

Starting Out Right: A Guide to Promoting Children's Reading Success. Ed. Susan M Burns, Peg Griffin, and Catherine E Snow. Washington, DC: National Academy Press, 1999.

United States Dept. of Education. *The Final Report of the National Mathematics Advisory Panel.* 13 Mar. 2008. U.S. Dept. of Education. 3 July 2008 <http://www.ed.gov/about/bdscomm/list/mathpanel/report/final-report.pdf>.

- - -. Office of Special Education Programs. "Strengthening the third 'R': Helping students with disabilities achieve in mathematics." *Research Connections in Special Education.* Vols. Number 11. Arlington, VA: The ERIC Clearinghouse on Disabilities and Gifted Education, 2002.

What Your 4th Grader Needs to Know: Fundamentals of a Good Fourth-Grade Education. Ed. E.D. Hirsch, Jr. The Core Knowledge Series. New York: Doubleday, 1992.

Wilson, Elizabeth A. *Reading at the Middle and High School Levels: Building Active Readers Across the Curriculum.* Arlington, VA: Educational Research Service, 1995.